The Disabled Child
And The Family:
An
Exceptional Parent
Reader

EDITED BY

Maxwell J. Schleifer, Ph.D.
University of Massachusetts–Boston
Boston, Massachusetts

Stanley D. Klein, Ph.D.
New England College of Optometry
Boston, Massachusetts

EXCEPTIONAL PARENT PRESS

Copyright (c) 1985 by The Exceptional Parent Press. All rights reserved. No part of this work may be reproduced or transmitted in any form or by any means, electronic or mechanical, including photocopying and recording, or by any information storage or retrieval system, except as may be expressly permitted by the 1976 Copyright Act or in writing by the publisher. Reguests for permission should be addressed to Permissions, The Exceptional Parent Press, 605 Commonwealth Ave., Boston, MA 02215.

Printed in the U.S.A.
Library of Congress Catalog Card Number:
ISBN: 0-930958-02-0

Excerpts from the following material have been reprinted by permission of the publishers:

Lisa Blumberg, " The Right to Live: Disability is not a Crime." Copyright (c) 1985 by Harvard Magazine. Reprinted by Permission.

James J. Gallagher, "Unthinkable Thoughts." Copyright (c) 1984 by ACLD Newsbrief. Reprinted by permission of the Association for Children and Adults with Learning Disabilities.

David Militzer, "Choosing a Summer Camp." Copyright (c) 1984 by the New Hampshire Developmental Disabilities Council. Adapted from Camping for All: A Guide to Camping and Outdoor Recreation For People Who Have Disabilities. Reprinted by Permission of the New Hampshire Developmental Disabilities Council.

Harilyn Rousso, "Fostering Healthy Self Esteem." Copyright (c) 1984 by Human Services Press. Adapted from an article published in Child and Adolescent Social Work. Reprinted by permission of Human Services Press.

Nancy Wall, "Microcomputer Activities and Occupational Therapy," p. 1, Developmental Disabilities Special Interest Section Newsletter, Vol. 7, No. 1, 1984. Copyright (c) by the American Occupational Therapy Association, Inc.

TABLE OF CONTENTS

FAMILY

Reactions to Disability

1. Grieving Over the Lost Dream
   Audrey T. McCollum — 3

2. Parenting an Infant with a Disability—A Practical Guide for Interaction
   Jeanette McCollum — 6

3. Meeting Parental Needs—A Neverending Dilemma
   Judith Weatherly — 10

4. Parent-to-Parent Support
   Sue Scott and Phyllis Doyle — 12

Self Esteem—Parents and Child

5. Helping our Children Accept Themselves
   Mae Gamble — 16

6. Social Skills and the Disabled Child—A Guide to Appearance
   Ellen Kahan — 19

7. Shawntell and Tanya—A Story of Friendship
   Jeffery and Cindy Strully — 21

8. Fostering Healthy Self Esteem
   Harilyn Rousso — 24

9. The Young Adult: Self Determination and Mutual Respect
   Editorial — 31

10. Wheel A While
    Maren L. Peterson — 32

Relationships and Dynamics

11. "I Feel like I'm dealing with these problems all by myself." Demands on Single Parents
    Family Life — 33

12. "I'll Never Learn How to Play with My Son." Problems of Fathering
    Family Life — 38

13. Professional Expertise and Children With Disabilities. A Problem for Marital Communication
    Family Life — 42

14. Life With My Sister—Guilty No More
    Julia Ellifritt — 46

Community

15. An Open Letter to Pastors and to Parents
    Henry and Elsa Ellis and George T. Warren — 49

16. Media and Attitudes Toward People With Disabilities
    Editorial — 53

17. The Public Library—A Practical Guide for Parents of Disabled Children
    Michelle D. Bowdler — 54

18	A Parent's Statement to a County Board *Bonnie Ziemman*	57
19	Preparation, Persistence, Pressure—Strategies of Moving to a New Community *Beth Ann Kelly*	58
20	Every Vote Counts *Editorial*	61
21	Not Fitting In—The Real Advantage *Linda Mischley*	62

Recreation

22	Taking Recreation Seriously *Gerald S. Fain*	63
23	Choosing a Summer Camp *David Militzer*	65
24	Parents Creating Recreational Experiences: Kamp for Kids *Michelle J. Bowdler*	67
25	Fun Stuff—Magnets	70
26	Fun Stuff—Dressing Up	72
27	Fun Stuff—Cooking	74

GROWING UP

Practical

28	Love, Lead and Let Go—Advice to Parents *Lois Wencil*	77
29	Persistence—A Father's Response to His Son's Hearing Impairment *Joseph J. Kulakowski*	79
30	The Story of Noah—A Rural Family with a Multi-Handicapped Child *Theresa Donar Riniker*	84
31	Selecting and Adapting Toys and Games	88
32	Entering the World of Work; My Daughter is Succeeding *Ann N. Stearns*	91

Education

33	Related Services and the Supreme Court—A Family's Story	93
34	Parent Advocacy Network *Dianne L. Ferguson*	97
35	Unthinkable Thoughts—Reexamining the Concept of Learning Disability *James J. Gallagher*	100
36	Helping the Visually Impaired Child Succeed in School *Patricia Ann Davis*	103
37	"I'm not going to high school if you don't take me the way I am." Mainstreaming in the High School *Family Life*	105

38 Have We Pushed Too Hard? An Adolescent in High School
    Family Life **110**

39 Vocational Training and Employment: Guidelines for Parents
    Sherril Moon and Andrew V. Beale **114**

Health Care

40 Understanding the Whole Child—The Key to Coordinating Services
    Irene Lester **117**

41 Learning from Megan—Adapting to Orthopedic Surgery
    Rita Spillane **119**

42 Coordinating Medical Services—An Eternal Problem
    Editorial **122**

43 Surgery for the Adolescent—The Impact on the Family
    Family Life **123**

44 Help for Drooling
    Alison Ouellette and Bruce M. Gans **127**

45 The Right to Live—Disability is not a Crime
    Lisa Blumberg **129**

Sex Education

46 Sex Education and the Disabled—Teaching Adult Responsibilities
    Theresa Varnet **131**

47 Sex Education—A Commentary From the Advisory Board
    Betty Pendler **134**

48 Sex Education: Let's Not Pretend
    Katherine Barnes **136**

Residential Care

49 Abuse of Children with Disabilities—Time to Stop Pretending
    Editorial **138**

50 Talking About the Best Kept Secret—Sexual Abuse and Children with Disabilities
    Janice Daar Watson **140**

51 When It's Time to Let Go
    Joan K. Blaska **144**

52 A Teenager Comes Home—A Dilemma for the Family
    Family Life **146**

53 Residential Placement—A Problem for Parents
    Paula Haramis **151**

TECHNOLOGY

Communication Devices

54 "Can You Imagine Feeling That Way About Your Own Helpless Kid?"
    Mixed Feelings about New Opportunities
    Family Life **154**

55 Hi! My Name is Daniel
    Nancy Schmalz **158**

56 Communication Devices and an Enriched Life—An Autobiography
Lake N. Kissick Jr. — **160**

Adaptive Devices

57 New Products—Problems and Prospects
Editorial — **163**

58 Wheelchair Design Changes—New Opportunities for recreation — **164**

Computers

59 LOGO is for All Children—Learning with the Turtle
Cleborne D. Maddux and Rhonda E. Cummings — **167**

60 Microcomputer Activities and Occupational Therapy
Nancy Wall — **169**

RESOURCES

Information

61 What's Happening — **172**

62 Directory of Organizations serving the Disabled — **180**

PREFACE

We have been publishing The Exceptional Parent magazine for over fifteen years. From the first issue, we have attempted to provide practical information and guidance for all those who are involved in promoting the growth and development of children with disabilities, parents as well as professionals.

During this period, there have been dramatic changes effecting the life experience of these children and their families. Parents have gained increasing respect as "experts" in the lives of children and important partners with professionals in any program.

The Education of All Handicapped Childrens Act (PL94-142) was passed. We have described the implementation of this important guarantee of educational rights of disabled children and the variety of problems that have occurred in implementing these regulations.

And, finally, we have witnessed and shared with our readers the dramatic application of contemporary technology to the problems of individuals with disabilities. Whenever we have admired one new development, the next seems even more breathtaking.

Many parents and professionals have asked to have the articles in book form. They have told us it is simpler to give a book as a gift or have as a reference or even pay to bind one year's subscriptions. We have responded by organizing the best articles from our 1984 issues in this one volume. We hope this will serve you and your network of friends and colleagues.

The Editors
Maxwell J. Schleifer
Stanley D. Klein

FAMILY

The family plays a central role in promoting the growth of children. Parents and professionals have all been made aware of the impact that the birth of a child with a disability can have on the parents' ability to meet the special needs of the new child, as well as other family members. Although there is literature on stages of family reactions to this crisis, there is little information that actually describes what happens to the family on a day-to-day basis and what they can do to help the child and themselves.

This section presents the psychological mechanisms that underlie the family's reactions; then how to help parents deal with the stress of childrearing. Self esteem in parents and children, central to everyone's effective functioning, is presented in the next group of articles.

Understanding family relationships is presented as a guide to the utilization of resources both inside and outside of the family. And, finally, we present practical guides to using community and recreational resources.

CHAPTER 1

Grieving Over Lost Dream

by Audrey T. McCollum

Parents grieve for themselves in their state of loss.

In pondering the meaning of loss, the religious philosopher Kierkegaard wrote, "Despair is never ultimately over the external object but always over ourselves. A girl loses her sweetheart and she despairs. It is not over the lost sweetheart, but over herself without the sweetheart. And so it is with all cases of loss . . ."

To understand the losses we experience when our child's health is sufficiently impaired to affect the quality of his/her life—and our lives as parents—it is useful to think first about why we ever choose to have children.

Choosing To Be A Parent

There are many different things that motivate us when deciding to have children.

A couple may want to emulate their own parents—to parent a child as they were parented—and vicariously to re-experience their happy childhood years.

Conversely, new parents may desire to compete with their own parents, to care for a child as they wish they had been parented. They may want to give their child what they never had, whether in affection, opportunities, or material goods—and vicariously to experience a childhood they never had themselves.

Men and women may want to prove their sexual adequacy by producing a child. Or, they may feel destined or pressured by their ethnic or religious beliefs to bring forth a child to perpetuate the race or the family name.

They may be trying to give meaning to lives that seem empty and without purpose. Some people have children because they are seeking a form of immortality. We all share a wish to survive our own deaths by leaving an imprint on the world, often in the form of our own children.

Or, men and women may simply wish to nurture, to shape guide and cherish another life—their child's.

Expectations

Any of these motives (and there is usually a mingling of several) contribute to the daydreams we have about our offspring. We dream about the child—how s/he will look, feel, sound, behave. We dream of the teenager and adult—who s/he will be, what s/he will be—gentle or boisterous, dainty or virile, artistic, intellectual, athletic, political, a professional football player, a famous author, a brilliant scientist, an astronaut.

Usually, parents and their offspring interact in such a way that gradually parent's dreams and expectations are modified by recognition of their child's actual capabilities. As the fantasy of the dream child is replaced with day to day living, parents will hopefully accept the child for what he or she is and wants to be.

When a child's health is impaired, parents can be confronted harshly and abruptly with a reality that allows little or no hope for fulfillment of their dreams. A child with muscular dystrophy is not likely to become a pro football player; a child with Down syndrome is not likely to win a Nobel prize.

So the fantasied child is lost and a process of grieving begins. Of course, most parents do feel genuine sorrow for the child whose health is impaired. But, parallel to that, as Kierkegaard reminds us, parents grieve for themselves in their state of loss.

Grief

Acute grief can have strong physical manifestations. It may include shortness of breath and frequent sighs, loss of appetite and empty feelings in the abdomen, lack of strength and feelings of exhaustion, along with restlessness and aimless activity, a loss of warmth and detachment from other people, irritability, anger, and guilt.

These, then, are normal responses to the sudden, total loss of a loved one. In my experience, they are also felt by parents of children found to have significantly impaired health, whether physical or mental. Their grief gains momentum when the diagnosis of the disability or disease really begins to sink in.

Most such parents experience depression. I am not speaking of a pathological reaction, an illness, but of depression as an expectable response to significant disappointment and loss—the loss of a dream. I am speaking of depression as it has been viewed by psychoanalyst Elizabeth Zetzel. It includes depressive emotion which is "a sense of lack of nourishment, fullness, warmth, energeticness." But depression is more than a cluster of emotions. It is a psychological state marked by helplessness and loss of self-esteem.

Self-Esteem

In the parent of a child with a disability, loss of self-esteem comes from many sources.

From the time we begin thinking of conceiving a child, most women and men have doubts about the outcome. But these are usually dispelled by the assumptions we make about our capabilities, often without much conscious thought.

Most of us expect to contribute unflawed genes to the embryo which will cause it to develop into a healthy baby. Both parents expect themselves to surround their child with a cocoon of care and protection to ensure its happy and healthy development, to ensure the fulfillment of at least some of their daydreams.

A child's impairment, whether inherited or acquired confronts us with a sense of having failed to live up to our expectations. We are helpless to undo the faulty development, and our sense of competence and self-regard can be shaken drastically.

Loss of self-esteem is fed by guilt. Most parents painfully review any acts of omission and commission that might have caused the child's impairment. We review our thoughts and feelings as well. Any negative feeling about the pregnancy or about the child before her or his problem developed can seem unforgivable. A parent can experience guilt and remorse over any mixed feelings.

Only secretly do parents allow ourselves to recognize the anger we feel at moments toward the disabled child because s/he is afflicted. Such anger can feel totally unacceptable.

All too readily we find cause to accuse ourselves, since we are all imperfect. When the sense of guilt is unbearable, it may be expressed as hostile blame of others—doctors, nurses, our own parents, and quite often our spouses.

Even as the hostility is felt and expressed, the internal critic that operates in each of us—our conscience—may judge the hostility to be unjustifiable, even unforgivable. How can we feel that way towards our *own* children? So from still another quarter, the self-esteem is lowered.

From a sense of inadequacy or blame, feelings of helplessness, guilt, and hostility, the boom is lowered on our faltering self-regard. Depression enfolds us.

The intensity and the duration of our grief and depression will vary. Each new major disappointment and loss that we experience through a lifetime tends to re-kindle the feelings associated with earlier losses and disappointments. For example, the birth of a baby with brain damage may unconsciously revive all the sadness, frustration, helplessness and rage associated with the terminal care of our own parent after a stroke. The feelings about the baby in the present are greatly reinforced as they are fused with the feelings about the parent in the past. There is always some chain of connections in our experiences.

The consistency of our self-esteem varies among us. Self-esteem is nourished in childhood by our parent's love and acceptance; it is shaped by their expectations of us, and our capacity and desire to meet those expectations. Self-esteem reflects the congruity or the incongruity—the fit, in other words—between the ideal self we aspire to be and the actual self we experience in reality. When we have come to accept both our limitations and our capabilities, when our ideal selves are in reasonable harmony, our self-regard is likely to be secure and resilient. It can absorb some bruises.

Those who lack adequate nourishment of their sense of goodness and worth, and who have transformed critical judgements from others into harsh self-judgments; those who cling to ideals of power and perfection and who depend on extraordinary performance and external recognition to feel worthwhile—such people have precarious self-esteem. When gaps between their ideal and actual selves are exposed, when they are threatened by helplessness, they plunge. In such people, normal feelings of depression which everyone feels from time to time, may develop into depressive illness.

Experiencing Pain

Some parents are unable to tolerate the grief and depression precipitated by their child's affliction. Sometimes, there actually may be an absence of grief. Although to outsiders this may seem to express courage (smiling in the face of adversity, keeping a stiff upper lip), in fact, it does not serve the parent of the family well at all. When the conscious experience of grief has been postponed, it is likely to erupt unexpectedly and inexplicably at a later time. Or it may be completely avoided, but the avoidance can draw the parents' emotional energy away from family and friends. A parent may become distant and detached, absorbed in work and emotionally unavailable to the other spouse who may want support for his or her own struggles with the situation.

"Blessed are those who mourn, for they shall be comforted." Even those who can tolerate their grief and depression proceed with the work of mourning slowly and unevenly to protect themselves from being overwhelmed, and to preserve their capacity to function in daily life. Grief can smoulder, to be rekindled again and again. Each time it flares, steps toward mastery can be taken.

The anger can be recognized and vented in appropriate ways. The sense of guilt and disappointment can be explored and expressed so that harsh self-accusations can gradually yield to self-forgiveness.

There can be a gradual giving up of the attachment to the lost dream—the dream of a fantasy child—and a reconciliation with the reality of the actual child's impairment.

The sense of helplessness can be examined. What cannot be modified can be accepted for what it is, but this acceptance can be paralleled by the mobilization of problem-solving efforts on behalf of the child and the family.

It is now well recognized that psychological growth and development continue throughout our life times. We bring to each new crisis the unresolved conflicts and the emotional baggage from our past. But each new crisis involves the reopening of a book, so to speak, and the chapter endings can be rewritten.

Grief is intensely painful. But psychological distress that is experienced and mastered results in the growth necessary to deal effectively with life's adversities and also to experience its joys. The lost dream can be transformed into a new vision. ∎

Audrey T. McCollum has written extensively in the child development and mental health fields. Her most recently published book is entitled, *The Chronically Ill Child: A Guide for Parents and Professionals*. Ms. McCollum has had prolonged experience counseling parents of children with emotional problems, developmental disabilities, and chronic illness at the Yale University Child Study Center, and the Department of Pediatrics of the Yale University School of Medicine. She works as a therapist in private practice.

CHAPTER 2

Parenting an Infant with a Disability
A Practical Guide for Interaction

by Jeanette McCollum

Playful, enjoyable interactions with one's baby occur relatively spontaneously. They provide some of the most delightful moments of early parenthood. Parents and babies seem to "fit" with one another almost naturally. Each behaves in ways that are most likely to capture and hold each other's interest and attention and continue the interaction. This happens so effortlessly that we rarely question what makes it work so well. This "goodness of fit" between a baby and a parent is important because early social interactions play a major role in early language, cognitive, and emotional development.

These social interactions with disabled babies are often less spontaneous, less fun, require more effort, and even become less frequent than with "easier" babies. As a result, parents have to be more alert to the cues the baby gives, more aware of their own characteristic behaviors, and more active in order to learn more helpful ways of interacting with their children.

The success of the parent-baby matching process is very dependent on the characteristics and capabilities of each of the two partners. Many of the interactive differences which have been found in babies with different types of disabilities and delays are the very capabilities which are important for relatively effortless and enjoyable social interactions. These capabilities include the baby's ability to communicate and reach out to adults via sounds, gestures, and "looks" and to demonstrate her specific interests in the world about her.

For example, a baby with a disability may not be able to enagage an adult by reacting with a smile, sound, or excited movements to an adult's greeting. Or the baby may not be able to attend to or manipulate toys or other nearby objects and attract adult attention and interest. Babies with a "noticeable" physical handicap may not be as physically appealing and likely to attract interactions with adults. Adults may have to work to overcome their initial upset with the baby's appearance.

As a further example, consider the behavior of an older "normal" baby sitting on the floor playing with a toy. He may simply be banging on it or batting it around, or he may be using it in its intended manner. One of the things that a parent does automatically is to watch closely both the baby's face and actions, looking back and forth between them. The second thing that a parent does is talk, and because he or she is so aware of what the baby is experiencing, his or her words are directly related to what the baby is seeing, hearing, doing, and feeling. As the baby experiences an action or a feeling, he is being supplied with the words that describe it. Third, a parent's language exaggerates for the child what is important—typically using very short sentences, and often simply labeling objects or actions. As the baby repeats his actions, the parent repeats the labels ("bang, bang"), providing repeated opportunities for him to attach a word to his actions.

At each point in this description, the interaction with the baby with a disability may be much more difficult. First, the child may be delayed in sitting or unable to sit unsupported and have great difficulty manipulating toys or objects. If the child cannot hear or understand the parent's language, then the parent is likely to be discouraged from the kind of repeated verbal interaction described.

Not all disabled babies show all of these differences, and some show none at all. When they occur, however, they can have a dramatic effect on the interactive partner.

Certain specific disabilities such as blindness will mean that the baby's parent may find it difficult to determine what he is interested in, making it harder to join his activity. Because the eyes play such a major role in expressing emotion, it may also be harder to tell how the baby is feeling about what you, the partner, are doing, giving little guidance about whether to continue. Greeting and luring you into an interaction will be less obvious, too. Think about the use of gaze in turntaking...how will you, the partner, know when it is your turn or when the baby is inviting you to comment on his toy play?

As another specific example, think of a baby with a physical disability. Social behaviors such as smiling or reaching toward a parent may be much harder for her to accomplish, and may lead to an abnormal movement pattern (such as a grimace) that may disguise what she is feeling. Her interaction patterns may also be less under her own control, so that turntaking is less easily accomplished. She may pass more quickly and without warning from pleasure to overexcitement, and may begin to cry. The parent will be less able to predict what effect his or her efforts will have.

It is useful to explore how a child's disability

might influence each of the qualities of a "good" social partner, and how these in turn might affect the adult partner. Any baby with medical or physical problems may have difficulty controlling his own level of arousal, and may be harder to rouse and/or more easily tipped into overexcitement. This is perplexing to parents—should the partner repeat what he or she is doing, change, introduce something new, or stop for a while?

When a baby rarely explores or plays independently with toys, or does not clearly show that he is engrossed in his own actions and interests, it will be difficult for his parent to use his interest as a topic for interaction. If the baby does not follow the "rules" of social interaction by providing few pauses (or by rarely acting or vocalizing) or by not looking at his mother or father, turntaking around a common topic will be very hard to establish.

Any baby who does not possess a full range of emotional expression will put us at a disadvantage in determining his readiness for or response to an interaction. The baby who changes little as he grows older will not continue to be a very interesting partner. Thus, regardless of the specific handicap, specific behavior in the baby will influence the fit between partners.

Adult Partners Need to Adjust

In any interaction with another person, we adjust to the situation and to the unique characteristics of our partner. Given a baby with a disability, if social interaction is to occur, the parent will have to adjust. The parent not only must take the burden of responsibility for the interaction, but may have to do so with fewer cues from the baby.

When a baby has problems, it is understandable that the parent might be more hesitant to engage the baby, tend to fill up silences with verbalization, turn social interaction into teaching situations, or even withdraw from the interaction, thinking that the baby does not enjoy his or her company. And that is exactly what has been found. Studied in interactive situations with their disabled babies, some parents have shown more inactivity ("do nothing" more), while others are muchmore active than parents with normal babies. Still others tend to alternate between these two extremes. One common pattern is for the parent to take the role of director of the interaction. Interaction with disabled babies is simply harder work.

Parents can become discouraged and/or exhausted when a good "fit" does not occur. And when a really good "fit" does not occur relatively automatically and without specific effort, partners must adjust their own interaction to compensate. But this is more complicated than it sounds. Some adjustments are very beneficial, and result in much more pleasurable interaction. Other adjustments, while they may be natural and unconscious responses to the baby's interactive characteristics, are not necessarily beneficial. One adjustment which is usually not beneficial is to stop trying and withdraw from the child.

The line between what is beneficial and what is not is less clear. How much to direct the interaction is an excellent illustration of this problem. On the one hand, if the baby has difficulty in playing constructively with toys, instruction and demonstration (adjustments which ordinarily seem to occur naturally) may help her to focus on the toy and explore its possibilities. On the other hand, if social interaction is always directed by an adult, the baby loses a type of experience very important for her development—the experience of having her partner join her, elaborating on her interests and feelings. There is thus a fine line between what is a "good" adjustment and what is not.

Another possibility is that there are adjustments which would help, but which do not occur because they are not automatic—the baby's cues do not "instruct" the parent to make them. For example, if the baby rarely vocalizes, her interactive partner may naturally adjust by talking more. But this in turn may make it harder for the baby to vocalize. An adjustment that might help the baby participate would be for her partner to slow down and wait longer for a response. Hence, adjustment may need to be conscious, and may even be opposite to what the partner would naturally do.

It is important that we are as conscious of our own and the baby's interactive behaviors as possible, so that we need not rely completely on nature to provide the most appropriate adjustment. Each time an interaction occurs, it is between two very unique partners, and is dependent on a very unique fit. While it is fit between partners that is critical, it is the adult who will do most of the adjusting. The partner who can make this a conscious process will still work hard, but the effort will yield more enjoyable outcomes.

Some General Strategies

Remember to relax and have fun with your child. Having a disabled baby is a serious business, but it is human nature to seek enjoyment with other people. Rest assured that the baby will learn many things from playful interactions.

Another general strategy for accomplishing more conscious adjustment is to approach each interaction as a very interesting problem to be studied and solved. To do this, the adult must be very observant of him or herself.

When the interaction is working, why is it working? What am I doing that is capturing and holding the baby's attention and interest? Am I using a lot of facial expression? Am I doing funny and unexpected things?

When the interaction is not working, what am I doing? Am I being overly active or overly inactive? Am I changing too quickly or not enough? Am I being overly directive?

The adult must also be very observant of the baby. What makes him cry? Why is she looking away? Sometimes it can be useful to try to take the baby's point of view to figure out why he or she does certain things. One researcher, for example, found that adults often misinterpret a blind baby's stillness as a lack of interest, when it may actually indicate that the baby is very attentive and interested. Other researchers believe that babies look away from interactions as one way of controlling their own level of excitement so that they can then come back for more—a baby who easily becomes overly excited might need to look away more often, especially if his or her partner is being very active.

Another general strategy that is part of this problem solving approach is to ask, "What else could I try?" and then try it and see what happens. One way to get ideas is to spend time with other babies, and again, to be very observant.

How does the interaction differ from those with my own baby and why? What is the baby doing that is different and what reaction do I have to this? Are these behaviors of mine something that my baby might respond to?

Practical Suggestions

Another way to get ideas is to think "variety." Variety comes in many forms, including what you do and when you do it. First, there are several specific strategies you might want to try. Just a partial list includes : repetition ("Gonna *get* you...I'm gonna *get* you"); changing speed (fast/slow); turntaking (anything where the child does something, you do something, she does something, etc.); exaggeration of your facial expressions; imitation; phasing (giving him more time to respond, waiting for her to do something you can respond to); introducing something new and unexpected; and elaborating (the child seems interested in your hair, so you shake your head to make it jiggle, and say, "Hair, that's my hair".) Then vary what you do.

The success of the parent-baby matching process is very dependent on the characteristics and capabilities of each of the two partners.

Remember the baby's attraction to "theme and variation," and aim for a good mix. You want to expand what he experiences and maintain his interest, but not lose him by using too much repetition and too much change. One very powerful specific strategy that is almost too obvious to call a strategy is to reposition yourself and the baby in relation to one another. Try to avoid sitting so that both of you are facing outward and the baby cannot easily see your face or reach toward you.

Now think of the different senses that you might use; have you tried capturing the baby's interest by appealing to her vision? To her hearing? Have you tried touching her or moving her body around?

An interesting way to think of things to do is to combine each of the specific strategies listed above with each sense. For example, are you providing exaggerations for her to look at? To hear? When you are repeatedly walking your fingers up her leg toward her belly, have you tried changing the speed? Have you tried imitating her sounds, her facial expressions, her movements?

Common baby games such as "patty-cake," "peek-a-boo" or "ride horsie" often contain many of these combinations, as do the more personal rituals that you and the baby may have developed yourselves. One father and his baby go through a nightly game in which the baby repeatedly opens and closes the kitchen cabinet, while his father accompanies his actions with, "Open...shut...open...shut."

Another type of consideration in conscious interaction is to vary when you do it. Think of different situations in which you and the baby are often together, and apply the combinations of what to do with each of these. In play situations in which no toys are involved, you can engage in "pure" social interaction, and can try out any or all of the combinations to see what happens. A type of situation which can become more social is caregiving, when you are dressing, bathing, or feeding the baby. For example, "You feed me, I'll feed you," introduces turntaking into snack time. A big surprise face after a sock goes on or a head pops through the neck of a shirt introduces social interaction into getting dressed, and finger walking games fit very nicely into bathing.

In the situations described above, *you* are the object of the baby's attention, and are free to make yourself as interesting as possible. Situations in which the baby is interested in something else (a toy, cars going by the window) are different in that they are not purely social. Your challenge is to add a social aspect without being so intrusive or so interesting that you draw his attention away. The one big secret to doing this is to join his focus of interest. You want him to learn that you are a source of information about the world but that you want him to be interested in and try things on his own.

When the baby is playing with an object, it is fairly easy to tell where her interests lie, and you can join her by quietly repositioning the toy to make it easier for her to get at, by demonstrating a new action, or by taking a turn too. You can also join by expressing approval (You're banging it!"), or exclaiming when she happens to glance at your face, ("Hey, you!"), accompanied by a face full of pleasure.

When the baby is not engaged with a toy, her gaze of direction or a pointing finger are your major clues, and you can join her by labeling what she is looking at ("Cars, cars are going by"), or by bringing the baby and the object together and briefly demonstrating or labeling. The trick is to be very attentive to the baby's focus of interest and to build a social encounter without taking over. Often, you will have to use your best guess. If you are not sure what she is interested in, act as if you do; you will often be right.

Instructional situations are somewhat different. Here you have a purpose, and a very important one—to teach the baby something that he is unable to do or unwilling to try (rolling over, imitating vocalization). However, instruction can profit greatly from the addition of some social play, making the hard work more interesting and fun for both parties, and motivating the baby to try again.

Why not, for example, accompany his rolling over with some repeated verbal nonsense syllable, and a big surprise exclamation when he finally makes it?

Remember, too, that the ultimate goal of instruction is for the baby to be as independent as possible. Whenever you can manage to follow his lead to accomplish your purpose, you will let him know that he can affect the social behavior of another person. Whenever you teach labels for objects and colors by using whatever he is already interested in, you can be more sure that he is paying attention and that the labels will have more meaning for him.

Social interaction with disabled babies can be very hard work. But, it can also be more enjoyable if the adult partner will take a problem-solving approach to consciously providing to the interaction that nature would normally provide. The outcomes of this effort will be interactions that are so much more fun that both partners will want them to happen more often. These interactions will also meet a wider variety of developmental needs.

Relax, observe, try a variety of strategies in a variety of situations, be deliberately conscious...and enjoy. ■

Jeanette McCollum is the coordinator of a program in Early Childhood Special Education in the Department of Special Education at the University of Illinois. Her primary research interest is in parent/infant interaction.

CHAPTER 3

Meeting Parental Needs
A Never-ending Dilemma

by Judith Weatherly

New parents are often advised that remembering to attend to their own needs as well as their newborn's is a vital ingredient for healthy family life. This advise is often forgotten or neglected when a child is born with a disability. Judith Weatherly describes her efforts to solve the never ending problem of finding the balance between meeting her needs and those of her chronically ill son.

My nine year old son was born with serious kidney problems and has been on dialysis for most of the last six years. Sometimes people ask me, "How do you do it?" This question annoys me. For one thing, I have never been too sure what "it" is. But I have finally come up with an answer. I do "it" by being selfish. In fact, I have decided that selfishness is a highly desirable—perhaps essential—personality trait for the mother of a chronically ill child.

Not a "Saintly" Mother

When we found that our son had a chronic illness which meant that he would require extra care, I assumed that as his mother, I would cheerfully provide that care. I measured myself against the stereotype of a devoted, saintly mother, living night and day in service to her stricken child. And, inevitably, I found myself falling far short of my imagined role model. I got tired, yelled at my child, and occasionally wished for the peace of a deserted island.

Society now recognizes feelings of anger, resentment, and isolation as a part of normal motherhood. Parenting books and counselors urge getting away, maintaining outside activities and friendships, and reserving time for the marital relationship. But too often, this understanding attitude is reserved for "normal" families. I felt that our family should be immune to all negative feelings about this child.

"Normal" Feelings

The more I read and the more I talked to other parents of children with disabilities and normal children, the more I found that feelings and emotions about children are very much the same in all families. The accident of illness or disability serves only to intensify feelings and emotions, not to change them.

Both positive and negative feelings may be magnified by a child's chronic illness. Love may be stronger, but so may be resentment. Overwhelming joy over the child's accomplishments may be offset by depression caused by self-imposed isolation. Mothers or fathers who feel that life must be devoted to the afflicted child may find themselves overcome by physical exhaustion, frustration and depression.

The isolation common to many mothers of young children is intensified by the feeling that "no one understands" and no one can help. I found that my excessive attention to my son's needs led to a loss of perspective. For a time, I almost stopped seeing him as a child, a separate person, and saw only a disease, a handicap, a collection of symptoms. Most of my life was lived through my child; his successes and failures became my own. Neither of us could succeed or fail on our own merits. In many ways, I was more dependent on my son than he was on me.

The Problem of Interdependence

Almost accidently, I began to realize that our relationship was not a healthy one. When my son was two, I took a temporary job for just a few hours a day. Gradually, I noticed how much more we seemed to be enjoying each other and how much more rapidly he seemed to be developing. Perhaps we both needed a change.

Our interdependence was caused partly by my own inability to let go of my child's care and was partly a natural extension and effect of society's expectations of the roles of disabled child and mother.

The problem has no easy solutions. Seven years later, I am still struggling with the issues of his independence and mine. Like that of many disabled children, his care requires extra time and attention. But a dose of selfishness (not necessarily guilt free) has sometimes been a catalyst in finding some solutions and alternatives. And surprisingly often, what is good for me turns out to be good for him as well.

Similar advice comes from others who have come to terms with their own special needs and those of their children. Mary Lou Weisman, the mother of a son with muscular dystrophy was advised, "It's hard enough for determined women to have lives outside of their children's. It's going to be especially difficult for you." (Mary Lou Weisman

The accident of illness or disability serves only to intensify feelings and emotions, not to change them.

Intensive Care, New York, New York: Random House, 1982, p.152)

Suzanne Massey found one way to cope with the anxiety produced by the uncertainty of living with hemophilia, "Sometimes after Bobby's cerebral bleeding, as the pressure grows more intense, I realized that to keep my mind intact, to keep from turning around in my cage like a panic-stricken animal, I had to do something hard, something mentally challenging. It had to be something so difficult that it would, by its own force, wrench my mind away from the unresolvable mysteries that tormented me everyday." (Robert and Suzanne Massey, *Journey*, New York: Warner Books, Inc., 1975, p.204.

Helping Myself

Self-help solutions for mothers abound in today's feminist influenced culture. And just as the problems of normal and exceptional parents are remarkably similar, so are the positive steps to alleviate them. At different times over the years I have started a regular exercise program, returned to school, worked part time, and become active in church and volunteer work. Sometimes, the solution itself has not been as important as the fact that I have done something that I wanted to do and from which I benefited.

Making arrangements to do any of these "selfish" activities was not always easy. Again, the problems are the same encountered by any family, merely magnified by the child's exceptionality. Finding an appropriate caregiver is always difficult, whatever the age or condition of the child.

It is still very hard for me to let go of the idea that I am the only one qualified to take care of my child. Maybe no one can do it better, but surely someone else can do it well part of the time. And I may do it better when I am not on duty twenty-four hours a day.

There have been many times when things have gone wrong. Guilt is quick to overwhelm me—why wasn't I there when he needed me? The temptation to do it all myself, to be sure it is done right, not to give up control, is often strong. But when I give into it, I am soon tired and resentful and things really do not go any better or more smoothly. Any home with children moves from crisis to crisis; ours may just be a little more frequent and unusual.

Lisa Cronin Wohl has written, "In a book that I read before my daughter was born, one mother said, 'I never gave up anything for my child.' At the time that woman sounded selfish to me. Now, in the wake of experience, I think I know what she meant. Of course a mother gives up a lot for her child: blood, sleep, tears, not to mention time, money and peace of mind. But a mother must not feel obliged to give up herself. Not unless she wants to raise a motherless child." (Lisa Cronin Wohl, Book Review, Ms., April 1982).

I believe that in the long run, my selfishness will benefit the whole family. When I am not available or willing to do everything for him, my child finds that he can do more for himself than either of us had imagined. When I feel that I am achieving something on my own, and am enjoying my life, my special child becomes more of a special joy instead of a special burden. Our son's problems will always be a part of our family, but they are no longer its focus. ■

Judith Weatherly lives in Tallahassee, Florida with her husband, George, and their two children, Robert and Christopher. Mrs. Weatherly has a masters degree in Russian language from Florida State University. She works as a free-lance editor, and contributes to her church newsletter and alumni association.

CHAPTER 4

by Sue Scott and Phyllis Doyle

Parent-to-Parent Support

I was the mother of a child who could grow, walk, talk, learn, and love as others, only at his own special pace.

When parents learn that their child has a handicapping condition, they may want to talk to someone who understands how they feel. In many parts of the country, support groups have begun to meet this need. Seattle's Parent-to-Parent Support, under the auspices of and funded by the King County Advocates for Retarded Citizens, offers a one-to-one "match" between the new parent and one of the parents from their team of trained "helping parents," who have disabled children. Since June, 1980, when the first group of helping parents completed their training, the program has served parents who are referred to them, often within hours of hearing about their child's diagnosis.

A Diagnosis

Mark's birth was an exciting and joyful experience. He came so fast that, except for a nurse, only his parents were present to welcome their third son into the world. His mother, Cathy, was elated by her marvelous accomplishment, feeling that no one else could do what she had just done.

Living on an island that depends on a ferry schedule for access to Seattle can complicate events such as a baby's birth. When the local pediatrician arrived, she examined Mark, and then suggested they take him to a hospital in Seattle for a checkup. The doctor was hesitant, and Cathy sensed her deep concern about Mark. Unable to get a clue from the pediatrician's manner, Cathy half-jokingly blurted out, "What are you trying to tell us? Our son's not mongoloid or something, is he?" That was the worst thing she could think of, and she was losing her patience.

"I don't know. A specialist will check him at the hospital," was the doctor's answer. Cathy was stunned. Her annoyance with the physician turned to panic, as she and her husband, Donald, took Mark to Seattle and checked into the hospital. When a pediatrician came into their room and said that Mark might have Down syndrome, Cathy told him he was in the wrong room. She felt robbed of the joy she had experienced at Mark's birth, and she was angry.

For five hours, Cathy and Donald waited to talk with a genetic specialist who had been called in. Donald ran back and forth between the hospital's library and their room, first reading about Down syndrome, then looking Mark over carefully for the symptoms. After what seemed like an eternity, the geneticist came in to talk to Donald and Cathy.

"Give me my baby," Cathy said as she took Mark protectively in her arms, hoping to shield her son from those who might accuse him. "Does Mark have Down syndrome?"

A "Match" for Mark's Parents

Yes, Mark did have Down syndrome. Everyone cried—parents, doctor, and nurses. As the doctor explained about Down syndrome, Cathy imagined a strange-looking child, someone she would have to be chained to for the rest of her life.

"I pictured myself wiping drool off his chin forever! And I never cried harder in my life." Finally, the room was silent and Cathy closed the door. The nurses, however, would not allow her to have privacy and kept opening the door. "Why won't they just leave me alone?" she thought.

Later, one of the nurses offered to call Parent-to-Parent Support so that Cathy could talk with another parent who had gone through the same thing.

"I didn't really want to talk to anyone, but I didn't want to hurt their feelings. I was too numb to protest. When Helen called me, I felt like telling her, 'Hurry up and say what you want to say.' But Helen made me listen, let me cry, and most of all, gave me information about Down syndrome. When I finished talking to Helen, I felt confident and strong, almost lucky. I was the mother of a child who would grow, walk, talk, learn, and love as others, only at his own special pace."

Helen and Cathy talked on the phone for an hour or so, and after that, Cathy's tears stopped.

A few weeks later, Cathy sensed that Donald had been feeling somewhat left out, and gave him the phone number of a father Helen had told her about. Donald practically ran to him, thinking that he had finally found a place where he could cry and let down a bit. Much to his surprise, Donald came home with a completely different outlook. "There is nothing to cry about. It's going to be okay." he said. In fact, he felt elated, his fears having been greatly relieved.

Mark is now a year and a half old, and is a healthy, responsive baby. He has joined the infant intervention program at the University of Washington. Asked about her opinion now of Parent-to-Parent Support, Cathy replied, "Educate the nurses and hospital personnel to call and get someone to talk to those parents right away!"

Learning to listen carefully for feelings is one of the main goals of the eighteen hours of training.

Background

A small group of parents of children with various disabilities and professionals working with these families began meeting together regularly in 1978. They wanted to find a way to fill the gap where services for children with special needs left off and services for parents began. There was nothing available in the Seattle area to meet the parents' needs for emotional support when they learned that their child had a disability. The parents in the group began identifying what was needed by describing what it was like to learn about their children's diagnoses.

These parents and professionals became the advisory committee of King County Advocates for Retarded Citizens' Parent-to-Parent Support program. During development of the program, they read brochures and manuals from other support groups and finally, by adapting the programs of other groups to their ideas, they wrote their own program. The committee's search for funding sources was successful; funding came from a variety of public and private agencies. Maintaining funding is a continual concern of the program.

Promotion in the community began after the committee had carefully developed the goals for the program. A medical advisory committee helped to pave the way by suggesting criteria for selecting helping parents, and by advising the group on ways to get referrals from physicians and nurses.

Staffing

When the program was ready to begin, a coordinator was hired. The advisory committee had decided that the position of program coordinator should be paid rather than volunteer, because of the demanding nature of the work. Duties of the coordinator included: recruiting and training helping parents, receiving new referrals and matching them with appropriate helping parents, acting as a resource for both helping parents and new parents, and making certain that the medical/professional community and general public know that the program exists. Qualifications that were especially important for this position were experience in dealing with a disability, good communication skills, a warm and caring way with people, and leadership ability.

Helen Armour Pym, the parent of an adult daughter with Down syndrome, met all of these requirements and was hired. She became the first salaried member of the Parent-to-Parent team, and continued with the program. By the Spring of 1980, the application forms and information packets describing the training for helping parents were complete.

The program was launched when the first group of parents completed their training in June, 1980. As Parent-to-Parent Support continued to expand, they hired a professional counselor to plan and direct the training of new helping parents and to facilitate the monthly support group meeting for already active helping parents.

Parents Helping Parents

"Helping parents" are volunteers who have children with disabilities. They are trained to communicate effectively with parents recently informed of their child's handicapping condition. In their training, they learn that grief plays a significant role in adjusting to being the parents of such a child. They also learn to make referrals to community resources and to use communication techniques. Learning to listen carefully for feelings is one of the main goals of the eighteen hours of training.

Each parent looks closely at his or her own experience and feelings around the discovery of their child's disability. Small groups of parents sharing with each other and a facilitator their "stories" of how they learned about their child's diagnosis is a powerful part of the training. To listen to each parent and then to realize the cumulative effects of the sorrow, frustration, and eventual adjustment is both moving and inspiring. The group can see how far it has come by looking back at where it started!

The philosophy regarding the role of a helping parent may best be summarized in this statement by the coordinator, Helen Pym:

We are "helping parents." We have unique and valuable skills and expertise in our roles as parents of children with handicapping conditions. We propose to share our skills and our caring with parents who are newly experiencing the traumas we have somehow survived. We hope to make the experience a little easier and a little less traumatic by our loving support. We are not counselors. We are not therapists. We are not adversaries to other support systems. We propose to add to the parents' experience, the richness of an empathetic, sensitive, skilled listener who can offer friendship and shared experience.

What motivates parents who sometimes feel drained and baffled themselves—by the demands of their own disabled children's care and training—to reach out to help other parents? Some never had the opportunity to share with another parent who really understood the trauma surrounding their child's diagnosis, and want to see that other new parents do not suffer alone. The parent who did have an empathetic listener, wants to pass on that support by being available to another new parent.

Some of the helping parents feel as though their own pain and difficulties during the early adjustment to their child's special needs can be used constructively by sharing their experience and skills with another parent. Or, perhaps a parent who is going through a particularly difficult time him or herself feels a need to be of service in some way, while receiving help from others. The helping parents have found that they function better when they are not only receiving, but also are giving.

Potential helping parents are required to apply for the job by completing a questionnaire that reflects their attitudes and feelings toward their role as the parent of a disabled child. An interview with the coordinator follows to insure that they understand the program and that it is the right time for them to undertake this project. They must complete the entire eighteen hours of training, and any missed sessions must be made up. Each helping parent makes a commitment to be available to work with new parents, and to attend the monthly support group meetings for one year. After that, the agreement may be renewed.

Sometimes there is a problem in attendance of the monthly meetings, particularly for those who have been involved for over a year as helping parents. That issue has been addressed by trying to give parents a more active role in determining the make-up of the program.

A contract report is required every month for each match, to keep track of the total volunteer hours given to the program. Also, helping parents report to the coordinator any travel and telephone expenses they incur. The program reimburses them for long-distance phone calls and mileage necessary for contacting the new parents.

Once they have decided to volunteer their time and talents to Parent-to-Parent Support, participating in this program offers many rewards—the communication skills they learn and practice are useful in other relationships as well. Those involved have found their lives enhanced by the skills learned in their training. The monthly support group meeting is a time to learn more about helping the new parents, as well as to become better acquainted and build friendships with one another. While improving skills, they also share successes and problems with peers who can listen with empathy to them, laugh with, and encourage them. Most of all, the personal satisfaction of being there with something to offer when somebody needs you provides the incentive for helping parents to say "Yes," when the coordinator calls to offer a new referral.

How Matches Work

When matching a new parent with a helping parent, the coordinator considers several questions. What are the special needs of the new parent? What is the disability and how severe is it? What are the strengths of the helping parent? Where do the two families live?

Matches do not always work, especially when new parents are in need of professional help. Marital problems stemming from the stress of having a disabled child, or child abuse are two critical areas in which helping parents defer to those more qualified. It is important that a helping parent have the skills to recognize when it appears that a match is not working, either for them or the new parent.

Once a match is arranged, the helping parent contacts the new parents within seventy-two hours to introduce herself and to set a time and place for their first face-to-face meeting. The helping parent then reports back to the coordinator, and together they plan for continuing contacts.

In building a relationship, helping parents take responsibility for being non-judgmental and non-critical. They are concerned primarily with the family's adjustment to its child's needs and with obtaining services. Except for suggesting specific resources, such as books to read and services in the community, helping parents do not give advice or try to instruct new parents. However, sometimes they do refer parents to counseling if they seem to have problems beyond the scope of the helping parents' expertise. Helping parents are not therapists. Being able to say, "I know what you're going through," is their main strength.

Someone to Talk To

This was the kind of help Myrtie needed when her three month old son, Kile, was diagnosed as having cerebral palsy. Myrtie tried unsuccessfully for several days to find someone who could understand what she was going through. Myrtie finally dialed the operator. "Who can I call?" she asked in desperation, explaining that she had just found out that her baby had cerebral palsy and needed to talk with someone who knew what that was like.

The operator spent twenty minutes on the phone with Myrtie and finally looked under new listings. There was Parent-to-Parent Support's new phone number. Myrtie called immediately and talked with the program coordinator, who listened to her concerns and promised that another parent would call her soon.

A couple of nights later, Myrtie's phone rang, and a man introduced himself as Bob, a parent of a child with cerebral palsy. He let Myrtie ramble on, asking question after question, sensing that Myrtie needed to vent her emotions. Bob did not start answering her questions right away, he just listened.

Some of Myrtie's questions reflected her concern for the future. "Will Kile be able to play or go to normal school? What are we going to do? Is this going to get worse? Will Kile even survive? What will he be like as an adult?"

When Bob began sharing some of his experiences with Myrtie, he had empathy, yet he was honest about what he did not know. These two qualities gained Myrtie's trust and confidence. Myrtie was relieved to talk to someone with experience comparable to hers, who was able to clarify certain concerns that she had.

Myrtie had felt hurt by the rejection of strangers in banks and stores resulting from Kile's frequent vomiting. Bob had a good answer for that. "Those people have not walked a mile in your shoes. If they don't understand the situation, it's their problem, not yours. Take one thing at a time, one day at a time." Bob told Myrtie about resources for evaluation and treatment at the University of Washington's Child Development Center. He described speech, physical, and occupational therapy, and gave her the names of two developmental preschools for babies like Kile.

Finally, after midnight, they finished talking. For the first time since Kile's diagnosis, Myrtie sat back in a chair and relaxed. Bob's phone call was a turning point for her; it had given her hope. "No matter what happens, we can handle it," she thought. Now that she knew someone who had successfully put problems similar to hers in perspective, she felt she could too. She no longer felt alone.

Most matches continue for several months. When a network of continuing support for the family has developed in their community, the formal match may stop. Many families keep in touch, though, because they have become close friends. The experience helps new parents gain confidence and adjust to life with their disabled child, while the helping parent grows from meeting a need that might otherwise have gone unmet. In the process, each parent gains something valuable.

Conclusion

As a service to professionals in the community, Parent-to-Parent Support offers speakers and information programs to various agencies, clinics, and hospitals—wherever professionals working with families of children with developmental disabilities want to understand more clearly the needs of parents of newly-diagnosed children. These parents experience many feelings, such as shock, grief, and helplessness, that they may need to share. The services offered by Parent-to-Parent Support can ease the burden felt by many professionals when a new parent needs someone who can take time just to listen.

Referrals continue to come from nurses and physicians, as well as from friends, the parents themselves, and various professionals within King County. In the first two years of operation, the program served 127 families, and trained 69 helping parents, who volunteered 5,140 hours of their time. In fact, the program has been so successful that other counties have asked for assistance, and have started similar parent support groups. ∎

Sue Scott is currently a senior in the School of Occupational Therapy at the University of Washington. She is active in the Parent-to-Parent support program. Mrs. Scott lives in Bellevue, Washington with her husband, Bob, and their children, Robert and Shari.

Phyllis Doyle lives in Seattle, Washington, and is a Doctoral Candidate in Early Childhood Special Education at the University of Washington. She is a member of the Volunteer Advocates for Retarded Citizens in Seattle.

CHAPTER 5

Helping Our Children Accept Themselves

by Mae Gamble

It was eight years ago when my husband, William, and I learned that our youngest son, Jesse, had muscular dystrophy. For the first few months we were dazed with confusion and ignorance. We knew that he did not look like "Jerry's kids" whom we had seen on the Labor Day Weekend Telethon, and we realized that we knew very little about muscular dystrophy.

After the shock wore off, we began the process of learning everything that we could find out about the disease. We visited medical doctors, read books and pamphlets, and learned that our son probably had the Becker variation—a muscle disease that affects all the muscles in a progessive manner. This form of muscular dystrophy progresses more slowly than the most common type.

After the facts of the disease became clear, Will and I went through a period of vacillating between grief and denial. We spent many nights crying and holding on to each other, feeling completely helpless. At other times, we refused to acknowledge that Jesse had muscular dystrophy, hoping that if we did not give it a name, it might go away. Why think about it since nothing could be done anyway?

As the years passed and Jesse's condition worsened, our denial could no longer prevail. It was replaced with anger. Will and I were angry with the medical profession that they had not found a cure. We were angry with all the well-meaning friends whose heartfelt wishes did nothing to make the disease go away. We were angry with the other friends who only acknowledged Jesse's condition by uneasy blanks in the conversation, not knowing how to talk about it. And yes, we were angry with all the able-bodied children we saw. Why was it our son and not them?

Adjusting

Eventually, the anger wore itself away like a sand storm in the desert. Then the weary, calm acceptance set in. We started to feel lucky that the form of muscular dystrophy that Jesse had was extremely slow in progressing. He would live a long life, though much of it would be spent in a wheelchair.

Our family moved from a duplex apartment to a simplex, and planned our new home so that everything was accessible by wheelchair. We subscribed to magazines for disabled people and joined activist groups. My husband and I observed that our grief and anger had dissipated. Instead, we had started to accept the fact that Jesse was physically disabled, and worked at making his life as rich as possible.

Jesse's Feelings

Jesse was not feeling as accepting as we were. He was not interested in reading magazines on independent living or attending meetings of the Muscular Dystrophy Association. He was still denying that he had muscular dystrophy—even to himself.

We became very concerned. With his denial came a refusal to do exercises or anything else that might help slow down the disease. It also meant that Jesse started hiding from others. When his walking became difficult and different, he would walk only when no one was watching. Eventually he stopped going out, refused to go to school, and insisted on home instruction. When a wheelchair became convenient for in-home use, Jesse began using it, but would stay in his room if someone were visiting. If he heard a visitor coming and could not get to his room, he would fall off the wheelchair, throw a cover on it, and pretend to be doing something on the floor.

Naturally, my husband and I were very upset. It was bad enough that Jesse was losing muscle strength and ability. It was far more serious, though, if he were to become a recluse because of his disability. But, what could we do? How could we help Jesse accept his disease? Before you can fight something, you must acknowledge that you have it— and Jesse was doing neither.   Jesse was ashamed of his disability.

We knew that the attitudes of society toward people with disabilities left much to be desired. Jesse was part of that society, and consequently, held the same attitudes. He thought that to be physically disabled meant to be ugly, deformed, and not "normal." Jesse also believed that a person with disabilities was naive, incompetent, unsophisticated, and to be pitied. Naturally, he did not want to be a part of *that* group.

The Family's Attitudes
What were the attitudes in our home? Had the attitudes of the family been the same as that of society? We thought back over the years. In so doing, we discovered that there were many actions taken and words spoken which communicated that to be disabled with muscular dystrophy was to be avoided at all costs. The following are some examples:

We first learned that Jesse had muscular dystrophy when he was ten years old. It was over two years later before we told him that he had the disease. We were being protective of his feelings. He was so young. How could he handle it? The underlying assumption of our behavior was that having muscular dystrophy was a fate too terrible to think about when you are ten years old.

*We went to every kind of doctor and healer imaginable. Jesse visited a chiropractor two or three times a week. For two years he had acupuncture treatment once a week. We visited a nutritionist who put him on a mega-vitamin program. We also went to a psychic healer for a three month period.

We saw psychiatrists, psychologists, and social workers individually and as a part of groups. We tried everything and spent thousands of dollars attempting to fight off the disease.

It is natural and right that people fight illness and disease, but we were hysterical in the way that we approached it. Again, the underlying assumption of our behavior was that muscular dystrophy is something so terrible we were willing to spend countless hours of time and thousands of dollars to fight it. Imagine how frightened Jesse became as he observed our behavior and did not even know the real cause of his walking difficulties.

*We started treating Jesse differently from the other two children. If the children came in too late or did not do their homework, the usual punishment was that they had to stay in their room and not see their friends. Not for Jesse. No matter what rule he broke, he was allowed to go out and have friends in. We believed that someday our son would not have friends, would not be able to go out, and that his social life would be limited. Having muscular dystrophy meant that Jesse would become isolated and friendless sometime in the future. How could we deprive him of such experiences now? Although we did not state those beliefs outright, our behavior communicated them to Jesse, and he believed us.

*We kept Jesse from learning anything about the disease. Even after we finally told him that he had muscular dystrophy, we continued to hide the most painful facts. We avoided going to any meetings or places where we might meet someone with the disease. We insisted he stay in the mainstream of the school system. He never went to a party, summer camp, or any event sponsored by the Muscular Dystrophy Association. We even managed to keep the family busy on Labor Day so none of us, especially Jesse, could watch the Jerry Lewis Telethon.

Evaluating Our Actions
As we analyzed our actions we saw that we were giving out many messages, and all of them said that the disease was something to be dreaded and avoided at all costs. If the disease could not be avoided, it should be put "out of mind," because the truth was too painful. Is it any wonder, therefore, that Jesse was still denying that he had muscular dystrophy? He was terrified because we were terrified. And worse than that, we were robbing him of experiences which would help him learn to accept the disease and live with it.

Jesse's feelings have changed with the passage of time. It has been a slow, difficult and painful process, but the denial is being replaced with acceptance. There is a definite improvement in Jesse's attitude, and there is less rebellion, anger and depression. The changes came about somewhat naturally, yet there were specific actions taken that caused all of our attitudes to improve.

Changing and Confronting
We told Jesse everything we knew about muscular dystrophy. We brought pamphlets, magazines and books into the home and left them where he could read them if he wanted. We asked doctors to explain everything to Jesse. When they would start to talk about him, we would include Jesse in the conversation.

As Jesse learned about the disease and its many varieties, he became less afraid and more realistic. There was information that made him sad, and he cried sometimes. Some information made him feel fortunate. The more Jesse learned, the less anxious he became. A known condition, no matter how difficult, is less frightening than an unknown.

We found other parents who had children with muscular dystrophy and met with them on a regular basis. This told us more about the disease than any book, doctor, or social worker we had previously encountered. Parents live with the disease on a day to day basis. They can discuss the inconveniences, the problems with school, the difficulty of transportation, and other issues concerning living with a child who has muscular dystrophy. They can also tell about solutions, successes, and achievements.

The more we learned, the less terrified we felt. Muscular dystrophy was no longer a dreaded disease to be avoided at all costs. It was a disease that caused physical dysfunction, but people afflicted with it could still live very full lives. Our change in attitude was communicated to our son in both our words and in our behavior. We became more relaxed, and so did Jesse.

Another action that helped Jesse to accept the disease was getting him to meet other people with muscular dystrophy and other physical disorders. This was very difficult to accomplish. Jesse wanted no part of it. He did not want to be physically disabled, and did not want to associate with people who were. We used bribes, threats, punishment, and cajolery, but we could not get him to attend a social event or meeting where he might meet other children in the same or similar circumstances. Although he attended school with disabled children, he always remained aloof and uninvolved.

Last year, after surgery to correct deformities in his legs, Jesse spent four months in treatment at the Institute of Rehabilitation Medicine in New York City. He met children with spinal cord injuries, spina bifida, cerebral palsy, and others. Since he was confined to the hospital, he was forced to interact. And he did. With interaction, there came increased knowledge and acceptance—acceptance of other people with disabilities, followed by increased acceptance of himself. Jesse began to realize that a person with a disability is a person first. Realizing this, his disability became less important.

Some of the young people he met were large, some were small, some were emotional, others were cold. He developed close ties with some, and had little in common with others. Jesse's attitudes changed. The physically disabled were no longer naive, ugly, and to be pitied. They were human beings who happened to have a physical dysfunction.

Treating Jesse as a capable, independent, responsible person who could take care of himself was another action that helped our son accept his disabilities. We were very over-protective of Jesse in our rush to protect him from the disease with which he was born. We watched him carefully, trying to avoid any unpleasantness or difficulty. If he had not done his homework, or was afraid of another child in his class, he was allowed to stay home from school. If a task was too hard for him, we did it. He was given no responsibilities at home. The other children washed dishes, emptied garbage, or did other household chores. Jesse was "excused."

While on the one hand we allowed him to avoid any difficult or unpleasant task and gave in to his weakest tendencies, we gave him absolutely no say in the important decisions of his life. My husband and I picked his doctors, his school, and his treatment. He could not be trusted—even though he was growing up into an adult—to make choices, since his disease was so serious.

Letting Jesse Decide For Himself

Naturally, we had great difficulties. Jesse started to rebel against all decisions we made, even if he hurt himself in the process. Like all adolescents, his own independence was the most important condition of his life. In asserting that independence, he had to reject our suggestions, even if he knew rationally that they were good ones.

We had no choice but to allow him to make his own decisions, even if we thought they were wrong. This was the only way he could learn. Trying to "soften" the blows of life through our over-protective behavior was robbing our son of valuable learning experiences, and making him feel weak and incompetent. His rebellious behavior let us know that he was not a baby that needed to be protected and advised. He was a responsible, mature, and capable person with health problems.

When decisions had to be made regarding health care or school, he could make them. We allowed Jesse to pick the wheelchair he wanted. We encouraged him to talk to the doctors and make decisions about health care. He decided where he would complete high school.

Jesse became responsible for *all* his actions, even the negative ones. If he threw something in the middle of a temper tantrum, he was sent to his room. His behavior was no longer excused because of his "condition." This, of course, had a positive effect on the whole family.

Results

Just because Jesse has a physical weakness does not mean that he is emotionally weak, unable to control his behavior, or unable to make decisions for himself. As we have changed and expected more from our son, he has shown that he is much more capable than we realized. He is strong enough to handle his health problems. The problems are not larger than he is. And if he is strong enough to handle difficulties, there is no need to hide from them.

Fortunately, we learned a great deal over the years. The staff at the Rehabilitation Institute, other parents, our children, and Jesse himself taught us to accept the disease as a fact of life. Jesse is also growing in his acceptance of the disorder. He is insecure at times. He wishes he did not have muscular dystrophy, and has a difficult time watching himself lose ability. In spite of all that, we believe now that he can "make it," that he can live a complete, full life. And that is really what we care about for all our children. ■

CHAPTER 6

SOCIAL SKILLS AND THE DISABLED CHILD

by Ellen Kahan

During my early teaching days, I had a wonderful teenage girl in my class named Donna. She was friendly and pleasant, a willing worker, and one of the most responsible adolescents I had ever met. Donna was only moderately mentally retarded; but, unfortunately, she "looked" retarded. Her appearance created negative reactions and closed many doors to her. One day, this became clear to me.

Donna had been trained to work as a messenger. Her first real job experience was to be in the county hospital. We talked at length regarding the potentially disturbing things she might see within the hospital corridors. People on gurneys, in wheelchairs, injured or crying must all be treated with respect and without curiosity by her.

On the first day at work, Donna was perfect. I trailed her as she made her rounds through the hospital. Not once did she stare or react negatively to anything she saw. At the end of the day, heady with pride for a job well done, we started back to school. As we were leaving by the elevator, Donna crossed to the other side to push the button for the first floor. Somewhere along the way, we stopped and picked up a very rude woman who was a hospital employee. She did not see that Donna and I were together so my prescence did not restrain her from staring at Donna until we escaped on the first floor.

Donna's pride for a job well done was gone. She was completely demoralized by this woman's behavior. I was furious. All the careful teaching I had done with Donna to make her behavior irreproachable did not protect her from being the target of the unkindness of others.

Better Than Anyone Else

Now, many years later, I have a beautiful stepdaughter. Laurie is friendly, kind, outgoing, loving almost to a fault, and cares for everyone. But she does not look quite "right" to most people which makes her the recipient of both subtle and direct cruelties.

A regular 5th grader, Laurie has neurofibromatosis which for her means orthopedic abnormalities, an asymmetric face, and speech and coordination problems. Laurie needs to be better than everyone else. Because of her appearance, small things can cause her to be the recipient of name calling, cruel glances, and outright teasing. When she carries herself with pride and when her appearance and manners are impeccable, her peers treat her well and adults admire her.

It hardly seems fair that she should have to work so hard to be accepted. Some people would say that the reactions and opinions of others are of no concern. That may be true for the rare child who has a skin of iron and enough self-confidence to get through any adversity. Laurie does not. Most handicapped children do not; many crave language problems, were the constant cause of negative attention.

You and Your Child

Look carefully at your child's clothing and compare it to the clothing of his or her classmates. Does this clothing help your child blend with the peer group or does it attract attention?

Look also at the way he or she walks and stands. Sometimes posture and walking are affected by the disability itself; but sometimes immaturity or lack of social awareness causes walking habits to carry over from childhood into adolescence.

Observe the gait and posture of your child with an open mind. Is there anything which attracts attention and can be corrected? If you alone purchase their clothes, pick out what they wear, or permit them to wear any old outfit they choose, you are missing a valuabe participatory learning opportunity. Take your child out to buy clothes and talk abut what to pick and why. Provide guidance so they develop the skills to make good decisions for themselves. When your child puts on something completely inappropriate to wear to school, gently tell them why it does not work and help them correct the problem.

Changing Behavior

I wish it were not true but many people are uncomfortable around children with disabilities. This discomfort can cause misplaced pity or even anger and an over-reaction to your child or mine in a public setting.

It is easy within your home to become used to a

19

child's voice or a laugh that may be too loud, or immature. In public, this same voice may attract attention to your child. People stare and start talking about "what's wrong with that child." Even when you may not be able to hear their unkind words, your child may sense the unkind feelings.

Help your child avoid these unhappy situations by being sure his or her voice, table manners, laughter and other social behaviors do not attract negative attention. Many children with learning disabilities have difficulty acquiring the good manners and social skills they need without specific teaching from you. All children benefit from having good manners and social graces taught to them as they grow up. For the special child, it is much, much more significant because these behaviors help acceptance. As parents we do not need to protect them from everything, but there are some practical efforts that can be helpful.

Clothing

We all know that adolescents are "into" clothes and labels. The Calvin Klein jeans or the Nike sneakers can go an amazingly long way in attaining acceptance and popularity for a child among his or her peers. Several research studies show that teachers also judge children by the way they dress and their appearance. Accordingly, clothes that are flattering, age appropriate, and perhaps even "in" are important for the special child. Clothes that draw attention to a physical abnormality, make a child appear immature, or are worn looking should be discarded.

Children's clothes are expensive and the undue importance placed on brand names may irritate you as much as it does me, but others think it is important. The great plus is that it encourages acceptance as "one of the gang". Help your child to learn what looks best on him or her. Give advice on which colors, styles or even fabrics are most flattering. Provide a full length mirror to assess his or her appearance each morning and to spot the more subtle dressing problems or overall neatness, length of pants, a color combination that is not quite right, etc.

Inappropriate Attire

Cathy's mother obviously focused a great deal of attention on the clothes her twelve year old learning disabled daughter wore. They were perfectly coordinated, the latest fashion and very attractive, but they were still not appropriate. The clothing Cathy's mother had selected were too tight and better suited to a sixteen year old. It made Cathy the focus of sexual attention and remarks from older boys. Her clothing conveyed a message that created situations this young girl could not completely understand nor react to appropriately.

Daryl, a young student with learning disablities, was very bright and capable. His use of language and the difficulties he had processing what others said to him sometimes set him apart from his fellows, but the problem that truly disrupted his peer relations was his appearance. Everything he wore was one size too small—as if he had outgrown it the year before. His too tight pants always showed three inches of white socks as the pant legs ended above his ankles. The other kids constantly teased him about his "highwater pants", teasing about "when the tide was coming in." Each year, teachers tried to help Daryl with his personal appearance but the problem rested at home. The only resolution possible came when Daryl's parents helped him buy more appropriate clothing. Until then his appearance, not his them to move into society without ridicule or rejection.

Experience is the best way to teach your child the skills they need to acquire. Provide opportunities to practice manners and social skills. Being taken to dinner, to the movies or a museum can be a very positive and enjoyable learning situation for your child. They do not have to know the outing has other purposes than just recreation but you can use these times to gently guide them and modify their behaviors.

Teachers Can Help

Sometimes it may help to seek advice from your child's teachers. We become so used to our children and so blinded by our love for them that we may not see them as others do. Ask the teacher if there are habits or behaviors that draw attention to your child.

Listen carefully to what they say for they have the benefit of seeing your child daily in his or her interactions with peers. They will know if certain habits of your child are creating unpleasant situations of teasing or rejection among peers. These behaviors can be worked on at home as well as at school.

Teachers are also in the position of viewing your child with far less emotional involvement than you. Their assessment may be more realistic than yours and very valuable.

It Is Unfair

It is unfair that our disabled children should have to "go the extra mile" to be accepted. It is unfair, but it is reality. The special training we provide them in their social development may be even more important to a happy well adjusted childhood and adult life than all that emphasis on reading, writing, and arithmetic.

Keep the doors of life open to your child by providing him or her with the skills to walk through them with grace and dignity. ■

CHAPTER 7

Shawntell and Tanya
A STORY OF FRIENDSHIP

by Jeffrey and Cindy Strully

This is a story of friendship between two girls who care about each other very much. The children view each other as important people, and see themselves as a part of one another's lives. What makes this story a little different is that one of the children has developmental special needs. We need to start realizing that children who are "typical" and those with special needs *do* want to share their lives in bonds of friendship with one another.

Shawntell

Our daughter, Shawntell, is almost twelve years old. She is a beautiful young lady who enjoys swimming, playing video games, watching movies, listening to records, watching television, and playing with her friends.

Shawntell also happens to be disabled. She has learned many new skills over the last few years. She is now able to walk for short distances with no external supports. Shawntell has a small vocabulary that includes, "yes," "no," "daddy," and "hi," and she also makes her needs known through body language.

For the last five years, Shawntell has attended the local, neighborhood elementary school. She has spent part of her time in a class for children with severe and profound challenges in learning. Shawntell has also spent part of the day with "normal" children learning skills that will help her to live and participate in the local community. Shawntell is a very friendly child who enjoys life and the people with whom she comes in contact.

Of course, Shawntell has her mom and dad who care about her and love her very much. She also has a brother and sister who feel the same way. In addition to her family, we hope that she has a circle of people who will be there to help her, love her, and assist her to participate in the community throughout her life. We hope that people will want to be involved with Shawntell because they care about her. We do not want professional human service workers to be the only relationships that she has.

Forming Friendships

It is sad to see people with or without developmental special needs who have no friends or family to care about them except those who are paid to perform that work. Have you ever thought about what your life would be like if the only people who would interact with you were paid to do so? I doubt if any of us would feel good about ourselves if that were the case. We want ordinary people to share their lives with Shawntell.

There are no easy answers or short-cuts to building friendships. It is hard work with many pitfalls, but there is nothing in this world that is more important. Just because someone has labeled Shawntell "severely mentally retarded" does not mean that we do not want the same things for her as any other parents. We want our daughter to experience the same joys and wonders that all children experience as they grow up—to go to parties, have friends, travel, learn new things, interact with all types of people and enjoy life to its fullest. Parents need to believe that friendships are something that are worth encouraging, working on, and striving to achieve. Though there is always the risk of rejection or that a relationship will end, trying to develop relationships is worth the risk.

Because Shawntell attended the neighborhood elementary school, rode the regular school bus, and participated in the local neighborhood activities, she met and started to become friends with a host of typical children.

Shawntell met Tanya two years ago at their school. They met as a result of Shawntell's teacher who has worked to integrate the children in her class into the regular education environment via a buddy program.

Children volunteer their time to work with Shawntell and the other kids in her class. They not only assist Shawntell and her classmates in learning new skills and competencies, but started to develop friendships—first in school and then later back in their neighborhoods. Over a few years, a number of children have started to form relationships with Shawntell outside of the school environment.

Tanya, a Close Friend

Tanya has become a close friend to Shawntell. We believe their story provides a vision on which to build a better community for all of us.

Tanya was ten years old and in fifth grade when she first met Shawntell. She is now twelve years old and has finished her first year in middle school. Tanya is a bright, articulate, attractive young lady who is interested in children (she babysits to earn money), animals (she wants to work with them when she finishes school), swimming, cute boys, parties, horseback riding, music, and a whole lot more. Tanya is a sensitive, caring person raised to respect and care about people.

Over the last two years, the girls have grown closer and closer. Their relationship, which started in the buddy program, has become just like any other good friendship between two girls. There has been a growing understanding and respect on both their parts as they learn more about each other. This has taken time and is a continuing process. The girls see each other often and enjoy their friendship. They do many things that are typical of children who are twelve years old— going to the movies, buying records, watching television, listening to music, and playing video games.

Vacation Trip Together

When school let out this past year, my wife and I decided to take our family on a summer vacation to Hilton Head. We knew that Shawntell would want to take Tanya with her on vacation. Tanya was really excited, not only to go on vacation, but to spend time with Shawntell. This was the very first time that the girls spent eight days and nights together in very close proximity.

The trip was great! The girls got along very well and enjoyed each other. They had fun swimming in the pool and ocean, and taking hikes on the beach at night. They even played miniature golf together where Tanya not only beat Shawntell, but her parents as well. We will never live that down. Friendship is sharing experiences together and making each other happy.

At a restaurant one evening, Shawntell and Tanya both located a young bus boy who they described as "real cute." Shawntell would follow him around watching his every move. She would get very excited at the sight of him coming around. Then Tanya joined in with Shawntell discussing their prospects of luring him. The two of them "talked" endlessly about this "cute guy." Friendships are like that—sharing private moments that only you and your friend can really appreciate.

We invited Tanya on vacation with us because we knew that Shawntell would want her to come with us, and we knew that Tanya would enjoy being with Shawntell. Friends like to spend time with each other. Parents of children with developmental special needs can help facilitate these interactions. Because Shawntell does not communicate very well, we have to think about what she would really want, and then help to initiate that action.

Messages for the Community

We need to work continually to enhance Shawntell's status and perceived value in the community. We do this by developing situations and activities that will increase the community's awareness of Shawntell and help others to see her as a member of the community.

One powerful message for the community is when a friend who is viewed as competent, valuable, and attractive is seen with Shawntell— walking down the street, going swimming, or going to the movies. Tanya can do something that her parents will never be able to do. She can say to the community, "This is my friend." How wonderful and beautiful that is. That message needs to be

---

Just because someone has labeled Shawntell "severely mentally retarded" does not mean that we do not want the same things for her as any other parents.

---

heard over and over again until it is a commonplace occurrence.

Shawntell needs to have a wide range of experiences that will enable her to live a full life in her community. In addition, if we are ever going to change people's behavior and attitudes, all our children need to learn from one another. This will never take place if we continue to separate, isolate, and prevent our children from being together. Perhaps it is not children who are scared of children with developmental special needs, but adults.

Many of us have never had the experience or opportunity to know a person who was perceived as different from us. However, our children can have these experiences. They can learn in the same schools, ride the same buses, go to the same parks, and enjoy life in a truly integrated community—if we give them the chance. We must all work towards having all children live, learn, and play together.

Tanya does not fully comprehend the significant influence she is making in the life of another person. More importantly, she is making a significant statement to the people of our community about the worth of another person—her friend, Shawntell. In her own way, she is making a contribution that is more important than all of the teaching that goes on in our school system and all of the contributions that paid human service professionals could ever make.

Sometimes we wonder if Tanya thinks we are making too much of this relationship. Why do we write and talk about it? We have tried to explain that the relationship Tanya has with Shawntell should be a very commonplace occurence that we all take for granted. Unfortunately, it is not. In many cases, children with developmental special needs have not had the opportunity to attend the local neighborhood school, live in the local community, and participate in community life. We believe that until all our children can learn together, our communities will not reach their fullest potential. So until that happens, Shawntell and Tanya's relationship will be viewed as something special—at least to us.

What Does the Future Hold?

What does the future hold for Tanya and Shawntell? Tanya is twelve years old. Over the next few years, she will be involved in many new experiences that will probably change her life. She will become more involved with boys, school, parties, other friends, and many new dreams and exciting adventures.

We believe that Shawntell will continue to have a place in Tanya's life. We know that Tanya has a place in Shawntell's life. The future for these girls can include a continued relationship that will only blossom and grow as time goes by.

Double dating may be a possibility in the future for our daughter and her friend. Just because Shawntell has some learning challenges and may never be able to do exactly the same thing as everyone else does not mean that she should live a separate life. Surely, this would require acceptance, adaptation, and support in order for Shawntell to participate in such events, not only on her parents' part, but from her friends as well. It would also require a strong and open support on Tanya's part. She will need to be able to stand up to peer pressure and proclaim to her other friends that Shawntell is her friend and has a place among them. Whether this will happen, we cannot tell. We believe that it is possible.

But why shouldn't Shawntell be involved in these activities? Don't we want all our children to experience life to its fullest even if there are hard times, risks, and possible failures?

Although Shawntell risks rejection or ridicule, life without risk is not life at all. Until an individual experiences some of those risks and takes some chances, he or she will never experience life to its fullest.

Children Are Caring

We think Tanya is an exceptional child, unique and one of a kind. She has been brought up to care about all people and to respect differences. She appreciates the unique gifts that each of us has to contribute to our communities.

Shawntell is also an exceptional child who is unique and one of a kind. However, is this not true of all our children? Each of them has his or her own unique qualities. This is the wonder and beauty of children. We would not want either Tanya or Shawntell to be anyone other than themselves.

There are a lot of children out there who, if supported, encouraged, and given the opportunity to interact with children with developmental special needs would do so. Until that is achieved, we will continue to perpetuate a separate mentality.

Children are not brought into this world disliking others that are different. They are not mean, nasty savages who are out to get your child because he or she is not exactly like them. Of course, there are some children—as there are some adults—who are not very nice to be around, but they are such a small group. The vast majority of children are caring, concerned people who, if given the right opportunities, would do the right thing.

A Lesson For Adults

The future is a scary and wonderous place, not only for Tanya and Shawntell, but for us. We will face the future with the firm belief that our daughter and her friend will make a difference in the way we care about and support one another. The girls have shown us more about what is important than all of the textbooks, professionals, research studies, and resources put together.

We believe that the girls have said to all of us, "You adults are really very silly, prejudiced, and narrow in what you think. We want to be friends. We don't understand why people make a big deal about two girls being friends. We accept each other for who we are and not for who others want us to be."

Tanya and Shawntell seem to understand and to know what is ultimately important. They know that people are people whether they can talk a mile a minute or not at all, or whether they have many competencies or very few. Their message is powerful and important for all of us. Maybe if we started treating all people the way these girls treat each other, our local community would be a better place for all of us. ■

Jeffrey and Cindy Strully live in Louisville Kentucky with their three children, Alex, Shawntell, and Sonja. They are both active in many community organizations—The Association for Persons with Severe Handicaps, the Council for Retarded Citizens, etc.

CHAPTER 8

Fostering Healthy Self Esteem

by Harilyn Rousso

Self-esteem is the pleasure, pride, and respect people have about their bodies, their selves and their lives. The issues of self-esteem for people with congenital disabilities (disabilities occurring at birth): such as cerebral palsy, spina bifida and a variety of other disabilities involving differently shaped and functioning body parts and limbs, are quite different from those of people who become disabled at some later point in their lives.

I do not think this distinction is always well-enough understood or appreciated. Using my personal perspective as a congenitally disabled woman, and my professional perspective as a psychotherapist, I would like to help clarify it.

Growing Up

In some ways, I grew up on the margin between the nondisabled and disabled world, or, using societal terms, between normality and abnormality. Although I had a physical disability from birth, cerebral palsy from insufficient oxygen during a delayed delivery, and always made needed accommodations to my limitations, I lived, went to school and played exclusively in a nondisabled world. I attended regular schools, had only nondisabled friends, and never actually knew another disabled person until my mid-twenties.

The specialist who diagnosed my disability at long last, when I was two, set the stage. He told my mother that I indeed had a disability, cerebral palsy, but, I was very smart. He warned her to keep me away from other disabled children and "raise me like a normal child."

My family and I followed his advice well. To some extent it was advantageous—schools and services are usually better for nondisabled than disabled children. But there were consequences. My parents and I never discussed my disability or how it might affect my future. Their silence caused me confusion and became a confirmation of the worst societal stereotypes about disabled people. So I learned to deny and pass, rather than integrate my disability into my life.

One aspect of my experience seems like a contradiction to all this denial and passing—an aspect which I did not come to understand until much later. My mother was quite concerned about the awkwardness of my walk—not only did it periodically cause me to fall but it made me stand out, appear conspicuously different—which she feared would subject me to endless teasing and rejection. To some extent it did. She made numerous attempts over the years of my childhood to have me go for physical therapy and to practice walking more "normally" at home. I vehemently refused all her efforts. She could not understand why I would not walk straight.

Now I realize why. My disability, with my different walk and talk and my involuntary movements, having been with me all of my life, was part of me, part of my identity. With these disability features, I felt complete and whole. My mother's attempt to change my walk, strange as it may seem, felt like an assault on myself, an incomplete acceptance of all of me, an attempt to make me over. I fought it because I wanted to be accepted and appreciated as I was. Teasing was painful, but not nearly as painful as losing a part of myself. I suspect that my mother then and perhaps even now has difficulty understanding my perspective, and not because she was uncaring. Rather, from a nondisabled perspective, . . . it is hard to realize or to believe that a disability, which seems like a liability, a defect, an eyesore, could be an okay, important part of a child's body and self. It is not that I would choose to be disabled, if one could do such a thing, but rather my disability, like other salient characteristics I was born with, is part of me.

Out of the Closet

It was not until my late 20's that I was able to "come out of the closet" as a disabled person in a direct way. Not only did this free up a lot of energy which I had used in passing, but it was an important, integrating experience—a matter of reclaiming a part of myself which I had disavowed.

I had learned in childhood to deny my disability, but not, I do not think, because I could not tolerate the limitations or the unique features involved—as I said, the latter were part of me. Rather, I think, I denied my disability because I could not accept society's definition of me as a freak, an inferior person. It seemed at that time that the only way to get around the freakish definition was to deny that part of myself which society viewed as freakish.

This story provides a sense of the dilemma facing congenitally disabled people. Internally, they feel okay and complete, disability and all. Yet, to the external world, often even to parents, they are perceived as defective, incomplete.

Remember the diagnosing doctor's words: "She's disabled but smart," as though the two descriptions do not usually go together. "Keep her away from other disabled children," as though disabled children are contagious and subhuman.

Somehow, congenitally disabled people must balance these two very divergent views of themselves while keeping both in mind, for both are part of their reality. Parents and professionals can either by very helpful in the balancing act or they can add to the difficulties inherent in the situation. They can be helpful if they can acknowledge and understand both sides of the balance, particularly that experience of intactness which I began to describe, an experience which is the core of positive self-esteem but is too often overlooked.

Elaborating the Dilemma

To repeat, congenitally disabled people are unique among the disabled population because they have never lived in a nondisabled body. Unlike the child or adult who becomes disabled after birth and thus experiences a loss or change in body part, functioning, or appearance requiring mourning and adjustment, the congenitally disabled person undergoes no such loss or change. Rather, the disability is an inherent part of the person's body and self. As such, like other salient body parts, the disability contributes to a sense of identity, is mourned if it is altered or removed, and is in need of acceptance, appreciation and affirmation from the environment.

While there is no precise way to prove this point, I hear it in the words of my congenitally disabled clients. A perky, school-aged girl with spina bifida expressed the sentiment nicely. I had asked her if she is disabled in her daydreams. "Of course," she explained, "in my daydreams, I'm me!" One young man, after a congenital tumor was removed, expressed his grief: "Something's missing, I'm not the same, a part of me is lost." Many of my congenitally disabled adult patients have expressed the sense of being truly understood and known when we talk about that notion of their intactness.

Body Image

Body image, the mental image we have of our bodies, is the cornerstone of any individual's identity and sense of self. Some people argue that people born with disabilities automatically have a defective body image and sense of self. But such a biological, "anatomy is destiny" viewpoint is narrow and limited, particularly in light of modern theories of development, which stress not the endowment of the child but rather the fit between the child and the environment, particularly mother, as most significant.

One of the earliest determinants of body image and sense of self is the child's own experience with his or her own body. Unless the disability causes considerable physical pain or severely limits self-exploration, there is no reason to assume that the infant disavows or distorts the disability in its earliest body image. The disabled or "defective" part is included in the body image but need not produce a defective image. At this early stage, the infant has not yet discovered that the disabled part is defective by external standards—the disability is just a part like any other part. From the infant's internal perspective, the body is intact and complete.

At some point, perhaps a little after one year of age, when children begin to notice and show interest in bodily differences, the disabled child will discover that his or her body is different from that of parents and siblings. This is not a one-time discovery with single meaning for the child. Rather like the discovery of genital differences, it is a discovery which the child keeps making at different ages, with different developmental meanings.

The child's assessment of difference at different ages and stages does not occur in a vacuum. Rather, it takes into account his or her perception of how parents and the environment perceive the difference. Indeed, theory and clinical studies tell us that one of the most important determinants of body image for any child is not the actual characteristics of the body but rather parental and cultural attitudes toward those characteristics.

Like little girls and children of racial minorities, at some points, disabled children inevitably discover that their difference, their different bodies—their disabled characteristics—are perceived by society as inferior. More so than the discovery of difference per se, this is the moment with the most potential for emotional trauma. Like any children subject to prejudice, the consequences depend largely on whether and how these children are helped to understand and deal with the negative societal view of them.

It may seem that I am minimizing the significance and impact of the physical limitations themselves on the emotional lives of disabled children. In part I am intending to do just that. I think we sometimes are too preoccupied with limitations in explaining problems in self-esteem. For example, although early Freudian theory told us that women grew up feeling inferior because they lacked a penis, we have fortunately come to appreciate that this is too simplistic a formulation in understanding female development. Similarly, it is too simplistic to say that disabled children inevitably feel inferior because they have physical differences and physical limitations.

Certainly, disabled children are likely to face frustrations and disappointments in their inability to accomplish certain tasks in the same manner as their nondisabled peers. How they handle these frustrations and whether they accept them as part of a negative self-image depends to a considerable extent on the reactions and responsiveness of their world. A young girl, who has never walked, rolls down the street in her wheelchair and the world stares, clucks and communicates through their looks that they view her life as a tragedy. As she is working and struggling in physical therapy to strengthen her muscles, her parents sit nearby, crying as they watch. Would not this girl's experience of not being able to walk, something she has never done in her life, be different if the world took a more neutral, less tragic stance?

Loving "Disabled Parts"

I want to return to the congenitally disabled child's initial experiences of intactness, completeness, because I believe it is so important. To sustain this feeling and have it grow and develop, disabled children need some nurturance from the outside world. In particular, disabled children need to have their bodies, disability and all, accepted, appreciated and loved, especially by significant parenting figures. This will solidify the sense of intactness.

For all children, disabled or not, the "gleam in the mother's eye" in response to all aspects of the child's body and self is essential for the development of healthy self-esteem. This includes the parent's ability to show pride and pleasure in the disabled part of the body, as one valid aspect of the child, and to communicate appreciation and respect for the child's unique, often different-looking ways of doing things. The result can be an environment which allows children to develop their potential and develop positive body and self-feelings. It makes children think: "Mother thinks I am great, so I must be."

Parents of congenitally disabled children may have difficulty loving the disabled parts of their child, often for many reasons. First, for them, the disabled body is not intact. Rather, it is a major loss from the hoped-for perfect child, a loss parents must mourn and come to terms with. Thus, right from birth, the parental perspective differs from that of the child. Also, it is helpful when parents see their own reflection in their child. However, with a disability, the child may look too different. As a result, a parent may seek to keep her distance or to find ways to alter or disregard the disability so that the child looks more like him or her.

In addition, the child's disability may have unique symbols for a parent, depending upon the parent's own sense of self. For guilt-ridden parents, it may seem like a punishment. Such symbolism can interfere with parenting. Furthermore, parents, socialized in this society, take on societal values. As was the case with my mother, it may be difficult for them to understand that a disabled body could be experienced by a child as intact when they have learned to view disability as a defect and a deviance. As a result of all these various reasons, parents too often communicate to their child, directly and indirectly, that the disability should be hidden or altered, if not purged—the child should strive toward appearing as "normal" and nondisabled as possible. This attitude can put the child into an identity crisis, causing him or her to push that feeling of intactness way underground.

However, I want to take parents off the hook if I can because we already blame them too much. In truth, I do not think the fault lies with them. The parents we see in our offices and agencies are by and large a committed group who would not wittingly hurt their children. They are often at a loss how to deal with not only their own pain, confusion and prejudices, but the cruelty and hostility of the outside world. Indeed, even when they are able to overcome their own issues and fully appreciate their child, they cannot always protect the child from taking in and accepting society's negative attitudes.

Parents need help in finding ways to explain prejudice to their children and to help their children distinguish physical facts about their disability from societal distortions about these facts. This is where professionals can play a crucial role.

Attitudes

Let me elaborate a bit more about societal attitudes. Throughout history, most cultures have put a high value on physical perfection—physical imperfection has often been equated with moral and intellectual imperfection. The Greek ideal of a sound mind in a sound body may be upheld today much as in antiquity. Research on the attitudes of nondisabled people toward the disabled reveals a preponderance of negative attitudes. These include that disability is punishment for sin, that it is contagious and that disabled people are sick, helpless, childlike, asexual and inherently socially and economically inferior. According to Goffman, disabled people are perceived as "not quite human." How can we explain these myths and stereotypes? Actually, we can understand them in various ways and on various levels.

In part, these attitudes reflect a lack of exposure to and realistic information about the lives of people with disabilities. Also, nondisabled people often use their own incomparable experiences with illness and temporary disability to make assumptions about the helplessness and dependency of disabled people. If a bad cold or broken arm renders nondisabled people miserable and immobilized, surely, they think, permanent impairments of movement or coordination must be impossible to overcome. Unfortunately, nondisabled people fail to appreciate the process of adaptation and creative problem-solving which can occur over time as the result of living with a disability. In addition, we must recognize that at the root of people's frightened and hostile feelings toward disability are their own unconscious anxieties regarding wholeness, perfection, loss and weakness, anxieties which are readily stimulated by contact with disabled people.

According to research, the attitudes facing people with disabilities in society often resemble those of other minority groups who face uncertain acceptance and often hostility and rejection in new situations, and in dealing with new institutions. In new social situations, daily occurrences like walking down the street or entering a room full of strangers, the disabled child or adult is likely to be responded to like a marginal or unwelcome person.

Coping With Prejudice

Thanks in part to the growing civil rights movement for disabled people, societal attitudes are changing, but these attitudes change slowly. Short of keeping them isolated at home, there is no way that parents can prevent their disabled child from experiencing daily doses of prejudice. But some factors can lessen the shock value of these doses.

I mentioned that my parents and I never directly discussed my disability. In fact, I never concretely knew the specific cause and nature of cerebral palsy until late in high school, when I did a research paper. My classic example is an older woman friend I have, a Ph.D. anthropologist with cerebral palsy. After getting her doctorate, she applied for a civil service job. On the form she was asked if she had a disability; she checked "Yes." Then the application form asked her for disability. It then suddenly occurred to her that she didn't know. Although she and her family had accommodated to her disability, they had never directly discussed it by name. So she had to then go to a doctor for an official diagnosis at age 24. Unfortunately, while extreme, this is not an isolated example.

Disabled children show a distressing degree of ignorance about their disabilities. Parents are reluctant to speak, for fear it will be painful to the child. This is a tremendous mistake. There is a powerful, often unintended message in parental silence and secrecy. Children learn early that things which they cannot talk about must be bad.

When parents do not make direct, matter-of-fact statements about disability, there is too much room for fantasy and confusion. Clinical studies tell us that parental secrecy about the disability is far more of a problem to children than the disability itself. Robert Furman describes his treatment with a three and one-half year old girl with one blind, deformed eye. Her parents never discussed the disability, but out of guilt and sadness, treated her "like a princess." At one point, she began looking in the mirror at her eye, with curiosity and confusion. Her parents knew she needed to know about it, but did not know how to begin. Furman found that as the result of the silence, her disabled eye became intricately interwoven in all her developmental tasks and fantasies. As a result, she reached the erroneous conclusion that she would not be able to cry or have other human emotions—indeed that she was not human because she was disabled.

Helping Children

Parental silence can feel like a confirmation of the societal stereotypes whereas parental communication can serve as a counterbalance. Children can handle simple facts. These facts can be clarifying and can be experienced by the child as an acceptance of the disabled parts of themselves. Direct statements can also help children sort out physical facts about their disabilities from feelings they have about those facts. This is a point which I have found very helpful in my work with children, and so I would like to clarify it.

As I mentioned, congenitally disabled children start out in life with basically good feelings about their bodies, including their disabilities. I can remember, for example, in my preschool years, being able to dance and run and laugh in public, with little feeling of self-consciousness. However, at some point, I learned to feel bad and self-conscious. For example, I learned to feel that the involuntary movements in my shoulders, arms and hands were quite disgusting, and I developed all types of strategies, ways of holding myself, to cover the movements. I took for granted that embarrassment and disgust were part and parcel of having movements.

One of the most significant moments in my own psychoanalysis was when I was making the transition from sitting up in a chair to using my analyst's couch. I was reluctant to make this change because my involuntary movements would then be more obvious. My analyst so simply asked me—"Why?" "Why does that bother you? What is so disgusting about movements?" He went on—"They are, after all, just movements, a neutral physical fact, with nothing inherently disgusting about them." At first, I thought he was being ridiculous, or naive. But as he pursued his curious stance, I came to appreciate that distinction between facts and feelings. Facts about a disability are unchangeable—but feelings about those facts are not fixed in stone or biology—they have been learned, superimposed on the facts, but they can and need to be separated out, because they are changeable. To make this distinction, however, children do need the facts.

Parents sometimes say that part of their difficulty

in being honest with their children about disability is that they do not always have their own facts straight either. They find that professionals are not always straight with them, so not only do they not have the facts, but they do not have a good role model for direct communication.

We can perhaps take things one step further. Professionals also sometimes do not have their facts straight about disabilities of clients they are working with.

In a study with cancer patients, Renneker found it striking how little the psychotherapists knew about cancer. Because cancer was anxiety-producing for the therapists, they preferred to remain only half-informed. I think the implications for professionals are clear.

I would urge that we continue along the same lines of direct communication, not only in terms of the facts about the disability, but also about future expectations for young people with disabilities, particularly social and sexual expectations.

Parents are often noticeably silent in stating their future expectations for their disabled sons and daughters. In a study of the parenting of thalidomide children, it was observed that parents were silent because they did not know what to expect. If they want to consider possibilities for the future of their nondisabled children, they can look in the mirror, at their own lives, or look at the lives of successful members of their family, community or people in history. When they try to think about the future of their disabled children, they are not sure what the possibilities are. They have no role models to look at for themselves or to offer their children. It is a curious thing that because of the stigma surrounding disability, people who are successful who have disabilities are no longer perceived of as disabled. In people's minds, disability and success do not go together.

In our society, it seems that successful disabled people are a contradiction in terms. In people's minds, disability and success simply do not go together. For example, why do we never think of Edison, Beethoven, Harriet Tubman or Elizabeth Barrett Browning as disabled, although they were? The lack of visible role models is one of the reasons why parents of disabled children tend to stay focussed on the present. They may think about the future, have hopes and dreams, but they are afraid to express them to their children for fear that their child will only be disappointed. Parental silence is too often experienced by youngsters as a confirmation of stereotypes about the future of disabled peole — and these stereotypes are bleak. These myths and stereotypes, among other things, can doom disabled people to remain asexual children, with no social or sexual potential.

My own experience illustrates this problem. My mother tells me now that when I was younger she always had hopes that I would date and marry. Perhaps I would meet a teacher of the disabled, someone who would really understand me — at least that was her fantasy. But it was an unspoken fantasy.

While I was growing up, my parents and I never talked about sex, dating, marriage, children. Not even the familiar warning not to get pregnant. I took their silence to mean that these things were beyond the scope of possibility for me. So I focussed on school and career, carefully avoiding boy-girl relationships, which only made me feel different. Not until I was established in my career, in my late 20's, did I begin to seriously consider the possibility of a social and sexual life.

A Social Life Is Possible

How does a woman in her late 20's, who feels more like an adolescent, begin? It was difficult, but not impossible.

To be sure, I had a lot to learn: how to flirt, mingle, kiss, when to say "no" and "yes". We sometimes forget that no one is born socially sophisticated. Social skills are things that all people — with and without disabilities — learn with practice.

I did face some special barriers, including painful rejections based on my disability. But these problems had solutions; they were not fixed as my disability was fixed. Needless to say, this process of discovering my sexuality was exhilarating — and also infuriating. I felt that I had missed out on years of pleasurable social and sexual involvement unnecessarily. Only the myth of asexuality in combination with parental silence had held me back.

Sexuality

Sexuality is no little thing. I am not just referring to acts of sex. I am talking about all the ways we think, feel, and behave as sexual beings. Human sexuality involves how we walk, talk, speak, dress, work, play, relate to others, feel about ourselves. To be considered asexual is to be denied a major part of oneself and one's life, for indeed, everyone is sexual.

I think we also need to realize that, for better or worse, we exist in a very sexually-oriented society. Everywhere we turn, there are references to sex, sexual relationships, enhancing sexual potential. Some of these references contribute to positive, joyful attitudes and a variety of sexual choices; others add up to new and restrictive sexual rules and regulations. Nevertheless, when disabled people are told that sexuality is not for them, it confirms the other existing stereotypes about disabled people: that we are abnormal and subhuman generally.

It is often a revelation for disabled people to discover that there is nothing inherent in the physical reality of cerebral palsy (or any other disability) that makes them asexual. Although certain sexual acts may be difficult or even impossible to perform, other equally creative forms of sexual and social expression always exist, regardless of disability. Facts about the disability can be helpful. But parents can do more then merely present facts.

Parents Can Help

While parents cannot single-handedly change stereotypes about disabled people, they can help counter them through direct statements which communicate positive and realistic expectations about their disabled children's future. Disabled children, particularly during adolescence, need to hear from their parents that they are indeed sexual people, with sexual thoughts and feelings, and that they can expect to socialize, date, even marry and have children if they wish.

Children also need to be aware that the social scene is frequently more difficult for disabled people — because of fear and ignorance. At times, they may experience unjust rejection based solely on their disability. Parents can continually provide opportunities for their disabled youngsters to talk about their pain. Parents can help adolescents sort out real prejudice from the typical frustrations everyone feels when negotiating social and sexual relationships. Socializing may be difficult, but it is not impossible. That is the main point that disabled children need to hear. Parents, remember that your children cannot afford your silence.

I will share with you a moving quote from an autobiographical book written by a disabled woman who was able to confront her mother's silence regarding sexuality only as an adult. Then she made a shocking discovery.

> (my mother) "said that the famous Dr. Bradford who had treated me once had spoken to her about the possibility of marriage for me, and he commanded her, 'If she falls in love, do not thwart her.' When she innocently repeated that sentence to me twenty years too late, I could not speak, I was so amazed. Then I said, 'I wish I had known he told you that, I would have felt differently.' She answered, ever so gently and remindingly, compassionately, 'But you were not thwarted...there never was anybody...' I didn't say anything more. Inside I was crying, clamoring, 'Oh, mother! The reason why there was never anybody was because I was so afraid. You did thwart me! If only I had known that he said that. If I had only known he did not think it was impossible. You ought to have told me. You ought to have let me know. You spoiled my life.'"

Expectations and Prejudice

In general, teenagers' social expectations closely mirror the expectations that their parents have for them. Current research with disabled adolescents suggests that parents of disabled children are an even more influential source of social and sexual information and values than the parents of non-disabled children. This is because non-disabled children are less likely to be isolated and consequently are effected by more outside sources of information. Parents are powerful! They need to use their power to prevent children from believing that prejudice is reality.

Parents need to communicate directly with their children about prejudice so that children are prepared to cope with it and eventually make satisfying choices for themselves. We know from studies of child development that language helps children develop a sense of themselves as individuals. Through labeling, children distinguish "me" from "not me". Similarly, when disabled children are helped to recognize myths and stereotypes about disability, they are better at preventing these myths from becoming part of their own self-image. Instead, they can succeed in recapturing their original, authentic experience of intactness, okayness.

In addition to labeling, disabled children need a game plan to handle prejudice when it comes their way. The world's prejudice is unfortunately not just the world's problem; it is also the disabled child's problem. He or she must learn to live with it, while not accepting it as truth. This may mean knowing when to "pass," when to make non-disabled people comfortable, when to ignore, and also when to confront. Learning survival strategies puts disabled children in the best position to make good choices.

Not all congenitally disabled people have self-esteem problems. Many have adequately resolved the intactness/defectiveness dilemma that they face. They have been accepted and respected as whole people, and have managed to preserve their original good feelings about themselves, all in spite of society's negative views. Such children and adults have perfected a valuable skill. They can navigate in the non-disabled world without disavowing their disabilities as a viable part of themselves. They recognize and, at times, are hurt and angered by prejudice, but do not accept it as an accurate assessment. They may seek to pass as non-disabled when necessary, but they do not need to pass to themselves.

Professionals' Attitudes Need Change

The suggestion I offered above for parents — direct, honest communication — is equally important for professionals. Unfortunately, many of the congenitally disabled children and adults professionals see in psychotherapy and various rehabilitation services have not achieved an adequate level of self-esteem. They may show little or no evidence of this sense of okayness, feeling instead despair and hopelessness about themselves and their lives. The professional's therepeutic stance can be extremely beneficial in work with such clients. What could be more valuable than curiosity and the capacity to ask "Why?" in the face of distress and confusion?

The Importance of "Why?"

"Why?" is an important question and attitude in the treatment of all people, disabled or not. It communicates to the client not only that his or her situation has logic and meaning, but more importantly, that there may be other, more hopeful ways to think and feel. "Why?" implies alternatives. It is a particularly significant question for disabled people, especially young children, who are likely to meet people every day who stare at them, call them freaks, and assume that their young lives are complete tragedies. Too often, disabled people and the world around them take their feelings of low self-esteem for granted, as if disliking oneself were the only possiblity. The question "Why?" may be the first time that anyone has seriously challenged the disabled person's feelings of embarassment and exclusion, rather than viewing these as an inevitable part of being disabled.

"Of Course" Does Not Help

Too often, professionals take a less helpful therepeutic stance. Instead of asking "Why?", the professional reacts with "of course," only confirming the inevitability of distress. "Of course" may offer a client momentary reassurance — at least the therapist agrees that his or her situation is difficult. But it offers no hope for change. When a therapist understands too quickly and accepts the client's pain without question, how can the client ever expect to feel differently?

When, as professionals, we find ourselves feeling too tragic, too despairing about our disabled patients' lives, when we are too fast to blurt out "of course," we need to look at our own attitudes and our own history regarding disability. We may be imagining how our lives would be if we were suddenly disabled. As newly disabled people, we would indeed feel shock, loss, even tragedy. But keep in mind that congenitally disabled people are not newly disabled. Their loss is not the loss of a body part or function, but the loss of their original sense of intactness and completeness as human beings, disability and all. When we are able to inquire "Why?", we are really wondering with our clients where this natural self-esteem has gone and how to recapture it.

Redefining Wholeness

Being disabled and being intact at the same time is an extremely difficult notion for non-disabled people to make sense of. I keep thinking of my mother's words: "Why wouldn't you want to walk straight?" Even now, it is hard to explain that I may have wanted to walk straight, but I did not want to lose my sense of myself in the process. Perhaps the best I can say is that my perspective on disability, from the inside out, is different from my mother's, from the outside looking in. In our work with congenitally disabled clients, we must always be receptive and respectful of that difference.

Differences in Common

If we think about it, this notion of intactness with disability can be personally helpful to all of us. Most people, disabled or not, have "different," sometimes deeply hidden parts of themselves which are important parts of their identities. These differences have been scorned and denied in response to parental and societal fears and prejudices. These differences might involve certain types or intensity of feelings, personality traits or styles, body features such as height or weight, ethnicity, race, gender, sexual orientation, economic status, and the like. Fostering self-esteem in our congenitally disabled children and clients means helping them reconnect and reclaim these scattered pieces of their identities and once again feel whole, as they deserve. As we encourage this process in our children and our clients, perhaps we will also be able to do it for ourselves and for all people. ∎

> Harilyn Rousso, A.C.S.W., is Director of Disabilities Unlimited, a counseling service for disabled people staffed by disabled professionals. She is also Project Director of The Networking Project for Disabled Women and Girls at the Y.W.C.A. of New York City. Ms. Rousso's work on this project was featured in *The New York Times* in December 1984.

This article is adapted from an article published in *Child and Adolescent Social Work*. We print it here with the kind permission of the publisher, Human Services Press.

See *The Little Locksmith* by Katharine Butler Hathaway, 1942.

CHAPTER 9

EDITORIAL

The Young Adult:
Self determination and mutual respect

The goal of parenting is to help children to grow up to become independent adults—adults capable of meeting their own needs and contributing to the community in which they live. Because of the demanding day to day challenges helping children with disabilities grow up, parents and professionals rarely have time and energy to actively think about how their current interactions with their children will contribute to the child's future life as an adult.

In addition to our time and energy limits, most of us have a very narrow range of experiences with adults with disabilities to draw upon. Fortunately, we are beginning to develop a broad base experience with individuals with many kinds of disabilities who are now adolescents or young adults. This is reflected in the recent focus on helping adolescents make the transition from school to the world of work.

We cannot wait until we know "everything" about adult development before we act. We can pool our experiences and put into practice our best current knowledge. This issue of *The Exceptional Parent* focusses on the adulthood.

The majority of our readers, parents of children, have always found these articles important to them. They are reminded that their children will become adults and they and their children can think about the future. Year after year, *The Exceptional Parent* has presented examples of the challenges of adulthood and the possible solutions available. This year there is an important change. We are able to focus on adults and achievement, not only in the text but by the example of four talented authors.

Harilyn Ruosso, a psychotherapist and a member of our Editorial Advisory Board, writes about body image and self esteem. Her contribution to both theory and practice will help inform and clarify the efforts of professionals and parent. Lisa Blumberg, an attorney, comments on the "Baby Doe" case. She addresses the issue of the rights of the infant with disabilities and the responsibilities of all of us based on her personal experience and shaped by her professional training. Utilizing her experience, Francis Barish has written a travel book for people with disabilities that will help enrich the lives of many disabled people, their families and friends. Finally, Dr. S. Phyllis Stearner has edited a book of biographies of disabled scientists in order to educate all of us about an exciting range of potential opportunities.

These authors, all individuals with disabilities, have achieved in different fields. They are "role models" for children and adolescents. In their articles, they also remind us that vocational achievement is only one aspect of becoming an adult. Caring for ourself and others is also important—whether we consider self care, managing money, or maintaining one's household; maintaining intimate relationships; learning responsibility for one's behavior and its consequences; and learning to find a balance between work and play and one's individual needs and the needs of others. None of us meet these challenges the same way, or manage each area with the same degree of maturity. Similarly we should not expect individuals with disabilities to be alike.

As we can define the challenges that adults must master, we can better define ways to help children manage the tasks of becoming an adolescent and in turn prepare the adolescent to meet the challenges of becoming an adult. The key ingredients at all ages are participation and opportunities. The earlier we allow children to be involved with decisions that affect their lives, the more able they will be to participate in the decisions that will affect their adult lives. The more opportunities we provide children, the more we will all learn about their ultimate capabilities and the more we and they will expand their horizons.

Our primary goal must be allowing every individual to determine his/her destiny to the extent possible. The goal is not "independence" because we are all intradependent. And we must pledge to insure that all children have opportunity for participation.

When people do not have a significant say in determining their own lives, they are likely to feel increasingly helpless and isolated. Twenty years ago, efforts were made in the poverty program to address similar issues of enabling control of one's own destiny by people who were "disabled" by poverty. President Lyndon Johnson, in 1964, in his State of the Union Address said: "The central problem is to protect and restore man's satisfaction in belonging to a community where he can find security and significance."

In 1985, let us hope we are all more ready to act so as to provide all adults with disabilities opportunities for self determination. This will require mutual respect for everyone's knowledge and experience—parents, professionals, and people with disabilities. ■

—S.D.K., M.J.S.—

Wheel A While

by Maren L. Peterson

Today is the first day I have given my lovely daughter the respect she truly deserves.

Boy, am I tired! It has been a long day, but a great one. This day has brought me closer to my daughter Barbara than any other day I can remember.

It began this morning when I took my eight-year-old son Matthew, who has Hunter's syndrome, to a respite care center for the day and left my 19-month-old daughter Kathleen with relatives. I got them "out of the way" for the day so I could embark on an extraordinary adventure with my oldest daughter, Barbara.

Barbara is twelve years old and has spina bifida. She is non-ambulatory and spends most of her waking hours in a wheelchair. Today I too became non-ambulatory: I spent five hours in a wheelchair, shopping with Barbara in a local mall.

So often I have nagged at Barbara because she moved too slowly, got her hands dirty on the wheels of her chair, needed help to open doors, or had trouble getting out of the way of others. What nerve I had! Here I have been the mother of this child for twelve years, nine of which she has spent in a wheelchair, and I have never really understood her situation. I have been guilty of focusing on educating the general public about children with disabilities when I myself was not adequately sensitive to my own child's limitations. How easy it has been for me to criticize her without any real basis for judging her efforts.

Today I found out for myself just how hard it is to push open a door and then try to get through it. I learned the difficulty of holding a tray of food on my lap while trying to wheel to a table (my white slacks would have been out of the question). I experienced the irritation of always having to look up at people when speaking to them. I felt the frustration of shopping in aisles too narrow and dressing rooms too small to accommodate people in chairs. I also realized very early in the day that I would want to be especially careful not to forget an item; going back to get it could not possibly have been worth the effort involved.

As our expedition neared its end, a wonderful and encouraging thing happened. There I was in the clothing store, my lap piled high with garments for Barbara to try on, when a young woman approached me and asked, "Do you have this in other sizes?" It took a moment for her meaning to hit home: she had taken me for a salesclerk, a salesclerk in a wheelchair! I was exhilarated by this sign that public awareness really is growing and attitudes are changing at last.

Spending five hours in a wheelchair was no great sacrifice on my part. I knew that I would get up and walk away from it when the afternoon was over. But the experience was the beginning of a much deeper, more personal understanding of my daughter and others in her situation. Today's adventure gave Barbara the opportunity to show me the obstacles she faces every day and created an equality between us that we had never before experienced. Now I understand the extra effort it takes on her part to accomplish all the things we ambulatory folks expect her to do as a matter of routine.

My arms ache with weariness, my hands are dirty, and the blisters hurt . . . but what a tremendous sense of satisfaction I feel. Today is the first day I have given my lovely daughter the respect she truly deserves. ∎

Maren L. Peterson lives in Portland, Oregon with her husband, Mark, and her three children, Barbara, Matthew, and Kathleen. She is a member of the Oregon State Developmental Disabilities Council, the Special Education Advisory Council for the Portland Public Schools, and the Columbia River Spina Bifida Association. This summer she began a masters program in special education at the Oregon College of Education.

CHAPTER 11

FAMILY LIFE

"I Feel Like I'm Dealing With These Problems All By Myself"
Demands on Single Parents

Billy Day, a child with learning disabilities, needed some special attention. Both of his parents wanted to help, but felt overwhelmed by the demands of being single parents.

Billy is having trouble playing with the other kids.

"**My son, Billy, needs** a special summer program so he can learn to play with other kids." Mrs. Miriam Day, a pale, thin woman in her early thirties seemed tired. "My ex-husband, Arthur, thinks I bug Billy too much and that we should leave him alone. That's what happened last summer, and it didn't work. I don't know how to convince him or where to begin to find a good camp.

"I'm exhausted. I'm doing all I can manage. Last week, the school people reminded me that it was time to plan for the summer. And then they told me how much trouble Billy was having playing with the other children. Maybe I misinterpreted it, but I felt they were saying I should be helping him even more. It made me want to scream.

"Sure Billy needs help, and he needs a good solid summer program. If I could actually depend on his father, my ex-husband, then maybe I would feel better.

"Five years ago, when my husband left me, you helped me come to terms with it. That was an awful time in my life. When I think about it now, I shudder.

"It was such a shock when Arthur took off the way he did. It seemed like it was the end of the world. I was so depressed; I felt totally worthless. I didn't know what I would do or how I would take care of the kids. Looking back, the kids more or less took care of themselves. It was all I could do to keep going. I remember thinking that if it hadn't been for them, I might have killed myself.

"I just hope you can help me now, because I'm starting to feel overwhelmed again. You said that being a single parent would be tough—but I never imagined it could be this difficult.

"Jill is ten now, and she's doing fine. She's in fifth grade, has a lot of friends, and is a terrific kid. Jill has so many things to keep her busy that she rarely makes me feel like I don't pay enough attention to her. I'm thankful for that.

"But Billy is a big problem, and I worry about him a lot. I remember the hard time I had when he was born. The delivery was difficult and I was scared. The pediatrician reassured me and said that Billy seemed healthy, but that we ought to keep an eye on him. I remember his words—'Billy had a hard time getting into this world, and might run into trouble later on.'

"Billy was slower than Jill in things like walking and talking, and I was very worried. Arthur always accused me of worrying too much. But after Arthur left, I don't think I kept much of an eye on either kid. I was such a mess.

"Billy has had trouble from the day he started school. Even in nursery school, they said he was infantile—he never got along with kids his age. Two years ago, when he started kindergarten, he still didn't mix well with the other children. The teacher said he had difficulty with the reading readiness materials. She called it a 'perceptual problem.' That's when he started special education.

"Billy is in second grade now, and doing so-so. He gets special help every day from the learning disabilities teacher in the resource room. It helps him. His reading has improved, and his writing is getting better, too.

"His teachers and I just had our spring planning meeting. We reviewed Billy's Individualized Educational Plan that we had put together last year.

"We sat down together and compared notes about how he's doing. His teachers came, and so

33

did the school psychologist and the special education director. They invited my ex-husband to come, but Arthur never showed up. He said he was too busy to come home from out of town. The learning disability teacher and his second grade teacher, Ms. Porter, said that Billy was making encouraging progress in academic subjects.

"But both Ms. Porter and the school psychologist said that Billy is having trouble playing with the other kids. He doesn't seem to know how. He seems to be afraid to play with kids his age, and besides, his coordination isn't that good. So with his fears plus his poor coordination, he even has a hard time when they play a simple game like kickball. The other kids tease Billy, and that doesn't help him at all.

"The special ed director said Billy needed help to learn how to play games. He said a special summer program would really help. I felt that it was all up to me. That made me very angry. I know that Billy needs help, and that he needs me. But I have a job, a house, and another child, to say nothing of the fact that I need some time for myself.

"On top of all that, I can't count on Arthur to do his share, either financially or emotionally, as a father to his own kids.

"Actually, things are better now. Arthur spends more time with the children than he used to. For the first year or so after he moved out, he was hardly available to them at all. Every other weekend he picks up the kids on Saturday morning, and takes them to his mother's house and they spend the weekend together. So twice a month, I get a day and a half for myself. I'm always trying to catch up on something—either my work, household chores, or just sleep.

"It's very frustrating. I'm on the go all day from the time I get the kids up at seven until nine o'clock when they finally get off to bed. Fortunately, both Jill and Billy go to a very helpful after-school program at the church. Billy plays there, but with kids two years younger. He likes the program, and he especially loves snack time. But the teachers tell me that he sulks whenever he doesn't get his own way.

"My neighbor down the street picks up her daughter and my kids at five o'clock and takes them to her house. Then I pick them up at six when I get home from the office. By the time we settle down at home and have dinner together, it's bedtime. I don't have energy left to do much with the children, except watch some dumb T.V. show. I feel terrible about that. I should do something more with the children than sit by the tube.

"I feel bad about not being able to spend more time with both my kids, but I worry more about Billy. Summers are a big problem because then he's not even busy in school. The school people are right—he needs to be in a special program somewhere.

"Last year, I arranged for Billy and Jill to go to the day camp program that the town recreation department provides. But Billy was very unhappy there. The program was very sports oriented. He didn't seem to fit in, and they didn't provide him with any special help.

"The counselors were kind of young and weren't particularly concerned about Billy not participating. He played in the sandbox quite a bit, or just sat around. Sometimes, he wandered over to wherever Jill was and made a pest of himself. Billy enjoyed the nature walks and the cookouts, and liked the water when they took the kids to the lake twice a week, even though he didn't make too much progress in learning how to swim.

"I'd like to find a program where they specialize in helping children like Billy. The people at school said that he does respond to individual attention. Billy just hasn't had much individual attention, and I don't think I can give him all he needs.

"I get three weeks off in the summer, and want to spend some time with my children, but I also want some time for myself. My roommate from college and I have talked about the two of us taking

I'm always trying to catch up on something—either my work, household chores, or just sleep.

a trip together. We're both single parents, and share a lot of the same problems. It would be great if I could really depend on Arthur to take care of the kids for more than a weekend.

"I feel like I'm dealing with these problems all by myself. Sometimes, I feel very lonely. My friend, Alice, has been encouraging me to think about dating, but I've been reluctant to do so. Alice says it would do the kids good if I got out more; she thinks I spend too much of my spare time with them and that I need adult friends. But I think it would be selfish if I started going out.

"Even though I feel selfish, I am tempted to start dating. Recently, at a church dinner, I met a nice guy who has just moved into the area. He's divorced too, and we talked about the problems of taking care of our kids. He seemed nice, and said he would like to get together with me sometime. We left it kind of vague. It might be nice to have some fun socially. I hate going to places alone when everyone else seems to be in couples.

"I want Arthur to be more active with the

children. I talked to him after the school conference, but it is very difficult for me to have a civilized conversation with him about anything. I feel like I have to do everything, and it isn't fair. He did say he would be willing to speak with you, as long as you only talked about Billy. Arthur doesn't want to talk about how we get along, or his present life."

"I guess I'm not the best father in the world, but I don't know what to do." Arthur Day, a well-dressed man in his late thirties, spoke dryly.

"It's hard to find interesting things to do with two kids who are so different. Besides, my ex-wife keeps leaving me notes about Billy's needs—'Billy needs this and Billy needs that.' I think she pesters both of us too much.

"I take the kids to my mother's because all I can afford is a small apartment, and I don't have room for them there. I'm trying to spend more time with them. Jill is a lot easier to be with. She likes to do things, and she does them well. With Billy, it's harder.

"I always dreamed of teaching my son the games I loved as a kid—baseball and basketball, especially. I wanted to be the father I never really had. My dad was always on the road trying to make a living. I was envious of the boys whose fathers were home every night.

"I was a pretty good ball player as a kid, and I still play basketball regularly at the Y. But I get so frustrated when I try to play with Billy. He can't seem to hit with a bat at all, and he can't catch either. He has a lot of trouble coordinating himself. I never had trouble and can't understand his problems.

"It's ironic, I suppose, when I look back. When Billy was born, I was so excited about having a son. I went out and bought him a little baseball glove and a ball.

"But I was never very good with babies—Jill or Billy. Miriam used to complain that I should do more with Billy, and she also used to worry about his development. I would say that he would grow up just fine, and when he was old enough to start playing sports, I'd be a big help to her. When I moved out, he was just beginning to get around the house by himself.

"But let's get back to what is going on now with the kids. I don't like to dwell on the past. Sometimes we play cards or simple table games—but I get bored. Jill will play with us, but she gets tired of these simple games, too. Jill and I will play more complicated games like Monopoly, or some of the other interesting games kids have. But Billy can't play those. He gets very upset when he doesn't understand all the rules. And if he isn't winning, he starts to cry. Then he usually goes and complains to my mother.

"My mother really gets on my case then. She's never forgiven me for leaving Miriam and the kids. Now, my mother blames me for whatever problems Billy has. She thinks that Billy has a learning disability because Miriam and I are divorced.

"Miriam is right when she says I should spend more time with the children, and really work at trying to be helpful to Billy. But the kid is difficult for me. I don't want to play favorites, but it certainly is a lot easier to spend time with Jill than with Billy.

"I know Miriam is worried about what to do in the summer. I've got a couple of weeks off from my job and could spend some time with the kids, but I'm not sure what to do. My apartment is too small for the three of us, and I don't want to spend two or three weeks at my mother's.

"I was talking to this fellow, Paul, at work, who is in a similar situation. He's divorced, and has a couple of kids he sees only once a month and during the summer. He talked about all of us going camping—his kids, my kids, he and I. Paul said that he's had a lot of fun going camping with his kids—that it's a way to have a nice vacation without spending much money.

"I'm afraid of the idea when it comes to Billy. I don't know if he can handle being outdoors and roughing it. It could be a disaster if things don't work out and Billy gets upset. He can be very difficult when he sulks. I don't want to finish my vacation feeling like I need a vacation to recover. Maybe I'm being selfish. After all, Miriam takes care of the kids all year and doesn't complain.

"I told Miriam I didn't want to talk to you about my life. I didn't want her to know, but I've had a tough time since we split up. I left my wife and kids for a relationship that didn't work out. I felt rotten. I couldn't get my work done, and I finally lost my job. It took me over a year to get another job, but it's in sales. Now, I spend a lot of time on the road. By the time the weekend comes around, I'm pooped. But every other weekend, it's time to pick up the kids. I wish I had more energy for them.

"Miriam doesn't know, but I got professional help. Completely by accident, I bumped into an old high school classmate who turned out to be a counseling psychologist. We spent some time together, and he was really helpful. Things settled down for me, and I got back to concentrating on my work and thinking about the kids.

"But let's face it. I was a failure in my marriage, a failure in the relationship that broke up my marriage, and now I suppose you think I'm a failure as a father."

Even when couples are happily married, parenting

is a difficult task. Being a single, divorced parent, under the best of circumstances, is very demanding and often frustrating and unrewarding. Conflicts between divorced parents about how time, energy, and money are distributed are very common, and often rearrouse the conflicts between individuals that led to the divorce. As a result, solving relatively uncomplicated tasks like making plans for being with the children can become major disputes.

A professional can play a valuable role by helping divorced parents establish guidelines for their relationships with their children, and by suggesting practical ways to resolve issues that take into account the needs of everyone concerned.

Despite the fact that Miriam Day was meeting the challenge of being a career woman, a single parent, and a homemaker, she worried that she was not doing enough for her children. When she thought of her own adult needs, she felt guilty and that she was being selfish. Now, under the stress of planning for the upcoming summer vacation for her son, Billy, Mrs. Day decided she needed some help.

Arthur Day wanted to be an involved father, but in many ways, he was like his own father had been—namely, not available to his children. He realized that Billy could benefit from his attention. Since Mr. Day had come to terms with his personal problems following the separation and divorce, he was interested now in being more helpful. But he was afraid he might fail once again.

Mr. and Mrs. Day were genuinely concerned about both their children. Although both parents had experienced severe emotional difficulties after the separation, each was successfully working to re-establish themselves. Both were willing to meet with me individually and then together so that they could communicate more clearly to one another about the children's needs as well as about their own plans.

In an individual session, it was very helpful to Mrs. Day to discuss how far she had come since the depth of her depression when her husband left her five years ago. She appreciated my acknowledgement that she was doing a worthy job and that her perceptions were common for women in her situation. Mrs. Day was relieved to know that she was not alone in her dilemma, but she also wanted to take some specific, practical steps to help her son.

At my suggestion, both Mrs. and Mr. Day met with Billy's teacher, Ms. Porter, to review the meeting Mrs. Day had attended. Ms. Porter clarified why it is important that a child learn how to make friends and to participate in activities with other children.

Mrs. Day then met with the youth director of her church in order to locate an older boy who might be interested in helping Billy during the after-school program. Through the youth service club, a teenage boy volunteered to work with Billy and another boy with similar problems twice a week during the after-school program. They would play games in the gym or on the playground with the idea of emphasizing learning to play together. Mrs. Day decided she could afford to pay the same teenage youngster to spend some time with Billy on the weekends when his father would not be available.

Mr. Day was referred to a father and son recreation program sponsored by a social service agency in a nearby community. This program had been designed to help fathers and sons learn how to play together when they had difficulty doing so. Every Saturday morning, a group of fathers and sons met at a YMCA with a recreation therapist.

Initially, Mr. Day felt embarrassed about starting this program, and was uncertain about whether he could find the time to attend each Saturday. Fortunately, once he and Billy got started, Mr. Day was delighted by the program because, at long last, he was starting to do what he had dreamed of doing with his son.

In this program, the boys, with the encouragement and participation of their fathers, played modified versions of games like softball, street hockey, and also "worked out" together with exercises and lessons on self-defense. With all of these activities, the goal was to increase the self-confidence of the boys about their bodies and about participation in group activities.

The recreation therapist demonstrated for fathers like Arthur Day how they could play together and enjoy their son's company. For example, the recreation therapist showed Mr. Day how by using a "fat bat" and a large plastic ball, he could help Billy begin to learn about hitting a baseball.

As a result of the positive experience with the recreation program with his son, Mr. Day decided to spend a day with his children and his friend, Paul, and his family. They all went on a picnic, and talked about the possibility of a summer camping trip. A few weeks later, Mr. Day took Billy and Jill for a stay at an overnight campground to see how things would work out for all of them. Mr. Day reported that the trip was not "perfect," but that it was still a lot of fun. He and his friend, Paul, decided to try a one week camping trip with their children in the summer.

In the meeting with both Mr. and Mrs. Day, we discussed the common dilemmas faced by many divorced families. The problem of individual children with different interests is faced by all families as soon as a second child arrives. However, in intact families, the on-going presence of two parents makes it relatively easier to address individual needs. For example, one parent can attend to one or more of the children while the other copes with competing household, community, career, or personal needs.

In contrast, the single parent with custody (usually the mother) must juggle many tasks and try to meet the unrealistic expectation of being all things to all people. The single parent (usually the father) who is only with his children for relatively brief time periods feels he has to entertain his children, or do several activities all at once. As a result of these and other issues, single parents like Miriam and Arthur Day often feel torn and exhausted. And when a single parent like Miriam Day considers her own needs and interests as an adult—which are independent of her role as a parent—she feels she is being selfish.

It was suggested that from time to time, Mr. Day take only one of the children for a weekend visit. In this way, both Mr. and Mrs. Day would have the opportunity to spend time with just one child and be especially attentive to the particular needs of that youngster. Even though such an arrangement meant less free time for Mrs. Day, she found that she enjoyed these days with just one child, and was willing to plan such occasions on a regular basis.

For the summer, Mr. and Mrs. Day decided to spend the extra money needed to enable Billy to participate in a day camp program directed by the recreation therapist from the Saturday morning program. Before agreeing to this, Mrs. Day called a number of parents whose children had attended this day camp in the past year to be confident that it would meet Billy's needs and would be worth the investment.

Mrs. Day was relieved and pleased with Mr. Day's willingness to take the children for an entire week during the summer. She realized that she was entitled to take some time for herself and went ahead and made plans with her former college roommate.

Billy Day had lost out from the lack of emotional availability of both parents during the years immediately following his parents' separation. Now, he needed their help to assist him in developing social skills and learning how to enjoy recreational activities. Both his parents were willing to try. As they felt some success in their work with Billy, they were more ready to devote more energy to the process as well as to enjoy participating. ∎

CHAPTER 12

"I'll Never Learn How to Play with my Son."
Problems of Fathering

Mr. Nash wanted to leave his family. This problem stemmed from his relationship with his son.

"**I don't know** what to do." Mr. Nash, a short, slender man in his late thirties sat back in his chair and spoke slowly. "I feel terrible about what I've done, and I don't know what else to do.

"Last week I wanted to leave my family—my wife, my child, my home. I had walked away in the heat of anger and told them that I'd had it. At the time, I knew it was better than winding up killing either them or myself.

"Doris, as she always has, calmed me down and persuaded me that we should come for counseling. I guess you could say our marriage was not that bad and we ought to sort out our problems. That's why we're here.

"I'd like to say it all began when our son, Jimmy, who is now eight, was born. He's an awkward, uncoordinated boy, but he's a good kid. He has a slight physical disability based probably on some brain damage.

"He's always trying to please me. In the last several years I've tried to do different things with him, but it never seems to work.

"I know my wife has probably told this story to the different specialists that she's talked to, but I've been reviewing it in my mind for the last week. How much is me and how much is the situation?

"I have always felt lucky that someone like Doris married me. I was a shy, lonely person who on the surface had friends but didn't quite know what to do with them.

"I was thirty when we married. I believed it was very important for me to establish my career before I even turned my attention away from myself. I met Doris at a company picnic and as reticent and reluctant as I was to participate in any of the games, she was the leader. I felt that somebody like her would never be interested in me. But she was.

"Because of my age, we were anxious to start a

> *It was important that I do more with him—that I act more like a father.*

family. A year later, Jim was born. Although the pregnancy seemed to be no problem—we were both very excited and very happy—it was a long, long labor. I can remember going in to see Doris and the pediatrician not looking very happy coming in after his visit to the nursery. He told us that he thought there was some problem. It didn't seem to be an extensive one, but he thought we ought to keep track of Jimmy. The doctor told us he was going to bring in a consultant. Our life was changed, not only because we had a child, but we now had a worry that has been with us for the last eight years.

"Jim's growing up hasn't been so bad that you'd say he's fallen on his face. But it hasn't been so good that we haven't worried about it every step of the way. He was a good-natured baby. There's no question that was because of how much love and attention he got from my wife. He didn't walk as fast as other kids; he didn't do most things at the same rate that other kids did. But this really was not a major problem until nursery school.

"It's such a paradox. He loved to go to school. It was never a problem getting him there and he seemed to be happy when the day was over. So we were sort of surprised in the middle of the year when the director of the nursery school called us in for a conference. She said that she thought Jimmy was having difficulty getting along with the other youngsters. She said that he was bit immature in all of his development, and that he would profit from an extra year of nursery school. That didn't really bother us. We knew he was slow and he was a little bit younger that the other children, so we

Other fathers can teach their sons, why can't he?

went along with that suggestion.

"The next year, things didn't seem to be getting a whole lot better. From the time Jimmy has entered school, his learning has been slow but steady. People have always talked about his trouble getting along with other kids.

"Then the story began. Everybody started to say that it was important that I do more with him—that I act more like a father, and teach him how to play games. That is, if he could only have the skills that would be helpful, he might start getting along better.

"First, I thought it was a good idea. I was spending too much time away from the family anyhow. I needed to be encouraged because I had never really had much experience playing myself. My father never played with me, or at least I don't remember him doing anything and calling it play. I wasn't somebody who hung around much with other kids. I was by myself pretty much, reading books all the time.

"That changed in high school when other kids had the same interests that I had. I joined the camera club and the chess club. I actually had a lot of friends from those clubs even though I did a lot of things by myself.

"Every time that I try to get something done with Jim, it never seems to work. He always winds up in tears. We can start either rolling a ball, doing something outdoors, or trying to fly a kite, but I'm just not good at it. First I start to try to let him do it. Pretty soon I get impatient and then I do it. Then I try to get him to do it again. Pretty soon, he's in tears.

"Last week was the bitter end. This year I've been trying to make an extra effort to spend time with him and do things with him. He was in a fall soccer program and I helped out. Soccer is a game where at that age, everybody can play some.

"Last week was Jimmy's birthday. We organized a party for a bunch of kids who he named and we knew, but who really weren't friends of his. In the middle of it, I decide to organize a kickball game.

I was the referee. Pretty soon, I began to talk about how poorly he was playing. Even though I knew he was trying hard, I looked at him and told him to do better. I couldn't stop myself. I really told him off. After that, he started to cry and ran off the field. Doris had to go after him. The whole thing was a disaster.

"I began to wonder what I was doing there and why was I spending so much time at something I wasn't good at. Why didn't we find somebody else to do it?

"For the past few months, I've been thinking a lot about Jimmy and his problems and my work has suffered. And my wife and I fight more. After the scene at the party, I finally decided that's the end.

"What a stupid thing to do at a birthday party. I'm ashamed of myself, and yet I don't know where I'm going to go with this."

"**B**ill is awfully hard on himself. I think Jimmy knows that his father loves him. He's made real efforts to try and do things but it doesn't seem to work. Bill's expectations seem to be too high for anybody—himself, sometimes for me, sometimes for the marriage.

"It really has been more and more of a problem lately. I think he starts out trying to play with Jim, and pretty soon he wants him to be the best. He has a funny way of expressing it to Jimmy. Bill seems to say, 'I want you to try to be the best you can at anything you do.'

"Well, as far as I'm concerned, 'best you can' has to be related to what your possibilities are, and also, whether you feel free to fail. In other words, I love to play games, and I know I was always pretty good at them. But I was never afraid to embarrass myself. I felt that if I fell down, I could get up and do it again.

"Jimmy is so unsure of himself just to start with. He takes a longer time before anything is going to happen. He has to take everything in very slowly and digest it. When he really feels very, very safe and sure, maybe he'll try it.

"I think Bill only has a limited perspective. He comes home and takes Jimmy out in the evening. He's got a half hour, and its all got to be done in that space of time. It's hard to realize that it is a patient, slow process. And then, Bill feels like he's failed. Other fathers are able to teach their sons, why can't he? There isn't a lot of pressure.

"Sometimes I cringe when I go to talk about Jimmy at school. The teachers want to know about his play problems. Sooner or later, no matter what specialist you talk to nowadays, they want to know if his father is involved. A part of me wants Bill to be involved; another part of me knows it's going to be a disaster. There's got to be some way out. I don't know where to begin.

"But, there is something else. I don't know what Bill thinks, but I think our marriage has been going downhill for quite a while now. I've been afraid to talk to him about it. But, I guess the birthday disaster forced me to say it was time to take action."

Summary and Conclusions

The Nashes came because of an outburst that Mr. Nash had had during their son, Jimmy's, birthday party. Mr. Nash had organized a kickball game at the birthday party and became increasingly critical of his son as the game continued. He had tried to stop criticizing his son, but could not stop. He had hoped that Jimmy would be playing better and be more involved in the game after all the time he spent with his son.

Mr. Nash had walked away from his family and considered not coming back. In the evening when he returned home, he was contrite and depressed. But he felt trapped by the marriage and his relationship to his son.

Mrs. Nash convinced him that something could be done about the way he felt. They both needed someone with whom they could talk about the current problem as well as themselves and their relationship.

Jim had been born with problems that affected his coordination and motor development. The problems manifested themselves early. He was a little slower to walk, to talk, and to be toilet trained. When he entered nursery school, his difficulties seemed to effect his playing with other youngsters.

From the beginning of nursery school, whenever there were school conferences, Jimmy's problems in relationships with other kids and the skills that might be helpful were always a part of the discussion. Inevitably, school personnel would ask about how much time Mr. Nash played with his son, and then strongly urge him to get more involved.

For a number of years, Mr. Nash made efforts to play with his son, but sooner or later, would get discouraged and stop. He never played many games while growing up. He himself had few of the skills that others expected him to teach his son.

After lengthy discussions with his wife, when Jimmy started the second grade, Mr. Nash decided to make an effort to play with his son during the entire year. He read all the books he could about child's play. He spent part of each Sunday playing with Jimmy. Before the birthday party, he decided to organize a game of kickball. He knew that he had higher expectations than his son could meet. But as he watched Jimmy continuously make mistakes during the game, he felt that he himself had also failed. He began to criticize his son. Although he realized that he should stop, his criticism mounted until his angry outburst.

In recent years, with the changing nature of families, more attention has been paid to the role of fathers. Fathers have been expected to become more involved in helping their children grow up. Not only are they involved in many of the issues of the routine, day-to-day care of the family, but have been especially encouraged to get involved in activities with their sons. Some fathers have had little experience in their own lives playing with their own fathers. Accordingly, these men have little to draw on as they try to play with their own children. As a result, they often have had to learn by trial and error.

Different stages of development make different emotional demands upon parents who are involved in the child-rearing experience. Parents also have different ways and abilities in interacting with children. For example, some adults are action oriented. They find it relatively easy playing with children when they are young and require a lot of direct physical contact and care. Other parents, particularly those who are more verbal, have an easier time as the child gets older and speech becomes an important aspect of the parent-child interaction.

When children are able to manage the issues of growing up without any great difficulty, different parenting styles are usually not a major problem. When children require special attention early in their lives and special kinds of interactions are necessary, the parents' ability to do becomes important.

Mr. Nash did not have a great deal of interaction with his father throughout his life and had little experience in play activities. He was very gifted academically and found his major friendships in high school at a time when intellectual activities were a link to other youngsters. He felt uncomfortable with physical play, and this kind of activity with his son, Jimmy, made him feel very inadequate.

Parents are continuously involved in using other people to provide opportunities for their youngsters to learn a variety of helpful academic and recreational skills. We turn to nursery schools, community centers and clubs to help our children learn the social skills necessary to get along with other youngsters. When a child has special problems like Jimmy, these opportunities may not exist or, when they do, they may not be sufficient.

Mrs. Nash had been a very action oriented person throughout her life. She had spent a great deal of time playing during her own childhood and working on those skills that were necessary in play. She had been disappointed that her own activities had not been more helpful to Jimmy. At the same time, she had experienced her husband's withdrawal of interest in both her and their son after Jimmy was born. When the various school people suggested that her husband become more involved, she hoped that this would lead to a greater interest, not only in her son, but herself.

Since parents cannot do all the things for their children, it is the child's belief about the parents' interest and investment that is crucial. It was this withdrawal of interest and attention that concerned

Mrs. Nash.

Furthermore, as a child gets older, adults are faced with the mixed wishes of a child for parental interest. Children increasingly turn to their peer groups for help in becoming independent of their parents. This turning to peer groups is part of an interesting paradox which changes as the child gets older. Elementary school aged children explore a variety of issues as they turn to play with their friends. They do so with the encouragement of parents. These friendships help a child assess his or her own abilities independent of the family. In adolescence, as a child can be independent and has greater freedom to move away from the family setting, he or she becomes more interested in challenging parents for independence.

Another aspect of contemporary life is that individual families are much less likely to be involved with their own family members on a regular basis. The everyday opportunities that extended family groups have in learning from one another in anticipating the stages in child development no longer exist. Children do not have extensive opportunities to play with their older cousins nor learn from their brothers, sisters, uncles, aunts, and grandparents. This means that parents now have to learn about child rearing from written material rather than what they observed directly while growing up.

The Nashes had a problem in their marriage. Slowly but surely, their relationship was less satisfying. The crisis at the birthday party was a reflection of their own deteriorating relationship. Neither one had known how to approach the other about this.

Mr Nash, although troubled in discussing the marriage, was relieved. Although the Nashes were concerned about Mr. Nash's relationship to his son, they wanted to improve their own relationship. The Nashes both wanted to understand what might help them both to return to the pleasures and satisfactions they got from each other before Jimmy's birth. They were both eager to begin counseling sessions for their marriage.

Mr. Nash also entered a group at the local community center that helped fathers improve their relationships with their children. Mr. Nash and his son joined in the activity program for fathers and sons once each week. Under the guidelines of trained professionals, fathers and sons played together and learned to be patient with one another. ■

—M.J.S., S.D.K.—

This case has been selected from private practice and consultation files. The names and situations have been changed to preserve confidentiality.

FAMILY LIFE

CHAPTER 13

Professional Expertise and Children With Disabilities:
A Problem for Marital Communication

The Kramers had different approaches to the information they were receiving from the "experts" who were involved in the care of their daughter, Judy. This conflict was creating difficulty in their marriage.

No matter what I do, or what I say, John always criticizes me.

"I've given up." Mrs. Kramer sat and held on to her chair while she spoke. "No matter what I do, or what I say, John always criticizes me. I can't seem to please anybody. It always seems like someone is angry at me.

"I don't know where to begin. Last week, I was meeting with my daughter's first grade teacher to discuss her problems in school. My husband had written out a list of questions that I should ask Ms. Winter, and I wrote down the answers she gave me. When I came home, John started to shout at me. 'This is nothing new. It's all useless information. You don't know how to ask questions. You really didn't get the answers I wanted. You should have confronted her more.'

"I thought I was going to faint this time. It's hard for me to answer when he gets so upset. I ran to my room, and John and I didn't speak for two days. We have spent very little time together since that happened a week ago. I spoke to my pediatrician, because he's the only one who knows us both and understands what I have to deal with. I know John doesn't trust Dr. Carlson, but I like him a lot. He suggested that we talk to you about our problems.

"John objected to coming, but I put my foot down. Our problems are getting too serious to ignore any longer. I told him that unless we did something, I wasn't going to continue in the marriage. That's not true, but it was the only way I could think of to get him to do something I wanted.

"We were happy when we were first married. Things were great between us. We were the envy of our friends. We spent a lot of time doing things together, and life was rosy. I had looked forward to being a mother, and I was happy when I was pregnant.

"Our problems started when my daughter was born. In lots of ways, Judy is a miracle. She is our first and, so far, our only child. Judy weighed only three and a half pounds, and for a long time we weren't sure whether she would live or die. It was awfully hard on all of us.

"We weren't able to take Judy home from the hospital right away. She remained in the premie nursery for almost six weeks. Judy still only weighed about four pounds when they let me take her home. I don't think the doctors were very happy about sending her home, even after all that time. I was nervous, too, but I really wanted her home. She didn't do very well, so a month later, Judy went back to the hospital for another three weeks.

"I really like our pediatrician, Dr. Carlson. My girlfriend had worked as his secretary, and I thought he was a great guy. He was very patient, and spent a lot of time trying to tell me what some of the issues were with premature infants. I would have done whatever he said, but he always patiently explained everything to me. While I always felt that Dr. Carlson was saying more than enough, John thought the doctor was cheating us—keeping information from us that he didn't think we'd be able to understand.

"John is a reader. He's one of these 'do-it-yourself' people. That has always amazed me about him. Whatever John wants to do, he does. He gets books on a subject, and keeps at it and at it, until sooner or later, he seems to understand what he needs to do. Then he might go pump someone for more information. He's not shy about getting other people's ideas, and then doing his own thing.

"John became an expert on premature babies. He read everything he could get his hands on. After he read all the books in the public library, he went to the hospital library and read everything there. Pretty soon he was challenging everybody who was trying to do anything for Judy. He had a real chip on his shoulder. It seemed to me that no matter what the pediatrician said, John would tell him that there were three reasons why he was probably wrong, and would push him to try some of the new ideas he had read about. It was really embarrassing sitting there listening to him fight with the doctor.

"We had a visiting nurse come for a while and no matter what she said or what she did, John would question her. He was suspicious of everything. Sometimes, I got really concerned about his behavior. He didn't trust any professional who was involved in caring for Judy. He was terribly rude to the nurse, and always seemed prepared for a fight.

"Dr. Carlson told us Judy's growth would be slow. Although our pediatrician thinks she has done very well, he couldn't give her a clean bill of health. One of the things he is worried about is the full development of her brain—that is my understanding of it. Dr. Carlson and my husband aren't getting along, having arguments about the latest scientific evidence, and things like that. I didn't want to know what the latest evidence is, or the old evidence. I just want somebody who I trust to tell me what to do.

"When Judy was almost a year, we took her to a neurologist. Now John had a new person to argue with. His nerve is really unbelievable. This doctor is the chief neurologist, and has studied for years. And my husband is telling *him* about the latest medical findings he's read about.

"Then there was a psychologist who tested Judy every six months until she was about three and has tested her the last two years. John wasn't thrilled with him, either. He has told us that although Judy is delayed in some areas, her problems aren't too severe. Everyone who works with her thinks she is a terrific kid. And that's what I think, too! She is friendly, and out-going. She likes people. I think she's very smart, although she is having some trouble doing some of the things other kids do.

"In first grade, for example, she's been having trouble learning to read—a little more than the other kids. Ms. Winter has tried to explain to me the kind of help they were going to give Judy. As usual, my husband has been critical. He's not sure whether they're up to date on the latest things, or if what they want to do is best for Judy. He doesn't trust Ms. Winter because she's so young.

"Whenever we go to visit these experts, I feel I'm in the middle. I'm afraid if you get angry with them, they won't help your kid. They don't need somebody yelling at them. They might get angry back and refuse to help. The more critical my husband is, the more defensive I get. Then I think everyone is looking at me like I'm an idiot.

"And all this time, I'm getting clippings from my mother-in-law. She used to occasionally send me clippings when John and I were first married about different things that newlyweds do, or things that she thought would be of interest to both my husband and me. It used to be fun getting mail from her. Now I get upset when I see an envelope with her name on it.

"Whenever she sees anything in the newspapers that she thinks is important for us to know, it's going to be in the next night's mail. I can't even talk to her about it. I always think she's criticizing me. I know it's not right, but whenever I see a letter from her I think, 'Here we go again. She's going to show you how you've failed.' I guess she thinks I need to read those things, but I hate getting them. And when she asks me if I received them, I feel like she's testing me to see if I have really read them.

"John's family believes that if you know enough, you can deal with anything. Also, if possible, you should deal with most things by yourself. Sometimes I think I have enough information, enough facts. I don't want to know any more. I feel overwhelmed.

"Maybe I'm like the person who wants to put their head in the sand, but it's so painful to have to know everything. I figure, take it a day at a time. If I get through today, there will be tomorrow to deal with. I trust the people caring for Judy, and it is their job to know.

"If there is something I really need to know, they will make me know it. I think that John is just absolutely the opposite. I'm drained, and I don't know what to do.

"Right now I feel like I'm a messenger, and both the people who send the messages and give the messages think I'm stupid. Or even worse, they feel sorry for me."

"**I know what Ellen is talking about**, but I can't seem to stop myself." Mr. Kramer, a tall, sturdy man in his early thirties, spoke rapidly.

"I like to be an expert in everything I do. Some people in school just would do their assignments, but for me, that was only the beginning. I wanted to know everything the kids in the class knew, and more. I used to get teased a lot because of it. It was certainly a part of my reputation growing up, and still is now. I guess people who work with me would say that if you need to know something, call John. Ellen has reminded me that some people think I'm a know-it-all. But, whereas Ellen trusts the experts, I'm not so sure. Some people I know in my own profession have reputations for being good. But I know their work, and they know nothing and make mistakes.

"When I was growing up, my aunt got very ill, and was misdiagnosed. The doctor gave her some medication that her system couldn't handle, and she died. That made me even more skeptical about doctors being experts. So when my daughter was born prematurely, I thought that it was important that Ellen and I know everything we could. I thought that, first of all, it would help us do a better job as parents.

"I'll be ever grateful to the obstetrician and the pediatrician. I know Ellen doesn't believe it, and maybe they don't either. I know that they were probably some of the few people in the world who could have managed such a difficult situation—knew what to do, and were optimistic. I never felt when I talked to them that they couldn't do the job.

"Somehow, when I get to talk to these professionals, the more I talk, the more I start to criticize them. The more I feel competitive, too. I don't understand it. And I can't stop.

"Ellen teases me and says that it reminds her of the arguing between my father and me. We enjoy it, but maybe other people see it differently. We argue about everything—world politics, sports, money, religion. I think it is sort of funny. If he says black, I say white. That's the way it's been ever since I was a kid. Everyone in our family likes to discuss and argue and thump and bang the table.

"As I got older, I wanted to read the same things my father had read so I could have the facts that he had. When Ellen and I first started dating and I brought her home to the house, she enjoyed it. She liked the 'liveliness' of the house. She thought it was very spirited. It was quite a contrast to the way she was brought up where people didn't show their emotions, and didn't encourage the kids.

"Ellen is awfully bright. She's one of these people who learns whenever she does something. If you show it to her once, she knows it. Ironically, I'm slower, and have to look at it and do it and do it and read before I've got something down.

"Ellen will start to do something even before she's read the directions. The next thing you know, she's got something that someone else will have to do over and over.

"I'm glad that she has the temperament to be patient with the people who have to take care of Judy. I think part of the reason Judy has done so well is because she has such a loving mother. It seems to me she should have professionals who are just as interested, and sometimes it makes me impatient.

"I love my wife and I love my daughter. I can see how everything I've done seems to be very critical of Ellen and seems to jeopardize what she does for Judy, and yet, I don't know how to stop."

The Kramers were puzzled and distressed by their marital problems. Mrs. Kramer felt she was constantly criticized and unappreciated by her husband. Mr. Kramer felt that his wife misinterpreted his comments, but he did not know how to stop making them.

Mr. and Mrs. Kramer's problems focused on their daughter, Judy, who was born prematurely, weighing only three and a half pounds. Both parents had different ideas about how they viewed and wanted to use the "experts" necessary in the life of their daughter. Mrs. Kramer felt that the various professionals were experts in their fields, and that they had a real interest in Judy's welfare. Mr. Kramer thought his wife was too trusting, and that she was unable to ask the professionals to justify the advice or treatment they were giving.

When Judy was very young, Mr. and Mrs. Kramer were able to go to appointments together. As Judy grew older, Mr. Kramer's work schedule made it difficult for him to attend these meetings. He began to send lists of questions he wanted answered. Mr. Kramer would cross examine his wife in the evening about the "expert's" responses, and was rarely satisfied with the information.

Mrs. Kramer found being in the middle between her husband and the professionals intolerable. After being criticized following a meeting with her daughter's teacher, she insisted that she and her husband do something about this problem, or she would end the marriage.

Problems involving experts and how to obtain and utilize the information they provide are common for parents whose child is born with a disability. They will often describe staff, doctors, nurses, and other consultants as cold, insensitive, and condescending. In turn, the professionals will insist that they *did* give the information to the parents, and cannot understand why the parents cannot remember. Often, professionals will focus on the emotional state of the parent as the source of the difficulty.

In the past, professionals had little training or information about the process of presenting information to parents of a disabled child. Some physicians did not believe that specific information would be useful. Others felt that little positive could be accomplished by leveling with parents about their child's condition. Finally, many had difficulty in presenting "bad" news to anyone.

More recently, we have developed a better understanding of the effect of stress on any interaction between parents and professionals around problems of the child with a disability. We have learned that information has to be presented carefully, clearly, and continuously over a long period of time if we expect the parents to fully understand, integrate, and actively use it.

We have also learned how overwhelming the birth of a disabled child can be to the parents, the "stages of mourning" they are likely to go through, and how much time resolving these issues can take. Professionals often have presented information at times when parents had difficulty in fully grasping anything.

In recent years, there has been an expansion in networks consisting of parents who have experienced a particular difficulty and who reach out to new parents from the moment of the birth of their child. These groups play a constructive role in helping new parents understand the total situation—information about the child's current and future life, what to expect from the various experts they will be using during the child's growing years, and other sources of help and information. When people are under stress, they turn to those ways of behaving that have been the most effective in handling difficult situations. There is often an exaggeration of the major personal problem-solving style of the individual. As the stress subsides, the individual will usually return to their more flexible ways of dealing with the issues of daily living.

When the stress continues as in the situation of parents with a disabled child, those personality traits that are adopted for emergencies can become problems if they are maintained for everyday living. Parents can remain so focused on the problems of their child that they overlook their relationship to one another, other members of the family, and the activities that may have given them pleasure and joy in the past.

The Kramers both looked upon their early years in the marriage as happy and productive ones. They traced their problems to the time of the birth of their daughter. Each of them represented different approaches to information. Mr. Kramer solved problems by gathering information by himself, and then using it to evaluate information from the "experts." He was interested in making long term plans.

Mrs. Kramer learned best by doing. She was afraid that too much knowledge would be difficult for her to manage, and was willing to deal with things one day at a time. Mr. Kramer was aware of the problem he had in dealing with professionals, and preferred when his wife dealt with them. He also understood that putting her in this position was not helpful either to his wife, or the marriage.

The problems the Kramers had involving their daughter made them uncertain about themselves as parents, and they had put off considering having another child. They spent so much time either finding out things about their daughter's condition, or doing things with her that they had stopped doing many of the things that had given them pleasure when they were first married. Their personal doubts made it difficult for them to discuss the problems with each other.

There had been a deterioration of the social fabric of the pleasures and joys of planning for the future that are necessary for any couple's growth and satisfaction.

The Kramers needed perspective on how well their daughter was doing. Both Mr. and Mrs. Kramer were pleased with Judy's ability to get along with other youngsters. Her learning remained above grade level, although she had some difficulties which her teacher had identified and was helping her with.

Children's growth and development are shaped, in part, by their relationships with their parents' behavior and attitudes. When children have difficulty in growing, parents as well as professionals search for those areas in attitude and behavior that they would like to change for the growth of the child. It was important for the Kramers to recognize that their child's growth and development was a tribute to their ability to be helpful parents.

Mr. and Mrs. Kramer were also reminded of the early days of their marriage, and their mutual commitment to one another. With this support, they were able to discuss alternative ways to deal with professionals and the information they provided. The Kramers also examined their wish to have another child and how each was frightened. They felt less reluctance to deal with the problems in other areas of their life—sexual as well as social. These problems had increased over the five year period of their daughter's life. They both were eager to resolve these difficulties and were referred to a marriage counselor who had experience dealing with couples whose problems were interrelated with the birth of a child with a disability. ■

This case has been selected from private practice and consultation files. The names and situations have been changed to reserve confidentiality.

CHAPTER 14

Life With My Sister —Guilty No More

by Julia Ellifritt

Being a sibling of a mentally retarded individual is complex since mental retardation affects everyone in the family. Everyone is a "victim" and yet there is no one to blame. Because there is no one to point the finger at, everyone in the family experiences some guilt. Guilt can be devastating to the sibling who does not know how to handle this.

> *I was supposed to be a good Christian and love and accept my sister when inwardly I did not.*

My sister, Bonnie Marie, is two years older than myself and has Down syndrome. She has influenced my life more than anyone else has or probably ever will. She manifests the true gentleness and unconditional love that comes only from God. Sure, I wish she were normal (although sometimes I do not wish she were normal, and that thought scares me). But I think that my experiences with Bonnie have made me a more tolerant, understanding person—one who does not judge people by outward appearances but who can see beauty in every person. However, maybe I am afraid to think that she has not been a blessing on my life.

My biggest problem in dealing with Bonnie has been guilt. I had not been able to forgive myself for the things I had done. I know that God has forgiven me. In fact, He is probably tired of me asking for His forgiveness. Maybe I would have felt better if Bonnie could have fought back—she never said anything bad to me, she never hit me. What is worse, when I would do something to her, she would stand there crying and say "I love you anyway." She was defenseless and I abused her. Now, years later, I cannot go to her and ask for her forgiveness—she would not know what I was talking about—so I have to live with my guilt.

I now know that there is sibling rivalry in every family—that bad feelings are not uncommon. But, as a child, I was told that those feelings were evil. I was supposed to be a good Christian and love and accept my sister when inwardly I did not. I concluded that there was something wrong with me.

It has been only recently that I have been able to come to grips with a situation that I had struggled with for twenty-two years without accepting.

My Own Identity
Part of my struggle in dealing with Bonnie was a need for my own identity, apart from her. When we were toddlers, Mom used to dress us alike. Maybe she was trying to make Bonnie look normal. From this early age, I was linked to a retarded person. Although I do not actually remember back that far, over the years whenever Bonnie tells people "we used to be twins,"—her way of explaining why we were dressed alike—I am reminded of this problem. I did not want to be associated with Bonnie.

My parents talk about my sixth birthday. I wanted a party without Bonnie. Bonnie loved parties and would be upset if she knew she was missing mine. So Dad took her to a movie while Mom had my party. I feel bad about that now. I know how much my actions hurt my parents but why should I still feel guilty about wanting my own identity; wanting a time when I was the special one without having a "freak" next to me?

It is interesting to me that I cannot remember any pleasant memories of Bonnie from my childhood. Whether that is intentional or not, I do not know. My earliest memory of her is when I was in the third grade and we used to "play house." I would always be the mother and make Bonnie the naughty child. During our play times I would spank her. Only I did not pretend, I really spanked her. Since I could not express my anger to my family, I expressed it to Bonnie, the source of my feelings, in a way that looked like play.   /During my grade school years I thought of Bonnie as a witch. She had long stringy hair and she was skinny. She drooled and twisted her fingers and had other unpleasant habits. My friends would come over to play, take one look at her, and some would actually turn around and leave. I felt like everything I did, Bonnie had to do also. I could not get away from her. If I took piano lessons, she had to take piano lessons. When I was in Girl Scouts, she was in Girl Scouts (Mom started a troop for retarded girls). She wanted to be like me, and yet I wonder what kind of a role model I was. And finally, the last straw—she was mainstreamed into my junior high school.

Adolescence

I wanted so much to be accepted by my peers, and yet no one would play with me because of my shadow—my "social disease" that would not go away. The kids at school would tease, take advantage, and play tricks on her and the other "special kids" in the lunchroom.

I remember on the bus, no one wanted Bonnie to sit beside them. One girl walked with a limp. Every day I would ask her if Bonnie or I could sit with her and she would always turn away and tell me the seat was saved. Day after day, no one sat beside her. She sat alone and we stood. One day I got fed up. I picked her books up off the seat and threw them at her. Then I sat on her and made enough room for Bonnie beside me. It was an uncomfortable ride home, but I was tired of standing and I wanted to show people that they would not "catch mental retardation" sitting beside Bonnie. When the girl got off at her stop, I watched her limp down the street and I cried because I had been so cruel. She was handicapped. Of anyone on the bus, she should have been understanding. She really hurt me. I wondered why no one understood my problem.

My biggest responsibility that year was to make sure Bonnie got on the bus each day after school. It was a simple task and not a problem until one day I could not find her. I panicked. She was not on the bus so I ran to her classroom. But she was not there either. I looked in the other rooms and ran back to the bus, but the bus was gone. I was so upset. I cried and cried. I would have to call Mom and tell her I had lost Bonnie. Bonnie was gone and it was my fault. I tearfully got through to Mom on the phone, just as Bonnie was stepping off the bus in front of our house. My mother wanted to know where I was. Why had I missed the bus?

Family

In my family, we were not allowed to discuss our feelings about Bonnie. After all, she was retarded and if we said anything negative, we might hurt her feelings. Well, what about my feelings? Who was concerned about how I felt? I hated my sister for ruining my life. She hurt me and I felt pain. I can remember one time having to sit next to her in the car and being so disgusted with her that I wanted to vomit, yet her feelings were at stake so I could say nothing. I remember being so angry at her, and then feeling so guilty. She was defenseless. She could not help the fact that she was retarded. How could I be mad at her? I lay awake at night praying that God would forgive me for having such thoughts about my sister. The range and intensity of emotions were too much for me to handle.

My parents never sat me down and said, "This is the problem. This is what's wrong with her. Do you understand? Do you have any questions?." My attempts to communicate with my parents were all in vain. I remember several times trying to tell my Mom how I felt and she would say, "Your feelings are wrong and you'd better change them."

It was devastating to always be told that my feelings were wrong, and yet still not be able to get rid of them. Besides feeling guilty about having angry feelings, I began to think there was something definitely wrong with me.

Right about that time, our family moved half way across the United States. This was my chance to start over. I was starting high school in a new town where no one knew me. I swore to myself that I would not let Bonnie hurt me anymore. In my mind, Bonnie suddenly disappeared.

"So, you're new in town. Do you have any sisters?" "No," was always my reply. Bonnie was not going to be my problem; she was not my sister. When other students would ask me about my brothers and sisters, I would simply lie. It was easier to lie than to explain. My plan worked for a few months until one night when I was at a Youth Group meeting at the new chruch my family had been attending. The leader introduced me, said I was new, and then told everyone I had a retarded sister. There went my alibi.

To my surprise, however, this group was different. They thought it was neat that I had a retarded sister. I talked about Bonnie and they were interested. They wanted to meet her, and to do something with retarded kids. So we planned monthly parties for the retarded kids in our community. I spent many hours phoning parents, planning activities, and putting together parties that turned out to be successes.

As my high school years wore on, I did a lot of volunteering and working in the field of mental retardation. That work continued until I went away to college. I enjoyed my work, yet I knew something was wrong. Something I could not put my finger on. After two years away, I transferred schools and moved back home.

I began to realize that I had all the patience in the world with profoundly retarded men, but if Bonnie looked at me wrong, I got mad. I was genuine and loving towards people more severely retarded than Bonnie, but my love for her was not genuine. I loved to tease her, even though I knew it hurt her and made her mad. It made me feel good. I knew then that I was not behaving rationally. Twenty-one years of unexpressed anger had built up inside me, and it was starting to come out in unfortunate ways. I was desperate to tell this to someone and get it off my chest but I had no one.

Without telling my parents, I went to a psychologist. I cried and cried and talked nonstop for one hour, paid sixty dollars, and left. He did not say two words to me the whole time and I felt like he did not really understand me, but I got it out. On the way home, I started thinking to myself, "You just paid sixty dollars to someone who didn't say much. You could have told all that to a friend and it would have been cheaper." Then I said to myself, "No, Julia, you don't have a friend that you could tell it all to. In fact, the walls probably wouldn't listen." I cried again.

Changes

I should have been glad that I won the admiration of peers and adults, but I felt they were not seeing the whole picture. They would tell me, "You sure are a patient person. I admire the work you've done," or, "You've handled your situation well. I would never have been able to live with a retarded sister." Politely, I would thank them. Inside my heart would cry out, "I did not choose to be in this position. If *you* had a retarded sister, you would learn to handle it. And maybe I haven't really handled it at all, but I can't tell you that now. You wouldn't love and respect me anymore. Why can't you let me be human?"

I began to realize that I had been doing all kinds of work with the mentally retarded partly to assuage my negative feelings for my sister. I felt that in God's eyes I was making amends—that good works made up for bad thoughts. That was a scary thought. I did not want to think that all those years of work were done in vain. On the contrary, I enjoyed my experiences, and my life has been enriched by some very special people.

I was a college senior majoring in social work. I knew I would never be able to help anyone as a professional unless I could deal with my own feelings. I knew then that I could not do it alone. With the help of an excellent therapist, I began a healing process that was very painful, but very much overdue. I went to a support group for siblings of the retarded, and for the first time in my twenty-two years, I talked to others who had a retarded sibling. The relief and joy I felt was

---

I am learning how to deal with my negative feelings and I am on my way to becoming a better communicator.

---

indescribable and will be forever etched upon my memory.

I am learning how to deal with my negative feelings and I am on my way to becoming a better communicator. I now realize that Bonnie possesses many of the qualities Jesus had—a gentle spirit, pure unconditional love, and selfless giving. I can learn from her. I am on my way to becoming more like her.

Dedication

This story is for Bonnie. With it, I pledge to do my best to educate other siblings as to the importance of feelings and family communication so that no other sibling need suffer silently. Bonnie may never read these words, but one day I know they will be inscribed in her heart and she will understand.

I have hopes that one day I will see her in heaven, and as we walk the streets we will embrace and cry, talk and giggle, and do the things that all sisters do; the things I have been deprived of in this lifetime. And we both will understand. Until then, I have my story. I can close the book on that part of my life, and I vow never to feel guilty about it again. ■

Julia Ellifritt is active in S.I.B.S.—the Society of Involved Brothers and Sisters of the Developmentally Disabled. She has recently graduated from Cleveland State University with a bachelor's degree in Social Work.

CHAPTER 15

AN OPEN LETTER TO PASTORS AND TO PARENTS

by Henry and Elsa Ellis and George T. Warren

Dear Pastors

Please understand that we are speaking for many people who are parenting children and adults whose physical, mental, communication, or behavioral problems have interferred with participation in "normal" religious activities.

In your sermons and programs, you have shown a deep concern for and have given priority to those who are isolated and alienated through poverty and hunger, sickness and death, racial prejudice, aging and divorce. *Why have you not included us*, permanently disabled people and our families? Your signs say, "Welcome!", but your steps and narrow doors, and your discomfort with our differences in appearance and behavior say "KEEP OUT!"

Your sermons explain the stages of grief anyone might expect to go through when experiencing a loss. Your congregation needs to know that loss due to a handicapping condition involves the same phases of adjustment as that experienced by those whose loss comes through death or divorce—shock, denial, rejection, pain, anger, guilt, then rationalization, compensation, and finally learning to live with what is left.

There is, however, a significant difference which needs to be recognized between adjustment to death and adjustment to disability—a difference which affects our lives in many ways. Death is final; disability is continuing and full of uncertainties.

In death, the bereaved are sometimes told, "God took your loved one away to do greater things in Heaven." Friends share their grief, and the family eventually is able to go on living their own lives.

Well-intentioned friends try to console us by saying, "God knows best," then leave us alone to cope with the disability and with the life-long changes it makes in our entire family.

When our disabled child was born, we had to give up the perfect infant we had anticipated. We learned to accept and love our baby as a different child. But at each stage of her life, we cannot help wondering what she would have been like if she had not been damaged by the birth process, or by Rubella during pregnancy, or by some other imperfection.

We cannot believe that God chose us to live with a disability, as the phrase "God knows best" implies. Had He done so, He would have chosen us from a congregation whose minister and members understood and accepted our child's unusual appearance and behavior, even though her presence might be disturbing at times. He would not have permitted others who were more "blessed" with attractive bodies and personalities to turn away when we needed the support of friends.

God did not take away the distorted limb, the disfigured face, the lack of ability. Disability is left with us. It is a daily reminder to us and to others of our loss. You say that the adjustment period for death and divorce can be expected to last for years. There is *no* time of adjustment to disability. We no sooner learn to live with one aspect of the trauma of disability when we are faced with another, especially at the "normal changing points" in life.

Sometimes the attitudes of other people in our lives create more problems that the disability itself. The ever-presence of disability announces our loss to every person we meet. Sensitive people are particularly vulnerable—they feel the loss almost as though it were their own. For us, it is as though the disability has just happened. We are forced to live the trauma over and over again as we try to help *others* adjust. We witness people's reactions constantly. They are shocked that someone can be so grossly different. They seem to turn away in disbelief and fear wondering how a person can live without a faculty which they have always taken for granted. They cry for us (and for themselves) long after we have been drained of tears and after we have learned to laugh at what humor we can find in our differences.

Can you imagine how we feel knowing the discomfort we cause others, simply by being in their presence? We try to rationalize that it is *their* problem if they are uncomfortable, but it is difficult to live constantly with adverse reactions.

We need you to help your congregation, the "others" in our lives, understand and accept us and our disabilities. You have an excellent opportunity to take action and dispell myths about disabilities. You can help your congregation to stop using

> We need you, our pastors, to help your congregations, the "others" in our lives, understand and accept us and our disabilities.

empty words which leaves families of disabled children feeling cold and alienated. We need support, not mere assertions.

Please tell them that it is O.K. to feel uncomfortable with the differences of our disability, but do not let that discomfort keep us away from *our* church or synagogue. In the past we have been asked not to bring our disabled family members to a service because "others" objected. But, Pastor, we need to come!

Please help them cope with their guilt. They need to know that it is perfectly normal to have negative feelings about disabilities. It is important to face those feelings and deal with them. Otherwise, these attitudes become our greatest handicap.

Assure your congregation that no one knows better than we do that a disability is not easy to live with or confront. A disability is only part of someone, though, and it must not keep us apart from our church or synagogue. A child of God can be a whole person in His image, even with a physical or behavioral difference from others. We miss what we have lost, but cannot dwell on that loss. Feeling alienated from a potentially supportive community makes that loss feel even more acute. Persons with handicapping conditions and their families must be allowed to live in peace with their fellow citizens.

Please let your congregation know we still need them as much, or more, than before disability came into our lives. We need them to reach out to us, not out of pity, but out of love and compassion.

Parents have been called "saints." We are *not* saints! We are normal people who happen to have a child with a disabling condition. We are good, we are bad; we are happy, we are sad; we are rich, we are poor; we are tender, we are tough; we are patient, we are impatient; we are weak, we are strong. We have one thing in common—we are all parents whose child happens to be disabled.

Some of our lives have been enriched by our experience of coping.

Some of us are bitter.

Some of us are tired.

Some of us have devoted our lives to our disabled child through adulthood—a responsibility normally shared early in a child's life by church, school, and neighbors. We have learned to hide our real feelings and to lie to ourselves and to others.

Some of us have tried to cope but failed. We deserted our families because we could not face the trauma of disability—but we carried our guilt with us, and we have no one with whom to share our guilt.

Some of us placed our severely disabled infant in a state institution without ever bringing him home, on the advice of our physician. Now we are being asked to take our adult/child out of the institution and bring him back to our home and community. And, we find our synagogue/church no longer has a place for us as a family with a severely disabled member.

We have the same need for spiritual renewal as other members of your congregation. Our awareness of disability, however, has given scripture and sermons a different meaning. For example, Pastors speak as though light is *good* and *holy*. Those of us who are blind need reassurance that God made darkness as well as light, and both are good. Pastors say, "Your faith will make you whole." Are you saying that it was a lack of faith that "caused" the disability, or our child's deformities could be cured with faith? Or is there some other kind of "wholeness" we should know about, in God's sight? Pastors tell us of the power of God to heal—but you do not help us understand why he heals some and not others. How will the congregation feel about my child when they find out his epileptic seizures cannot be controlled by medication? Even in this enlightened age, will they believe he is devil-possessed? Many act as if they think he is.

Like other families, our family needs someone who cares and understands our unique abilities and limitations, to share our joys as well as our sorrows—our joy in our ten year old's progress when he learns to tie his own shoes, our frustration when our teenagers and young adults watch their friends move away from their families to live more independently.

What an opportunity you have to enable your congregation to open the doors of your church/synagogue's building to those who have been alienated by ignorance and prejudice against disability. Please let your congregation know that prayers are not enough—theirs for us and ours for them—unless our prayers bring us together in a give and take relationship. ∎

Dear Parents

Thank you for sharing yourselves in such a frank and honest manner. It is important that the door you have opened for communication between us swing both ways, with each of us understanding that we speak from caring and concern. I shall try to be equally honest and open with you. I cannot speak for all pastors, for our varied religions and faiths have grown out of our differences in theology. Perhaps our theological concepts have not kept in step with medical and social concepts. Together, we need to re-examine our beliefs about the nature of disability.

I feel all pastors will agree, however, with the basic concept that we are all created to be with other human beings, and our very existence depends upon our relationship with one another. When any one of God's children is isolated from others for any reason, that cause should and *must* be addressed by the church.

You are on firm Biblical and theological grounds to ask, "Why do you not include us in your sermons and programs?" Jesus himself pioneered in reaching out to heal disabled persons and to restore them to acceptance within the community. He understood the trauma of isolation and rejection by the community.

God is not "testing" you or "punishing" you with disability. Yes, God can bring good out of suffering, but that does not mean he sent the suffering. No, suffering comes from accidents of nature, human ignorance or human evil, or from some source beyond the finite limitations of the mind. The church and synagogue seek to alleviate suffering.

You who live with people that have handicapping conditions are the authorities; pastors and congregations are the "laypeople"—many of us have never known a severely disabled person. Our church will benefit in many ways as we learn to apply our religion to the real life situations disability presents.

You have every right and responsibility to claim an equal place among the congregation—to serve and be served. We pledge our support to make churches and synagogues as available to families with disabled members as they were to those families before disability entered their lives. Our prayers are for pastors and congregations, as well as for persons with handicapping conditions and their families—for we are handicapped in our ability to reach out and include others who have been isolated and alienated by society.

The church and synagogue are in a unique position to inform, to educate, and to motivate people to become involved in the transition of severely disabled individuals from social isolation to "full participation in the least restrictive environment." However, neither pastors nor congregations have been prepared for the key role we need and *want* to play. We are expected to adjust and feel comfortable with each disabled person we meet, regardless of the nature and degree of the disability. We are admonished to "just be ourselves," but we are human and we need time and support while adjusting to the wide range of disabilities.

Living with a disability is a new life role for us. Our parents taught us how to be "acceptable" children. Our children taught us how to be decent parents. Friends taught us how to be friends. Divinity and rabbinical school taught us how to be pastors.

Now you who have learned to cope with a disability may need to teach us *how to be ourselves* in this new situation.

What should we say or do when we meet a disabled person? Or is there nothing "special" we need to do, except try to relax?

When we offer to help, we are accused of taking away independence. When we ignore the disability or do not offer to help, some think we are unkind, rude, or insensitive. When we focus on the disability, it seems everything we say or do is wrong.

How can we communicate with someone who does not or cannot talk?

How can we protect someone who seems vulnerable due to disability, without being "overprotective?"

We have so many questions. Whom do we ask?

Please understand that I am not trying to excuse pastors for our failure to meet the needs of permanently disabled people and their families. There is no excuse for putting disabled families last on our list of priorities. It is important, however, that the needs of pastors be understood as we try, together, to seek solutions to our communication problem.

We are not saints either! Pastors and members of congregations are human, with normal needs, feelings, and behaviors. Most pastors have more ability in one area than in another—some are exceptional speakers; some are expert theologians and teachers; some are adept at administration and fund raising; some are their best at personal counseling and problem solving. Few have expertise in all aspects of the ministry, although all pastors are expected to be capable and to serve in all of these roles, with God's help and with the help of our congregations.

We care! We want to share the responsibility of helping our congregation—the "others" in your life—understand and adjust to the differences of disability. Some of us have tried to remove architectural, communication, and attitudinal barriers, yet few persons with handicapping conditions attend our churches or synagogues. We have replaced steps with ramps, widened doors, and reserved parking spaces. We have had sign language interpreters for worship service and sponsored sign language courses at our synagogue. We have had films, speakers, and special programs to create awareness of people with handicapping conditions. We have tried to develop our own understanding and to reach out by attending meetings of parent and disabled groups. They, in turn, rejected us. We have been told that over ten perecent of the population is disabled. Where are they?

Pastors are motivated to be what God calls us to be to all of His children. Can you imagine the guilt and frustration we feel when, with our human frailties, we fail—as we apparently have failed the disabled community.

Ministers, rabbis, and priests receive hundreds of appeals for worthy causes. Is it any wonder that the sensitive pastor will choose a few that he or she is confident can be done well? Pastors who have attempted more than is humanly possible for one person to achieve have become "burned out" over the years. After seeing critical causes and programs fail or be rejected by the congregation, a new emphasis on mainstreaming the severely disabled may be perceived as one more in a long line of risks.

Pastors and congregations need the wisdom and understanding of those of you who have learned from experience to cope not only with the disability, but also with the feelings one might be expected to have when first faced with disability.

Will you come and share your experiences with us? Will you listen to our sermons and educational programs, then let us know what you have heard us say—the hidden messages we did not realize were there? Then together, we may find a way to help our congregation understand, and to speak more effectively to exceptional parents and their families.

We need this dialogue. Will you invite us to your home and to your parent and disabled persons group meetings so that we can get acquainted with you and the issues that concern you?

Religion must address the reality of disability, and the continuing needs of all who are involved. Together we can demonstrate God's power, not only to heal, but to restore to acceptance within the community. ∎

After seeing critical causes and programs fail or be rejected by the congregation, a new emphasis on mainstreaming the severely disabled may be perceived as one more in a long line of risks.

Henry and Elsa Ellis are founders of OUTLOOK Nashville, Inc. and OUTLOOK Central Florida, Inc., non-profit organizations whose purpose is to provide more normal community experiences for persons with handicapping conditions and their families.

The *Open Letter to Pastors/Parents* were written with the thought that these letters might be used by both parents and the clergy to open the door to better communication and greater understanding of one another.

Open Letter to Pastors is a compilation of concerns and feelings expressed to the Ellises by disabled persons and their families over the past thirty years.

Open Letter to Parents, written primarily by Reverend George T. Warren, attempts to respond to the desire for support and inclusion in the church or synagogue by families who have a child with a disability.

CHAPTER 16

EDITORIAL

Media and Attitudes Towards People With Disabilities

Controversy about television programming is part of an on-going dialogue in our country. Many different groups would like to have changes or restrictions in the nature and content of television programming. These groups cover the political spectrum, and the issues range from the depictions of sex and violence through the portrayal of different ethnic, racial, or religious groups.

Recent research has outlined the usual presentation of the disabled person on T.V. These characters are cast generally as victims of ridicule or abuse. Often, they are shown as submissive people with little to say, as stupid or uncultured, or as passive and weak. Sometimes they are seen as impatient, selfish, and self-pitying. When challenged, producers argue that T.V. programs merely reflect what people already think and believe.

We are concerned because television plays a major role in providing information and shaping attitudes. Attitudes influence what people attend to in their world, and therefore, what and how they will respond. Attitudes are very difficult to change. They develop over a long period of time, and single dramatic events like a television special are unlikely to change them significantly.

The attitudes of important decision makers—T.V. producers, elected officials, superintendents of schools, and parents—were shaped at a time when our understanding of individuals with disabilities was limited, and the views held were often negative. Laws were passed to change behavior because waiting for society to change its attitudes might have meant that people with disabilities would have to wait forever for opportunities for a richer, fuller life in the community.

Many still remain pessimistic that any real change has occurred. They can cite problems of implementing legislation, hostility within their communities, and problems in funding. Poor television has been seen as merely reflecting this poor state of affairs.

We believe that a revolution has taken place that has not received attention. Our children and other young people have had far more experience with children with disabilities than any other previous generation. Public Law 94-142 has meant that school children are likely to interact and be aware of children with disabilities in their schools and playgrounds.

Children's television has been a pioneer in leading the way toward a different presentation. There have been a number of specials in which individuals with disabilities are presented in a more realistic light. The programs present the individual's struggles to grow, and their needs for support. For example, a recent poignant episode on Diff'rent Strokes included a girl in a wheelchair, and her able-bodied classmate dealing with mainstreaming. Shows like Sesame Street, Zoom, and Mister Roger's Neighborhood have been increasing presentation of children with disabilities as everyday participants in their lives, and in the schools. In Fat Albert, the cartoon program produced and acted in by Bill Cosby, there is a systematic effort to present children's weaknesses, and provide ways of helping children whose behavior is negative.

We will not have to wait until our children reach maturity before their more positive attitudes and experience will affect society. Although we are aware of how parental attitudes shape children's behavior, we have not fully understood the extent to which children educate their parents. While we ask and discover what our youngsters learn in school, we are continually re-educating ourselves.

In the media section of this issue, we have included the names of films, books, and pamphlets that merit inclusion in the general resources of any community. We must continue in our efforts to encourage the media decision makers and sponsors to include people with disabilities and relevant themes in their productions. Each of us must continue to write and call those who are helpful as well as those who are not to encourage them at every level of media—local as well as national, via satellite and via neighborhood cable. It is in this way that we can all make a contribution to the more positive attitudes of this generation of children. To the extent that children educate their elders, we will all benefit. ■

—M. J. S., S. D. K.—

CHAPTER 17

THE PUBLIC LIBRARY
A Practical Guide for Parents of Disabled Children

by Michelle D. Bowdler

The public library belongs to all of us, and is responsible to provide the information we need.

People with disabilities and their families require information. Coping with the needs and adjusting to the progress of a disabled child is a difficult, on-going process. Parents need to understand their child's condition, to have reasonable expectations for their child's growth and development, and to know how to help both themselves and their child. Ordinary guidelines for parenting may not fully address the special problems parents of disabled children confront.

The information resources available for people with disabilities and their families are growing—more books, films, and newsletters are available now than ever before. It is unlikely, however, that one can walk into a bookstore or up to a magazine stand and find substantial information about disabilities. Many people overlook a wonderful resource in their efforts to find information—the public library.

The Public Library

Libraries vary in size. Depending on where one lives, the public library may be one or two small rooms maintained by a volunteer staff, or span an entire city block and employ hundreds of people. Libraries can be intimidating regardless of their size.

We probably remember from childhood that the library was a place where, if we were quiet, we could find books and read them. As adults, we can learn that libraries are excellent places to find information, and that their function is to serve members of the community. The public library belongs to all of us, and is responsible to provide the information we need.

The Staff

When you first walk into a library, you will see the staff at the front desk. The people at the front desk often work in circulation, and may not be able to respond to requests for information. If you are unclear about where to begin, it may be helpful to ask for the reference librarian. Knowing which staff person to ask for help will give you a solid place to start.

Try not to feel reluctant to "bother" the librarians. It is their job to help you. The reference librarian has been specially trained to be familiar with many information sources, and how to help people find the information they want.

Be as specific as possible when telling the reference librarian what you want. The more information a librarian has, the better she or he will be able to help you—saving you both time and energy. If you want a specific book, ask for it. If you want information on a specific disability or illness, let the librarian know.

Merely asking what resources the library has on disabilities may give you enough material to keep you reading for the next five years—and about a lot of things that do not apply to either you or your child. Sometimes, having too much information can be as overwhelming as not having enough.

The Card Catalogue

The reference librarian might first take you to the card catalogue, where you can look up resources by subject, author, or title. This system can be of value both if you know specifically what you want, and if you want to research more generally. The card catalogue can tell you whether or not the library has a specific book, or books by a particular author. Also, it enables you to see what resources are available under one category or subject. You will find many books listed under "handicaps." But, under specific disabilities like "Down syndrome," or "cerebral palsy," you will find fewer.

Card catalogues have limits. For example, you might not find anything if you look under "William's syndrome," or some other rare disorder. This does not mean that there is no information available about rare syndromes. Rather, it means that you need to look in a more general category for information.

Try not to feel reluctant to "bother" the librarians. It is their job to help you.

A good imagination helps while searching through the card catalogue. If you look in the card catalogue and there is nothing under "dyslexia," try thinking what other subjects information on dyslexia would fall under. There might be information under "learning disabilities," or "reading," or "childhood development," or "language." The more practice you have with the card catalogue, the easier this process will be.

Remember, if you feel stuck thumbing through thousands and thousands of index cards, ask the reference librarian for further assistance. Most libraries have subject headings list books. If you look up your subject of interest in the guide, it will tell you what categories it is listed under in this library's catalogue system.

Finding a Book

If a book that you want is listed in the card catalogue, that means the library owns it. Finding it is the next step. The cards in the catalogue will have a series of numbers on them that identify where books are located in the library. Most libraries leave ample scrap paper near the card catalogue so that you can copy down the numbers and begin your search. You can either give the numbers to the librarian and ask her or him to find a book for you, or you can ask to be taught the layout of the library so you can find books yourself.

If a book that you want is not on the shelves, you can check with the front desk when it is scheduled to be returned. Unfortunately, many people do not return their books when they are due. Someone at the front desk might be willing to take your name, and call you when the borrower brings it in.

If The Library Does Not Have What You Want

If the library does not have a book you want, see if it is still in print. Almost all libraries carry *Books in Print*. This reference source will tell you if a book is still being distributed by a publisher. If the book is still in print, you can order it directly from the publisher.

Even if a book is no longer in print, some other library in the area may have it. Most libraries have access to interlibrary loan. Your librarian can contact neighboring libraries to see if they have the book you want. If they do, they can send it. This process may take several weeks. If you want the book right away, you can find out which library has it, and either read it there, or see if you can check it out.

If there are books or periodicals that you think your library should have, suggest they order them. It will help the library staff if you can give the name of the book, the author, and the publisher. Sometimes it helps to attach a favorable review or brief summary to your book request.

The Reference Room

A library's reference room is another area in which to find information. The resources available in this section of the library can provide you with information concerning your field of interest, as well as refer you to various resources.

Many reference sources are compilations of materials available on a specific subject. For example, *Notes From A Different Drummer: A Guide to Juvenile Fiction Portraying the Handicapped by Barbara H. Baskin and Karen H. Harris* can be found in some library reference rooms. In books like this one, the research has already been done by somebody else. If you go to the library to find novels for your child to read about other children who have disabilities, this one reference source will provide you with the titles of hundreds of books, the authors, publishers, and a brief description of each piece. This saves you countless time searching through the catalogue and shelves of the children's section.

The following list provides a few examples of the kinds of books and materials that may be available in the reference room to help individuals with disabilities and their families:

The dictionary. A short definition and the correct spelling of something can help in beginning to find information on a specific subject.

A medical dictionary. This dictionary will give you a more specific definition of your child's disability. If there is anything written you do not understand or have not had explained to you by your doctor, write it down and ask about it.

Libraries are often delighted to have their space utilized, but do not have the time or resources to research and execute plans by themselves. Parts of the library can be used for posters and book displays from organizations concerned with the care of children with disabilities. This is just one more way the library can be used to educate the community.

Other Libraries

In addition to the public library, there may be other libraries in the community that can be helpful. Many libraries carry a reference book entitled, *Directory of Special Libraries and Information Centers*. This book lists special libraries by subject, and gives pertinent information about location, hours of operation, phone numbers, and access.

It may be possible to gain access to a local university library. Even if you cannot check out books without being a student, they may still allow you to use their reference or periodical areas, as well as reading books there.

Some hospitals have libraries. These tend to be smaller and geared to health care professionals, but it may be easier to find specific information and resources about disability and illness in one of these libraries.

Call specific organizations you know about—or have found out about from your public library—and ask if they have libraries. If you are specifically interested in mental retardation, the local Association for Retarded Citizens in your community may have a small library that has helpful resources. The March of Dimes chapter probably has several books or pamphlets about specific birth defects. United Cerebral Palsy will undoubtedly have resources concerning cerebral palsy, and so on.

Every state has an Easter Seal chapter. One of the primary functions of Easter Seal is to provide information to people with disabilities and their families. Even if they do not have a library themselves, they may be able to suggest organizations in your town that do have them.

Organizations that are not specifically for disabled people and their families may have libraries that are helpful. For example, Planned Parenthood is concerned about educating the community about sexuality and birth control. They would be a good choice to call and see if they have any books about sexuality and the disabled. Even if organizations do not have libraries, they may be able to suggest a few books to look up in the public library—use them as a reference source.

State library agencies quite often oversee public libraries and offer support in terms of money, consultants, and information sources. Usually, there is one person in the state library agency designated as the "special needs clientele expert." This librarian may be able to direct you to a variety of informational resources, as well as tell you where you can obtain "special" items like talking books for the visually impaired.

Support Your Libraries

Libraries exist to serve the need for information of the members of its community. They cannot be faulted if, with their limited resources, they are not being encouraged to buy books that will help the disabled community. The library staff cannot know what people in the community want unless we tell them.

Libraries need information, support, and encouragement from all of us. There are several ways to be active in helping the public library—giving money, serving on the library board, and telling friends and organization members the help we have found from the public library.

People with disabilities and their families can benefit by utilizing information and helping to expand existing resources available through the public library. If resources that exist to serve all of us actually help the disabled population, we have taken one further step in assuring an integration of the disabled community into the community as a whole. ■

Librarians ordinarily enjoy being able to share all of the information and resources that they have access to.

June Carrell, Reference/Community Services Librarian for the Reading Public Library, was instrumental in preparing this article. John Collins, Head of the Boston University Educational Resources Library, gave his assistance as well.

CHAPTER 18

A Parent's Statement to a County Board

by Bonnie Ziemman

I am the mother of two small boys and raising them alone. My son, Adam, is bilaterally profoundly hearing impaired. He is also hydrocephalic and requires an internal shunt to carry spinal fluid from his head to other body areas. He is not retarded, and one need not be with Adam long to discover that he is a bright child with much potential.

I have a special needs child, no one can dispute that. I am a special needs parent. The tragedy that occurred to my son has happened to me too, and will affect us for our lifetimes.

The child I hoped to have, planned to share and grow together with, and fantasized caring for, died at birth due to multiple birth defects. I felt grief as great as a death experience, but there was no funeral or final end point so that time might diminish this great emotional wound. This child has been cheated and I am cheated with him.

The least painful choice was for me to try and keep this child. Together we would struggle, hope for and try to find meaning and quality in life. My anger that wanted to rip walls from their foundation would channel itself to finding answers and not allow me to surrender as I faced with my child his eleven surgeries, hearing impairment, and meningitis, all prior to two years of age.

Early on I was forced to quit my job. There was nothing normal about my life and I felt fragmented, dangling somewhere but not any longer a part of the everyday world. I am a minority. I do not feel blessed or like some special goddess chosen by the Lord to do his work. I am not so special that my coping abilities are any better or worse than the next person. Statements to that effect take the everyday world off the hook so they need not participate or deal with it at all. Another line I have heard too often is "Take him home and love him." Love alone, like kissing away the hurt of a small child's scratch, will not make the impact families face disappear.

Parents of disabled children sacrifice a lot, often times our careers, financial stability, our own personal goals, and too often the breakdown of the family unit. A disabled child's needs can dictate where the family lives, making it necessary to find a city with suitable schools and medical facilities.

Our children are at risk to receive medical or life insurance. I know of families where the father turned down raises and job promotions simply to stay within the financial guidelines so their children can receive medical care under SSI.

Our futures, as well as our children's, are not financially secure. We are boxed into a financial catch 22. My child alone utilizes six different medical specialties. The financial, physical, emotional, and spiritual drain placed upon a family is astronomical. Extended support groups and counseling are skimpy to non-existent. It is a basic need and should be implemented.

My Adam is well adjusted, secure, out-going, and generally loved by those who know him. I love him no differently than you love your own children. He has given me far more than he has taken. Adam has established a rich vocabulary of signs, and his efforts to speak will probably allow him to be oral some day. His adjustment, hunger to learn and accomplishments have come from me. No school could have provided this alone for my son. I am his mother, father, nurse, physical therapist, advocate, and teacher. The support that I am able to give Adam gains its very foundation from the support given to me. Support is energy, though. What can I give to my child and still have left over for me?

Why do I devote myself to letter writing, speeches, and counseling other parents? I want to spread awareness, to impress upon others our great need, and to help existing progressive programs remain alive. I see the benefits today, but even more I visualize tomorrow when we have kept a child in the community—his or her natural environment.

If we nourish children and their families today, we all reap the benefits tomorrow.

When you consider priorities, please do not forget children. ■

Bonnie Zeimann is the mother of two sons, Adam and Matthew. She is a registered nurse who now devotes her time to her children and to volunteer advocacy work on behalf of the Association for Retarded Citizens, United Cerebral Palsy, and many other organizations. She and her children live in Madison, Wisconsin.

CHAPTER 19

Preparation, Persistence, Pressure
Strategies For Moving To A New Community

by Beth Ann Kelly

Moving is a stressful experience for any family. Families that include a child with special educational needs have concerns which add greatly to the stress of moving. Will the new school district have appropriate programs for my child? How long will it take to get my child into school? What if there is no program to meet my child's needs? What will we do if there is a waiting list? And how will our disabled child adjust to a new home and school?

I have moved several times since my son was identified as having disabilities. He has attended school in three different school districts in three states. With each move, I learned more about how to help along the process of changing schools with a child who has disabilities. I have found three necessary ingredients to the process—preparation, persistence, and pressure.

Learning

I was naive when I first approached a school district to have my son, Eddy, admitted. One of Eddy's therapists told me that a law—Public Law 94-142, the Education for All Handicapped Children Act—had been passed, and that the public school system was required to begin educating Eddy when he turned three. His third birthday would be in the fall. That spring, I made an appointment with a school psychologist and took a copy of Eddy's records with me. I fully expected the psychologist to accept Eddy into a program without questions. But he did not.

The psychologist informed me that Eddy would first be evaluated. Then the district would inform me if Eddy qualified for special education. I was very surprised that anyone would question Eddy's eligibility. I was appalled to think that the two years of home programs—physical and speech therapy—would be dropped when Eddy turned three, and there would be no alternative programs available. Eventually, the school district determined that Eddy was eligible. He entered a preschool special education program.

Delays

When Eddy was five, we moved again. I still did not know what Public Law 94-142 said. I assumed that all school districts were somehow connected, and operated the same way in special education. In hopes of avoiding the delays of his initial placement, I had Eddy thoroughly evaluated prior to our move. I approached the new school district for placement, confident that Eddy's specific educational needs were well documented.

This time I did not have copies of the recent evaluations. I had to insist that the receiving school district get those results rather than redo the entire evaluation. This caused a delay. Eddy missed eight full weeks of school because I had not prepared adequately for the move.

Our most recent move was smoother. I prepared for it and followed through using the three steps of preparation, persistence, and pressure.

Preparation

Long before contemplating a move, I learned about the federal laws that affect my son's education. Those laws are: The Education for all Handicapped Children Act (P.L. 94-142), and parts of Section 504 of the Rehabilitation Act of 1973 (P.L. 93-112) and the Vocational Education Act Amendments of 1976 (P.L. 94-482). Parents can read these acts and get further information about them from their members of Congress, or from many parent network groups.

While learning about those laws, I also learned that each state writes its own implementing rules and regulations for the federal laws. Every state (and all Department of Defense schools) must comply with the federal laws to receive federal funds for the education of handicapped children. The state of New Mexico does not receive federal funds and does not comply with P.L. 94-142. Each state may provide more rights and services to handicapped children and their parents than P.L. 94-142 requires if it chooses to do so.

Armed with that knowledge when I knew we would be moving again, I set about making preparations for a smooth and quick transition for Eddy from one school district to another. I wrote to the school district we were moving to—which I refer to as the "receiving school district"—describing Eddy's disabilities and educational needs. I asked about possible placement options, and what specific information that district required to determine eligibility for special education. In the letter, I also requested a copy of the state's special education rules and regulations.

I also wrote to a group for parents of handicapped children in the area, asking for a parent's view of the school district's services to children who have disabilities. This contact with a support group proved useful to me later.

School Evaluation

Several weeks prior to moving, I reviewed my son's educational records and noted that he was due to have a three year re-evaluation that spring. I requested that his evaluation be completed before we moved, with enough time to get the written reports so that I could hand carry copies to the receiving school district. I asked that the re-evaluation include all areas of disability. In other words, I wanted occupational therapy and speech evaluations as well as an academic one. Because these requests were made well in advance of our departure, the school district was willing and able to grant them.

At the same time that I requested the updated evaluations, I also asked that a new Individualized Education Program (IEP) be drafted before we left. This way, I would have an IEP that accurately portrayed Eddy's educational strengths and needs, and that gave an accurate picture of an appropriate educational program for him. Again, the school district personnel were very helpful.

Further Evaluations

I made an appointment with Eddy's pediatrician for a complete physical and a conference. Because Eddy's pediatrician was a specialist in child development and developmental disabilities, I asked him to write a summary of Eddy's development, and to include any recommendations he would want to pass on to school personnel and Eddy's next physician. The doctor's two hand-written pages were helpful to both the receiving school district and Eddy's subsequent pediatrician.

When the school district completed its evaluation of Eddy's academic, social, intellectual, self-help, physical, speech, and motor abilities, the IEP meeting was held. Eddy's teacher had assessed his progress toward his IEP goals and objectives, and presented that information at the meeting. Each person who had assessed or worked with Eddy during the school year contributed to the IEP process.

Even though I was up to my chin in packing boxes and tissue paper at home, I took care to have Eddy's educational and medical records in a place safe from the chaos. I put them in the car to protect them from helping friends who might have packed them inadvertently. The last thing I wanted was to have Eddy's entry to a new school delayed because his records were misplaced.

Following the IEP meeting, I went to the district office and had most of Eddy's file copied twice—one set of copies for the receiving school district and one for myself. When we boarded the plane—the packing and cleaning finished, our household goods well on their way, all the goodbyes said over and over—I carried Eddy's records in my handbag. I was determined that, this time, Eddy would be placed promptly in an appropriate program.

My initial contact with the new school district was when I registered my daughter in the neighborhood school. I asked there who I should contact about Eddy's admittance. I was told that the school counselor would handle it. This is where the second stage of the process began.

Eddy had fallen through the cracks in bureaucratic paperwork shuffles before; I was not going to let it happen again.

Persistence

Because Eddy's evaluations were current and complete, there was no need for him to have any preliminary meetings or evaluations. I did, however, take Eddy with me to the initial meeting with the psychologist. It is my belief that it is better to have Eddy known as a person than as a file of paper. I gave the psychologist the file I brought along, and asked him to begin the process of admitting Eddy. I suggested using that file until the official file was received from Eddy's former school district.

The psychologist recommended that I place Eddy in a regular classroom while the paperwork was being processed for his placement in special education. I did not think that Eddy should have to make two transitions, and decided I would keep him at home until appropriate placement was made.

The school people informed me that Eddy's case would be reviewed, and I would be notified as to Eddy's eligibility for special education. I asked *when* I would be notified.

I began keeping notes. I wrote down the name of each person I talked with and the phone number where that person would be reached. With each individual, I wrote down what we talked about, what should happen next, when it should happen, and the date of the conversation. This log helped me to keep track of the process of getting Eddy into an appropriate program. Eddy had fallen through the cracks in bureaucratic paperwork shuffles before, and I was not going to let it happen again. When someone from the school district told me that I would be contacted on a certain day and no contact was made, I called that person the next morning.

Eddy did qualify for special education, and a date for an IEP meeting was established. Because the receiving school district did not know Eddy, an "interim" IEP was proposed, to be changed after Eddy was in a program for a while. I agreed.

Following the IEP meeting, a placement decision was made and transportation was to be arranged. So far, all had gone smoothly. It looked like Eddy would be in a program two weeks after leaving his former placement. I was very pleased.

Just when I was ready to relax thinking that everything was all worked out, there was a miscommunication between the educators and the bus company that was to transport Eddy to school.

Pressure

When persistent phone calls did not get a bus to our door to take Eddy to school, I called the same parent group I had written to prior to moving, and got the name of a parent advocate. She had been in the area for a long time, and knew who I could call to get a bus rolling our way. A few conversations over the telephone with that contact person got the job done. Eddy was out of school only three weeks this time.

Conclusion

Moving is stressful, but parents of children with disabilities can alleviate some of their added stress by:

1. adequately preparing for a move from one school district to another;

2. being persistent in their efforts to have their disabled child placed in an appropriate program as quickly as possible; and

3. applying presssure when necessary. ■

Beth Ann Kelly lives in Kaneohe, Hawaii. In 1979, she received advocacy training from the Parent's Campaign for Handicapped Children and Youth of Washington, D.C. and from the Disability Rights Education and Defense Fund of Berkeley, California. She assisted in the formation of the PAVE Parent-to-Parent Training Project in Tacoma, Washington, and served as its first training coordinator.

CHAPTER 20

EDITORIAL

Every Vote Counts

Every four years since 1972, the major Presidential candidates have accepted our invitation to share their views about the care and education of children and adults with disabilities—issues which are not likely to be addressed in television debates, whistle stop statements, candidate advertising, or any other general campaign materials.

The Presidential candidates have used this forum because they know that thousands of voters will read their statements, that citizens who are personally involved with specific issues will be especially attentive, and that personally relevant issues determine voter choices. Similarly, we as voters know that a candidate's views on certain issues are far more important to us than his or her views on other issues.

We are now in the process of soliciting statements from the Democratic and Republican Presidential candidates for 1984.

We urge local groups of parents, professionals, and people with disabilities to create similar forums for state, county, and local candidates for public office this year. Although the national policy leadership of a President is important, it is local elected officials—school board members, state legislators, city councillors—who directly affect the day to day lives of children with disabilities and their families.

Reach out to candidates for public office and invite them to comment on the specific local issues affecting the lives of children and adults with disabilities and their families. Local candidates, lacking the resources to command mass media attention, know how critical it is to get their message to concerned citizens. Thus, candidates will respond when they know that their views will reach a group of interested voters.

Yet, no candidate for public office, "large" or "small," can be expected to be an expert on all topics. Individual candidates, while usually thoughtful and informed citizens, may be unfamiliar with various specific concerns of their constituency. These individuals, like all citizens not directly involved with family members who have a disability, need to be educated so they can develop responsible opinions. Local groups, already experienced advocates for children and families, can provide this critical election year education.

Successful candidates will have a direct say in what happens in the community. The opinions that they form with the help of local groups of concerned citizens may then become policy and action. As office holders, these individuals often turn towards those "educators" who have been helpful to them in the past. And, whenever necessary, we can also help our elected officials remember our "teachings" and their campaign platforms when the complexities of public life seem to cause forgetfulness.

Even those who are not elected this year are likely to be active, influential community leaders. As a result of their education, they will be community leaders with more informed opinions about issues concerning people with disabilities. They can also become active supporters of organizations. In addition, they may be successful candidates in future elections.

What about an individual citizen? How can he or she make a difference besides being involved in a "special interest" group that provides a forum for candidate's views? Volunteer to help the candidate most likely to be involved in decisions affecting your child and your family. In many smaller communities, campaign workers can be hard to find, especially in a year with so many different elections taking place.

Does such election year activity really make a difference? Can a few "ordinary" people matter? We had those kinds of doubts when we first approached Presidential candidates in 1972. We wondered whether their statements to our readers could make a difference. The most direct answer to our doubts came in February, 1982. At that time, when a proposed policy change seemed to threaten programs for children with disabilities, hundreds of members of Congress, representing both major political parties, reminded President Reagan of his campaign statement in THE EXCEPTIONAL PARENT magazine in 1980.

Each of us as a voter, with friends and fellow members of local groups who are also voters, can make a difference. Candidates need votes. Before election day, they need people to help them reach voters. We need only to look at the significant changes that have occurred in recent years to note the tremendous impact that individual citizens and relatively small groups have had in the development of a better life for people with disabilities. Much work remains to be done. ■

— S.D.K. , M.J.S. —

CHAPTER 21

NOT FITTING IN
The Real Advantage

by Linda A. Mischley

I grew up with a very "normal" childhood. I "fit in" to the middle group in school. I did not have any visable disabilities. I was of average intelligence. I was not beautiful nor ugly. It was perfect. I just "fit in."

I married my high school sweetheart. People used to say we were such a cute couple. I worked; he went to college. During this period of my life, I "fit in" to the college, married, and working wife scene very well. We were like every other young couple—struggling to put food on the table, paying the college bills, and postponing a family.

After my husband's graduation, our first child arrived. Shortly after, we had a second child. Now I had what I had dreamed of for five years of marriage—children. A boy and a girl. Just perfect.

Marital disaster invaded our lives. My dream included a husband and father for my children. Reality did not provide one. I stopped "fitting in" to the nice comfortable feelings of love and security I had before. I was now a divorced woman, a dating woman, a college woman.

I kept looking at my ring finger and feeling naked. Did everyone notice that I did not have a wedding ring on but that I had two children? Could I be the babysitter, divorced mom, or unwed mother? Did people assume I was on welfare? Should I tell everyone about me? I no longer "fit in" to the life I had imagined for myself. I felt different from everyone else.

After my graduation from college, I remarried. Finally, I would "fit in" to the secure role of being unnoticed—just casually floating carefree through life. Now I had a terrific husband, and my children had a loving step-father. We were a real family and my dreams seemed to be coming true.

My Third Child

Reality burst my bubble once again with the birth of my third child. This pregnancy was the best of the three. My new husband was expecting his first child, and was thrilled at the thought of being a new dad. He loved seeing me pregnant. He loved to look at me, wait on me, and talk about our impending arrival. It was the best nine months of my life.

Our new son, Bobby, was born and with his birth came new problems and a new world to explore.

Bobby was born with cri du chat syndrome which means that he is physically and mentally impaired. He was born six weeks prematurely with an inability to suck a bottle or nurse. We tube fed him for twenty-two months until he could eat enough to survive on baby foods. The tube went into his nose and down into his stomach. It was taped on his face so we did not have to change the tube after each feeding.

Bobby was certainly noticed in our small city. Again, I felt like everyone saw me as different. Now I was the mother of a disabled child. Did they think it was my fault that my baby was not blessed with being born "normal?" Did everyone think that I smoked, took drugs, or drank during my pregnancy? I did not! Should I tell them?

After months of agony trying to explain to the world that it was not my fault that Bobby was not born perfect, it suddenly hit me—I was no longer going to "fit in" to the space I had prepared for myself of being unnoticed, average, and part of a "cute couple." I was now the mother of a special needs child, and will *always* be his mom. I will always stand out and be noticed because I have a child who does not "fit in."

Freedom and Strength

For the first time in my life, I felt freedom. I could now be the outspoken woman I had held back inside myself. I could now fight for causes for which I had to fight. I have to be noticed now because I have to try and help my son within the new world he has opened up to us—the world of people with disabilities.

Since Bobby's birth, I have organized a parent support group and I am on a parent advisory committee board for the intermediate school district. My husband and I are involved in hockey for our oldest son and gymnastics for our daughter. I live a busy and happy life with my three beautiful children and wonderful husband. I may not "fit in," but I am finally glad that I do not. ■

Linda A. Mischley lives in Alpena, Minnesota with her husband, Steven, and their children, Randy, Andrea, and Bobby. Mrs. Mischley graduated from Alpena Community College with an associate in applied science degree. She is active in many volunteer organizations.

CHAPTER 22

WIDE WORLD OF RECREATION

EDITORIAL

Taking Recreation Seriously

by Gerald S. Fain

When our children are not adequately considered in recreational activities, we have the right and responsibility to complain.

Recreation provides many benefits, and has a value beyond the fact that it can be fun to play. It is because of these accepted values that, in recent years, we have developed expanded recreational opportunities for children and adults with disabilities.

• In recreation, the individual has the opportunity to explore, create, and nurture social relationships. In play, children learn about themselves and each other. This is particularly important for the disabled child as it can facilitate normalization.

• In recreation, people have the chance to be creative and self-expressive. The very meaning of recreation is tied to the creative parts of life pursued when one is free from the necessities of labor.

• In recreation, the individual is given the chance for respite. We "reward" ourselves with recreation after the work is done.

• In recreation, intact strength and available health are emphasized. The individual is asked what he or she can do, rather than focus on "curing" a problem. This allows the individual to progress at his or her own pace, and judge success and failure from a more personal set of norms. It also allows for the revealing of strengths, abilities, and uniquenesses possibly not covered through other means.

Recreation and Children With Disabilities

Many still do not understand the critical role of recreation in the development of children with disabilities. Because of limited employment and career opportunities, individuals with disabilities ordinarily have more free time, making recreation and leisure skills especially important.

We are beginning to accept that in an enlightened society knowing what to do and how to do it during leisure is the mark of an educated person. This type of education does not depend upon successful schooling, for many highly educated people are unable to live a quality life without a work schedule. Rather, it depends upon the individual's recreation or leisure abilities. In this sense, *all* people have similar special needs, giving education an expanded definition.

When children do not learn to read or write, we feel a loss. I feel the same sense of loss when a child fails to learn how to use leisure in health supporting ways.

For example, we can consider swimming. It is not unusual to find swimming programs for children with special needs. It is also not unusual to find rather cavalier attitudes toward swimming. If a child does not readily learn how to swim or come to enjoy him or herself, there may not be the same sense of loss we associate with more "serious" life skills.

Yet, we may change our attitudes when we stop to consider the benefits of swimming. It is an activity that can occur over a lifetime, as an indoor and outdoor activity, provides a good opportunity to develop social relationships, is available to all social, economic and cultural groups, and allows one to freely participate in the related activities of boating, water skiing, and other water-based activities.

Swimming needs to be approached with great seriousness and equally as great expectation. Not to learn how to swim and enjoy water is a great loss to anyone. However, the loss is even greater when we recognize that individuals with disabilities often depend more heavily than their non-disabled peers on leisure and recreation for meeting life quality needs.

Discrimination

When our children are not adequately considered in recreational activities, we have the right and responsibility to complain. Recreation can be used to discriminate against people. One of the most common forms of discrimination is when we separate people by ability in the construction of activities. This is a basis of stereotyping that must be avoided.

We need to challenge the community recreation department or YMCA to alter their ideas about disability. All too often, they respond to requests for recreation by structuring separate programs for the handicapped. Recreation people need to ask how they can adapt their programs so that individuals with disabilities can participate rather than segregating programs for disabled and able-bodied participants.

Possible Harm

While recreation provides the opportunity for "good" in the lives of individuals with disabilities, it can also provide the opportunity for "harm." In talking to adults, I have come to understand that some of the most traumatic life experiences they can remember occurred in recreation: the sadness of being humiliated by peers or onlookers when things did not work out on the playground; the isolation of being left alone without resources or skills to have "leisure"; being left out of the big event; and not being able to share special time with those they love.

A trained recreation staff can structure programs to avoid physical or psychological harm. Physical harm can take various forms. Excessive eating during recreation, or simply using food as recreation can lead to poor nutrition as well as obesity. Other forms of physical harm include hearing loss due to prolonged exposure to loud music, and the encouragement to take unnecessary risks in sports and games.

The nature of psychological harm resulting from recreation is not clearly understood. Yet, manifestations are easily witnessed. We see that a child feels hurt when he or she says things like, "I don't want to play today." "Do I have to play with those kids again," or "I don't think the leader likes me."

In play, the leader must use sensitivity in construction of activities. Each child will go at his or her own pace, and cannot be expected to conform to the leader's wishes or expectations. Moving from individual to team skills takes careful planning. The decision to "require" activity involvement must be made with the child's needs and abilities in mind. A leader must continue a careful and ongoing assessment of peer interaction while planning recreational activities. We know that the motivation for a child to participate is much more a function of trusting the support system and liking the leaders than is any particular activity experience.

Guidelines

Recreation is an essential human service. Yet it is clear that we ordinarily do not judge it by the standards we apply to other services. Let us contrast our attitudes toward residential summer camps with those toward schools. Communities require all the teachers who encounter a child to be properly credentialed and licensed. Even the educational specialist that may be with the child only a few hours a week must meet standards. In the course of the day, the child at school is in contact with a variety of these qualified adults, and only on rare occasions ever spend more than six to seven hours a day in school.

By contrast, we send this same child to a summer residential camp to live in relative isolation from their social/familial support systems, and supervised by people not always trained in recreation. The child does not even have the chance for respite, as one does at the end of the school day. The campers are living in a group situation in which meal times, sleep times, and activity times are usually well regulated. At the end of the residence, we merely ask, "Did you have a good time?" In short, we expect little from the camp experience.

More appropriate questions for the child might be:

"What did you learn?"
"Can you show me what you learned?"
"Did you make new friends?"
"Were there people there who hurt you or did not like you?"
"What did you do when you were unhappy?"
"What should be changed if you go back there again?"

Furthermore, questions to the staff should be concerned with the individual and include a detailed assessment of the child. What did my child accomplish? What did the child do when she or he was unhappy? How did you handle discipline? Did you notice any particular strengths or abilities? What kinds of recreation abilities did the child exhibit that I should be particularly concerned with supporting at home? Clearly, summer camp is not the only recreational experience in which we are ready to forget standards.

We need to consider our moral responsibilities to insure participants adequate protection against harm. One important way to do this is to encourage appropriate training of recreation and leisure professionals. Recreation is too important to be left entirely in the hands of volunteers or the uninformed. A significant factor in bringing about change is to educate the general public about the importance of recreation, as well as its potential hazards. ■

Gerald S. Fain is the Coordinator of Leisure Studies and Health Education Programs at Boston University.

CHAPTER 23

WIDE WORLD OF RECREATION

Choosing a Summer Camp

by David Militzer

Whenever any of our offspring venture from the security of the nest into the unknown, parents have fears and concerns. When our children have handicapping conditions, the fears and concerns are often felt more strongly.

Will they be homesick? Will they like it? Will people at the camp see all the lovable qualities we do and relate kindly? Will they be warm enough? If there are problems, can they be communicated so others will understand and respond?

Will the staff take adequate responsibility? Will our children be frightened? Will they be happy? Will they be able to make friends? Will they be picked on? Are we doing the right thing? Have we packed enough warm clothing, and clothing for all situations? Will they be able to keep up with the group or be left behind?

Will our children feel as if we have deserted them? Are we really sending them to camp for their benefit or for our own? Should we? If they get lonely, will the staff provide adequate support? What if something happens and we cannot be reached? Can we relax and enjoy having our children elsewhere? Can we do it without feeling guilty? Will the camping experience be a happy or unhappy one? What if . . . ? What if . . . ?

Round and round goes the internal questioning, all the "what ifs . . ." In one sense, the doubt and anxiety we face when considering sending our disabled children to camp is similar to that of sending our other children off to college. It gets easier, and we learn to feel less fearful each year. Our children have grown because of both happy and unhappy experiences. And somehow, through all of our fears and concerns, we too survive.

The Benefits of Camp

Children who have attended camp will describe the benefits they have derived from the experience. they might say enthusiastically, "I met loads of neat people, did some great things, and had tons of fun." If you have attended camp yourself, you have probably stored some happy memories and pulled them out occasionally to recall the joys of camp.

As a parent who is about to make a personal and financial investment in a camp for your child, you should want to know the values of camp, beyond what is recalled by an enthusiastic child or a nostalgic adult.

A camp whose program components comprise a well-rounded variety of activities has the potential to provide opportunities for mental, physical, and social stimulation and growth to your child. Each program in which your child participates—aquatics, nature study, cooperative games—offers unique chances to learn adaptive life skills, cooperate with others, and gain confidence.

The opportunities for your child to meet, share, and successfully work with other children and adults should be plentiful at camp. Rooming with others in a cabin or tent, "buddying" up for swimming, and helping out on a scavenger hunt team are only some examples of the activities which can help to build and reinforce positive social relationships.

The camp program you have chosen should provide a range of physical activity to meet the special needs and interests of your child.

From the possibility of scheduled physical or occupational therapy down through organized and adapted aquatics or sports, as well as less structured and popular past times of free swims and nature hikes, your child will find many opportunities for motor development at camp.

Camp activities have a way of being educationally stimulating without being associated with the negative feelings a child with special needs may have about school. Remembering the words to a camp song, taking part in an after dinner skit, or recalling the name of a wildflower all are examples of how a child may develop language, memory and learning skills at camp.

Camp can have the effect of introducing your child to a side of himself or herself never known before. Whether proving that he or she could try an activity and master it, or that cooperation with others gets the job done, or simply that camp is "tons of fun," your child will carry these values around for the rest of his or her life, and be a more confident person in the process. And in the life of a child with disabilities, a little confidence goes a long way towards further achievements.

Determining If A Summer Camp Is Right For You

Choosing a camp is similar in some regards to choosing any product. There are name brands, certified products, and advertising of all sorts. The consequences of making a poor choice of camp can be great—physical, intellectual, social, or emotional harm to your child. It would be disappointing for your child to miss out on the dynamic potential for growth in these areas which an appropriate camping experience could provide.

Camp "shopping" is important. As with other important shopping decisions—like a car or a home—you are better off with a specific idea of what you want as you search for a camp. Ask your child what he or she wants for activities, living arrangements, etc., and combine that with your own needs—respite, qualified staff—in forming a "wish list" for the ideal camp.

There are a variety of ways to get the answers to questions you need to know about the camps you are considering for your child.

•Interview the director of programs in person or by telephone.

•Request and review written information about the program such as flyers, brochures, staff manuals and program descriptions.

•Visit the site and observe the program being run.

•Talk to other parents whose children have attended the camp in the past.

•Attend parent orientation meetings that the program may sponsor.

•Encourage your child to assist you with the above activities.

Important Questions

There are several important questions you should be sure to have answered when considering a camp for your child.

1. What is the ratio of campers to staff? How old are staff members? What are their background and training?

2. Are personnel oriented to special needs of individual campers? What is included in staff orientation? Have the staff members worked previously with individuals with disabilities? How are individual precautions such as special diets or limits on strenuous exercise communicated to the staff?

3. What are the major objectives of the program? Have generalities such as "having fun" or "learning skills" been broken down into specific objectives? (e.g., participates in at least three cookouts; chooses clothing that is correct for weather conditions). What are some of the program's success stories?

4. What are the major activities included in the program? Are activities adapted to facilitate all skill levels? Do campers have a choice of activities? Are a range of activities available, including some areas new to my child?

5. Have safety and emergency procedures been established? What happens when someone is lost? How many of the staff hold First Aid or Water Safety Instructor certification? Are the facilities clean and in good repair?

6. Is there parental involvement in the program? Can you visit during the camp program? Can you phone? Can you provide information to the staff regarding behavioral characteristics, best techniques for personal care assistance, etc.? Will the camp inform you of any problems?

7. Are medical personnel on staff and on call throughout the program? How are the medications handled? Where is the nearest hospital? What supplies and equipment are available at the camp's infirmary?

8. What is the cost of programs to parents? Are scholarships or camperships available? Is transportation provided through the program? What about insurance? Are there extra fees for certain program activities like field trips, arts and crafts expenses or horseback riding? What is the policy regarding lost or damaged clothing, glasses, braces, etc.? What supplies are provided by the program?

9. Does the camp employ any staff members with disabilities? Is there any possibility that my child could be a member of the staff in a few years? Are vocational skills a component of the program?

10. Is evaluation used to improve the program and better meet the needs of the participants? Will you receive a report or checklist summarizing your child's stay at camp? Will your child and you have the opportunity to critique the camping experience?

Camping can serve the dual purpose of inducing fun and enjoyment while developing skills. The extent to which either of these occur is directly related to the extent to which a camp's potentials and a camper's interests and needs are matched. Be a wise shopper—both you and your child will benefit from making the best choice possible. ∎

The above article was taken from a booklet distributed by the New Hampshire Developmental Disabilities Council entitled *Camping For All: A Guide to Camping and Outdoor Recreation For People Who Have Disabilities*. The excerpts chosen were prepared by Mary Frost, Consultant For Community Living, Division of Public Health Services, Ann Wails, Community Services Council and Respite Services Coordinator, and Jeff Witman, Senior Recreation Therapist of Hampstead Hospital, New Hampshire.

A copy of the American Camping Association's *1984 Parents' Guide to Accredited Camps* provides detailed information about more than 2,000 camps. The book is available for $6.95. To order, write to *ACA Parents' Guide, American Camping Association, Box 100, Bradford Woods, Martinsville, Indiana 46151*.

CHAPTER 24
WIDE WORLD OF RECREATION

Parents Creating Recreational Experiences: *Kamp for Kids*

This article presents a recreation program that involves parents of children with disabilities in a variety of ways. The program described began because parents wanted to create a positive summer camp experience for their children, and continues to be maintained through their efforts.

Every summer in western Massachusetts, one hundred and twenty campers, some of them able-bodied and some of them in wheelchairs or on crutches, can be seen playing volleyball, doing arts and crafts projects, or going through an obstacle course that can be adapted for different levels of ability. Kamp for Kids, an innovative summer recreation program, stresses parent involvement, as well as the belief that the only failure any one of us can have is not to try.

In the history of Kamp for Kids, parents of children with disabilities have perservered to find summer recreation for their children. The camp is a model for parent involvement—from its fund raising activities to the family weekends held four times a year, attended by parents and their disabled and able-bodied children.

Summertime

Kamp For Kids began through the work of a small number of parents. They wanted to create a program that would enable their disabled children to enjoy a positive camp experience, as well as to provide able-bodied children with the opportunity to relate to a child with disabilities as a peer. They felt it was important to show children that even though they had some differences among them, they could all have fun together.

Many of the parents who helped create Kamp for Kids had been trying for years to involve their disabled children in recreation programs. Their efforts were often met with resistance and fear.

Judy Hoyt, one of the principle founders of Kamp for Kids, and her husband felt strongly that they wanted their son, Rick, to experience all the things that other children experience. Judy found that it was often necessary for her to offer something of herself—her time, energy, and knowledge of her child—to a recreation program, before it would allow her son to participate. For example, the local YMCA camp would not let Rick, who has cerebral palsy and is a quadriplegic, into their camp. They said they simply did not have the staff or proper training to care for him.

In order for Rick to be able to go to camp, Judy Hoyt had to volunteer to go with him, and care for any special needs he had. In this way, Rick was able to attend summer camp. The experience of many parents of children with disabilities has been that they have to give something to the community in order to get something in return. This has become one of the basic principles of Kamp For Kids.

The Beginning

When Judy Hoyt and other parents of children with disabilities got together and started talking about the summer, they realized they all had a similar problem. With no school to go to and few recreational opportunities, their disabled children had nothing to do during the summer. While their able-bodied siblings could go off and play with other children, they required their parents' assistance. The children were not accepted by most summer recreation programs, and the only way they could go was if they were accompanied by their parents.

As a result, the parents did not have the opportunity to spend some time alone during the summer like parents whose children are away at camp are able to do. Respite care was not an entirely satisfactory option, since it did not adequately provide for the children's needs. Out of a desire to create a valuable program for their children, a small group of parents decided to start a day camp program that would integrate disabled and able-bodied children.

The first year, the Easter Seal Society of Western, Massachusetts gave some seed money to publicize the camp, and the parents held bake sales and did other fund raising activities to help finance it.

Kamp for Kids developed out of that small day camp. It opened in 1976, and was funded initially by a federal grant from the Westfield Community Development Office. The camp stressed the right of every child to be free to learn and participate with everyone else, within the limits of safety, ability and personal satisfaction.

One of goals of those who began Kamp for Kids was to encourage disabled and able-bodied children to play together, and learn to accept one another. Many people in the community sent their children to the camp which was offered free. After the camp's grant ran out, the board of directors decided that the camp would have to close unless they found some way to pay its bills.

Paying For Camp

The directors realized that parent support was essential to maintaining Kamp for Kids, and that the program was going to die without it. They worked hard to come up with a budget. The board committee told parents that they were either going to have to start paying to send their children to camp, or work out some system to keep the camp alive.

They started with trade-offs. If a parent helped with fund raising, his child could go to camp. If a parent directed or taught a swimming class at camp, her child could come. The problem with this system was that some families felt they were being excluded. They said they did not feel they had the time to fund raise, or take time off during the day to teach a class at camp.

The next year, some families paid for camp or worked to have their children come, and others got to send their children for free. This system also caused problems. Parents who were paying or working resented that other children were going without charge.

Finally the camp steering committee, made up of parents, devised the point system. Parents can pay for as much of the camp costs as they want to—all

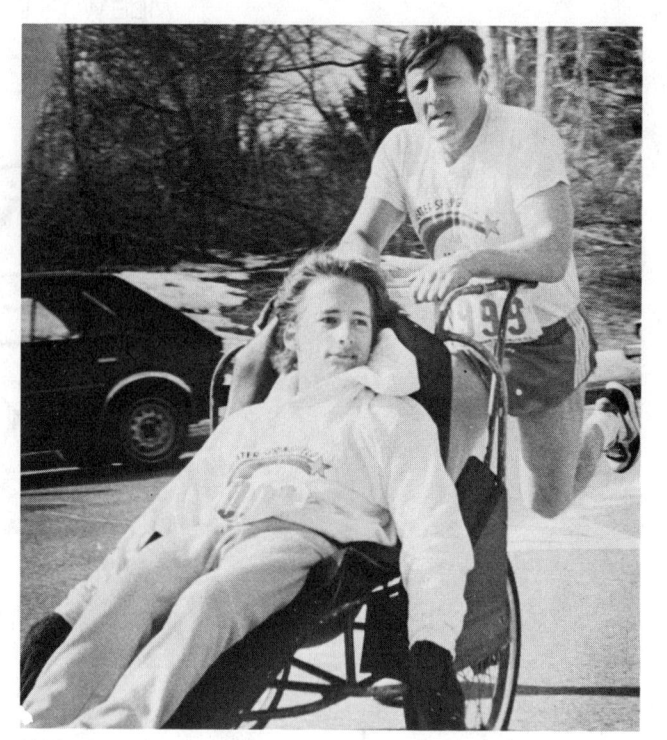

Ricky Hoyt and Dick Hoyt

of it if they choose—or they can work to earn points to send their children to camp.

Almost anything a parent does that contributes to funding the camp gets translated into points. In the past, the camp has run bake sales, clothing sales, etc. The hours it takes to bake a cake, drive it over to the sale, and sit and staff the bake sale table all count as time for camp. Even someone who has to stay at home can earn points by licking envelopes or making phone calls. Points are translated into dollar amounts which help to pay the cost of a child's time at camp.

There were many hidden problems when the point system was first implemented. Parents began to watch each other closely to be sure that one parent did not get more points than another for a similar job. This type of difficulty led the organizing committee to try and discover a new activity that would be equal in the eyes of parents, and would earn money for Kamp for Kids at the same time.

Bingo

In addition to the point system being used to give parents "camp credit" for activities like typing fliers, running errands and doing community outreach, the camp committee's newest idea for raising funds is to hold bingo games. One parent working one Saturday a month for twelve months will earn one child an entire summer at camp.

The local Boys Club is offering their building and bingo equipment to the camp. If the project is successful, the Boy's Club and Kamp for Kids will offer overnight camping together in the summers. Both groups are hoping the bingo will be able to fund this integrated activity.

Support From the Seabees

Kamp for Kids has received a great deal of community support. The Seabees have helped them out with a number of projects. They rebuilt a dam on the Kamp for Kids grounds, and repaired damaged concrete walls.

In addition, the Seabees constructed a "wheelchair" nature trail a mile and a half long. More than twenty tons of trap rock was donated by a local contractor, along with several hundred surplus railroad ties. The trap rock was installed by hand since the terrain made use of power equipment impossible. The recycled railroad ties became curbings and barriers.

Another project the Seabees worked on was a specially designed confidence course for disabled children. The course content and design were planned by specialists from Boston University, and the Seabees transformed the plans into reality.

The Seabees are currently working on constructing a half mile oval wheelchair racetrack. It is being built around a small farm on the property the camp operates on. And finally, they are planning to build several cabins designed for parent-child camping, a conference center, and an ampitheatre.

Parent Weekends

Another aspect of parent involvement in Kamp for Kids are the parent weekends run by the camp approximately four times a year—twice in the spring and twice in the fall. The purpose of the weekends is to have the entire family unit enjoy time together, and learn how to play together. In addition to the camp staff stressing integration of able-bodied and disabled kids at camp, they also attempt to teach parents the skills to integrate their child with disabilities into the family unit.

Several families get into Kamp for Kid's "green bus," and go off to a rented area for the entire weekend. There is only one rule at the parent weekends—if you go, you have to participate.

On Friday evening, each family participates in a "systems activity," to remind them that families are a system that can work together and share many common experiences. The counselors might have the whole family blow bubbles through a straw, or draw their house together. Afterwards, everyone gets into a circle and each family discusses how the activity went for them. Who led the activity? Did everyone get a chance to do something? Was it fun?

On Saturday after breakfast, everyone does adventure education—families play outside and have fun together. At Crotched Mountain, New Hampshire, an area commonly rented for the weekends, there is an obstacle course designed for varying levels of ability. In addition, there are cooperative games that have been designed so that everyone in the family can play them.

For example, "blanket volleyball," an adaptation of the original game, has each team member holding onto an edge of a blanket, and tossing the ball over the net with the blanket. This way, even individuals with limited mobility get to be a part of the team effort of tossing the volleyball over the net.

In the afternoon, the families are split up into different groups for discussions. Parents are in one group, teenagers in another, and younger children in another. Children under seven are watched by counselors in training who play with them. Topics of discussions range from, "Letting kids make choices for themselves," to "Independent Living," to "Mainstreaming." After the small groups discuss the topic of the day, the whole group gets together and has a general discussion.

On Saturday evening, all of the parents go out together. This is an important time for parents. Parent weekends stress ways that a family can learn to play together. At this point in the weekend, parents take the time to do something just for themselves. In this situation, it is not the rest of the family going out and leaving the child with disabilities behind. It is the parents going out together without *any* of their children.

Sunday is when all the work for the weekend comes together. All of the kids go off to play, and the parents talk informally. It is often at this point that parents share their feelings about the weekend, and the new skills for playing with their children that they have experienced during the weekend.

Camp staff reports that many of the parents who were unsure about attending the parent weekends now urge Kamp for Kids to have more of them. The staff believes that the weekends work because parents feel more comfortable when there are other people who have the same difficulties participating and learning to play together. Support is a key factor for many—if the other parents can do it, so can I. And we can do it together.

Kamp for Kids was created and continues to thrive through parent involvement. Its structure makes participation possible on several different levels. The point system is one way in which parents remain active in their children's recreational experiences. Parents work throughout the year to insure that their children will be able to enjoy a quality camp program in the summer. By offering an integrated recreation program and parent weekends, Kamp for Kids gives families that include a child with disabilities the opportunity to learn how to play and live together. ∎

—M.D.B.—

Judy Hoyt, Mark D. Havens, and Chris Roland gave their time and assistance in helping to prepare this article.

CHAPTER 25

fun stuff

Magnets

Children enjoy playing with magnets because of the strange and magical powers they seem to possess. Magnets can draw metal objects toward them, and can hang on metal surfaces without falling.

A magnet's power is in its poles. The poles are at the ends of a magnet—one on each end. The two poles of a magnet are not the same. If you take two poles that are different and try to put them together, you can feel the force with which they pull towards each other, and if you try to put two poles together that are alike, you can feel the force with which they resist coming together.

Kinds of Magnets

There are many different kinds of magnets, and they come in all shapes and sizes. Most of us have seen a horseshoe magnet, which has its poles on the two ends of the horseshoe. There are also bar and disc magnets, the kind many of us have on our refrigerators, holding up messages and grocery lists.

Games

Draw a racing strip on a large sheet of construction paper. Add any sort of roadway designs and obstacles you like. Place the strip down on a table that is thin enough for a magnet to attract through. Then take two small metal cars, or any metal objects—paper clips, metal buttons, etc.—and place it at the beginning of the course. Have your children run the cars or objects through the course by using the magnets underneath the table to guide the metal above.

A similar game can be played by drawing an island scene, a

jungle, a forest, or a park on construction paper, and placing it on cardboard. Your child can run metallic objects through the scene with a magnet guiding underneath the cardboard.

Make paper boats and attach paper clips to each one. Place the boats in a small tub of water, and sail them. The magnets will draw the boats to them. The same game can be played by putting a metal object in a soap dish, and using it as your boat.

Buried Treasures

You can have a treasure hunt using magnets. Hide several different metal objects in a sand box—safety pins, thimbles, paper clips, steel spoons, nails. You may also want to include non-metallic objects so that your child can see which objects the magnet can find and which objects it cannot. Have your child run the magnet through the sand until she or he finds all the hidden items.

After, you can run your hands through the sand to see what objects the magnet did not pick up.

Telling Stories

Draw different figures, color them and cut them out. Or use figures cut out of a magazine. Tape the drawings onto magnets. Then place the figures on your refrigerator, or any large metal surface to help illustrate a story.

Making Your own Magnet

Magnets are easy to make. Rub a nail with a magnet, making sure to rub it in the same direction each time. Now test the nail to see if it has become a magnet. If it has, it will pick up metal objects. If not, rub it some more and try again.

Magnets make fun toys when you use them to play with metal. Use your imagination to think of other ways to have fun with them. ∎

CHAPTER 26

fun stuff

Dress Up

"**Let's pretend**" is a game all children like to play. Children of different ages, abilities, and interests can enjoy the world of make believe and experience fun using imagination and a few items from around the house.

Hats

Hats can be the key ingredient to costume play, and they are easy and fun to make. Just a change of hats can make you go from a sailor to a pirate to a clown to a king or a queen.

Crowns are easy to make.

Take a piece of construction paper covered with tin foil and cut out a shape like the above.

Wrap it around your head, and fasten it by using heavy paper clips, staples, or tape.

Decorate the crown with old costume jewelry or color it with markers.

A sailor's hat can be made by folding up a piece of newspaper or construction paper like the one shown.

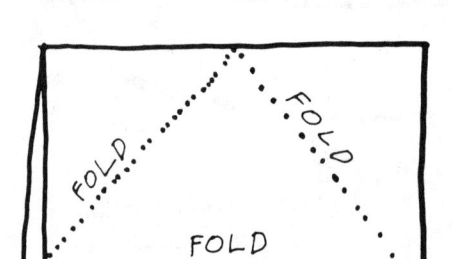

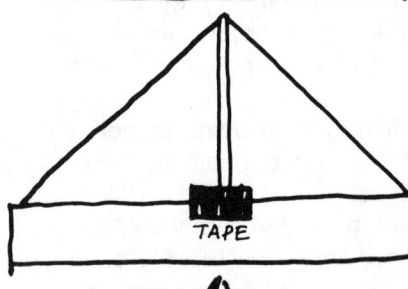

Take a piece that is 12 inches long and 18 inches wide and fold it in half.

With the folded edge at the top, bring two corners to meet at the center.

Fold up the bottom flaps and tape them.

Color this hat with pictures of the water, or write the name of your "sailboat" on it.

You can make a gentlemen's top hat—an Abraham Lincoln hat— from construction paper.

Take the paper and make a tall paper tube that fits over your head. 5Tape the sides together after you have made it fit.

Cut out a circle from the construction paper to fit over the top, and make a ring for the brim.

A party hat and a witch's hat are made almost the same way. Take a piece of construction paper and shape it into a cone.

Make sure the open side is big enough to fit your head. Decorate it however you like. To turn it into a witch's hat, just add a brim to it.

To be an indian chief, cut out a strip of construction paper. Measure it to be sure it fits around your head. Then, make feathers from the construction paper. Decorate them and glue them on to the strip.

A white hat with a red cross taped on the front can turn you into a nurse.

You can pretend to be a hard hat construction worker by wearing your bicycle helmet.

You can become a pirate by tying a scarf around your head. Or, you can use that same scarf and pretend you are a gypsy.

A clown wears all sorts of hats. Any decorated scarf, a bunch of flowers in your hair, or a brightly colored wig can be a great start for a clown costume.

You can be a policeman by taping a star to the center of a paper hat.

Treasure Chest

In addition to wearing hats when playing, you may also want to complement them with some accessories. You can make a "dress up" chest for whenever you play. Some of the following items from around the house can be kept in the chest.

an assortment of old clothes
coats, suits, dresses
formal gowns, tuxedos
aprons
dancing costumes
high heels, boots, old shoes
costume jewelry
mirrors
blankets
pillows
old handbags or wallets
pieces of bright material
gloves
old eyeglass frames
an umbrella
artificial flowers
a broom
a hand fan ■

CHAPTER 27

fun stuff

Cooking

"**H**ey Mom, what's cookin'?" At home, the kitchen is where the action is. And the action is cooking.

Children of all ages, and *both* sexes, like to cook. They enjoy the process of making something to eat—the mixing, sifting, shaping, decorating, and sniffing. And then they enjoy making the end product disappear!

Whatever children's skills or aptitudes or temperaments, sooner or later they will want to experiment in the kitchen and concoct *their* specialties. With thoughtful supervision, cooking can be a creative treat for everybody.

Like anything else, it's a good idea to start simple—melon balls, celery stuffed with peanut butter, whipped cream, your own granola mixed from natural ingredients, popcorn, cinnamon toast, milk shakes made in a blender with ice cream and an egg.

Some Recipes

Here are a few recipes beginners can handle. Some of these you can do without a stove or even an oven. Some take five minutes. Others—handshaped and decorated cookies, for example—can consume an entire rainy afternoon. Some cooking projects will require a good deal of guidance at first. Others, very little. For more recipes as well as more complicated recipes, check out the children's cookbooks at your bookstore or public library.

Peanut Butter Logs. Blend 1/2 cup peanut butter and 2 tablespoons honey. Knead in 3 1/2 tablespoons instant nonfat dry milk (as much as mixture will take). With fingers, add up to 1/2

74

cup raisins. Shape into logs, cookies, initials, any fancy shapes that strike your fancy.

Jello is a universal favorite. Just follow the recipe on the box. (Some children will need help pouring the boiling water.) Children like to make it with ice cubes since it's "done" quicker, and so you can eat it quicker! Put fruit, raisins, nuts and other surprises—even M&M's—in your jello for a treat.

Instant Pudding. Stir it up the usual way. Or make it in a large jar with a top on it. This way you shake it to mix it up.

No Bake Cookies. Mix together 1 cup peanut butter, 1 cup confectioners' sugar, 1/2 cup walnuts, 2 tablespoons margarine. Pinch off, shape into marble-sized balls and roll in coconut, finely chopped nuts, or chocolate sprinkles.

Rice Krispie Squares. The recipe is on the cereal box. It is a great favorite among children both to make and to eat!

Gingerbread People. Another one to mold with your fingers and fashion with your imagination. An easy recipe is to use one box of gingerbread mix and add just one-third of the water required for gingerbread. Use raisins or currants or chocolate chips for eyes and buttons.

Cookies. Making cookies with your fingers, playing with dough—any dough—is fun. Most standard recipes for sugar cookies and oatmeal cookies can be adapted for "hand making" by simply substituting more liquid shortening for the eggs in the recipe.

A Whole Meal. As your children grow up and get to feel more at home and experienced in the kitchen (using the stove carefully and knives safely, for example) why not let them try a complete meal, for themselves or the entire family?

For breakfast try that homemade granola, with fresh fruit cut up and prettily arranged in a bowl. Or, scrambled eggs, with parsley and green onion mixed in, or bits of tomato, ham and cheese.

For lunch or supper, put makings on the table for submarine sandwiches. Or the cold salad soup the Spanish call gazpacho, made with tomato juice thickened with cut up raw vegetables such as celery, scallions, cucumber and green pepper. And garlic bread, made by buttering thick slices of crusty bread, sprinkling them lightly with garlic salt and heating in the oven until the butter melts.

Have a good time. And don't forget, good cooks also learn how to clean up! ∎

GROWING UP

The disabled youngster faces the same challenges in growing up that other children encounter. The nature of the disabilities can influence the ways the challenges are experienced and met. Young children have been the focus of efforts; we are now confronting the problems of the adolescent. The articles in the education section reflect our growing concerns about older children with disabilities. The articles on sex education are also related to issues in making the transition to adult life.

Health care concerns influence the child and families' ability to focus energies in adaptive struggles. These articles emphasize understanding the whole child rather than thinking of the child as a symptom or a disability. Articles also deal with coordinating medical services, surgery and the right to live.

CHAPTER 28

Love, Lead, and Let Go— Advice to Parents

by Lois Wencil

How often my parents must have held their breaths through the skirmishes and squabbles of my childhood.

So many times, parents look at a disabled child and wonder what life will hold for them. Will they work? Will they be able to care for themselves? Will they have a family? Although these questions frequently worry parents, they are somehow set aside for the more pressing "here and now" situations that confront them and their children. Growing up as a blind woman—and to an even greater extent when I became a mother myself—I realize that it was much harder for my parents to watch me develop than it was for me to live my life.

I spent my younger years playing in parks and the neighborhood with my cousins and friends. I never noticed how my parents would show me the safest way to go, or would take my hand to guide me to the next piece of playground equipment. I only knew it was fun to run, roll, climb, and play with the other kids. The other children learned to take my hand or talk to me so I could come with them. I never heard the adults tell them they should "help" me when we played together.

At the age of five, following the advice of the educational counselor from the local state agency for the blind, my parents entered me into a braille class at a public school in my home town. Either an older child or my teacher took me where I had to go until I was ready to venture forth independently. I do not remember anyone telling me that either I must go by myself, or that it was dangerous. If my friends who could see asked me about my eyes, it was natural to answer them truthfully because that was all I knew how to do.

Having been raised around many boy cousins and friends, I learned how to get what I wanted and hold onto it. How often my parents must have held their breaths through the skirmishes and squabbles of my childhood.

Necessary Skills

It was in kindergarten that I learned to read and write braille. Braille has been and *is* the most valuable tool I possess. My family and friends and my children and their friends have been curious about my pages loaded with dots.

Utilizing braille, I have read books, taken my own notes, have lists of telephone numbers and addresses, learned to read music, sung in glee clubs and choirs, played games with my friends and children, helped my children with their homework, wrote speeches and articles, kept my own recipes and financial records, taught professionally and in Sunday School, and held many offices—both in college and in the community.

The current use of tape recorders for record keeping exasperates me because trying to find a certain piece of information can waste valuable time and energy. When cultivated, braille is quick, quiet, storable, retrievable, and portable.

My second most valuable and highly encouraged skill is typing. It is another means of communicating to the sighted world. Because of my typing skills, I was able to take tests myself. My papers and reports could be done independently within my time frame. Print handwriting is also indispensible to me for short notes, legal documents, and checks. By the time I was ten, I had my own braille equipment, braille print typewriter, phonograph, and television. I have always been encouraged to use them, and loved the freedom they gave me.

Parental Concern and Support

I think the most difficult thing for my parents was not knowing exactly what I was doing and with whom. They had to put me on a school bus each day, and could only drive and pick me up from the dances, games, movies, and clubs that I joined. They worried and waited while I played, participated, worked, and had fun.

They never showed their worry, or told me about it; they were happy with my excited stories about what had happened to me on various outings. When my fears came or I was apprehensive about trying something new, they listened and encouraged me to try instead of being afraid.

My fears mainly centered around the problems that everyone faces, perhaps intensified by my lack of vision. Each first day with a new class schedule was frightening. Traveling the crowded hallways "gracefully" bothered me terribly. I dreaded the thought that I might be late or lost. Social situations also have been a source of much apprehension. I have often worried about being shy or if I will enjoy myself. My worries usually disappear once I arrive where I am going, but they make getting ready to go some place less fun than it should be. My parents were there to listen to my concerns, and to reassure me. Now I plunge into an activity with less fear.

It has not always been easy or fun. But my parents led me slowly and gently to independence. Then they let go. It is better to let go than have any child, especially one who is blind, pull away or lose their spirit. Because of the way they raised me, my parents knew that I could make it independently. And I have!

My parents planned for my future with a bank account of happy memories and confidence in what I was and could become. It was unnecessary for them to plan for someone to take care of me. For me, blindness mainly has been a challenge that has necessitated my finding a way to do things rather than a burden, an insurmountable barrier, or an excuse for not accomplishing those things that would make me feel fulfilled. ■

Lois Wencil is an educational consultant and is on the advisory board for the St. Joseph's School for the Blind. She has a master's degree in special education, and has helped to develop a curriculum for multiply-impaired blind adolescents. Ms. Wencil lives in Millburn, New Jersey with her husband, Bill, and their children, Stephen and Elaine.

CHAPTER 29

P·E·R·S·I·S·T·E·N·C·E

A Father's Response To His Son's Hearing Impairment

by Joseph J. Kulakowski

All parents of disabled children face struggles in finding the best programs to help their youngsters. Not only do they have to find available community resources, but they must also confront their own fears and frustrations in dealing with their child's disability.

Joseph Kulakowski describes how important persistence was for him in dealing with these problems. In order to find help for his hearing impaired son, he had to transform his anger and pain into action. He refused to "give up," and eventually found a program that both he and his wife felt satisfied would help their son deal effectively with his hearing loss.

Daddy a bad boy," Joey says, voicing his disapproval at my scolding him for teasing the cats. How normal. But in Joey's case, it is more than normal. It is a miracle that he can talk at all. My four year old son has a profound hearing loss. It has been over two years now since that day when I sat in the audiologist's office, numbly listening to her grim diagnosis: "Profoundly deaf . . . bilateral . . . sensorineural loss . . . nerve deafness . . . no cure . . . never be able to speak . . . should start on sign language . . ."

In one sense it was a relief to learn of Joey's hearing loss. My wife and I finally understood his problem. A lot of things suddenly made sense, pieces fit. But then, we are like everybody else, and thought that this terrible thing could not happen to us and to our little boy. It *does* happen, and it did happen to us.

The Proces of Adjusting

Our first reaction was grief, sadness, and a hurt like I had never known before. My baby, deaf. I will never forget that day. Michele and I sat crying on our bed, while Joey played in his room, oblivious.

The hurt never really goes away. You learn to live with it, but the sadness lingers just below the surface. Little things bring it back. One day I watched out of the window as Joey played with some neighborhood kids. One child began counting, and suddenly they all ran off in different directions—hide and seek. Joey was left standing there, bewildered, looking a little forlorn and confused at being left out. I felt frustrated and hurt for him. There was little I could do to help, to make it better.

My second reaction was anger. A fury took hold of me, a need to lash out somehow against this terrible thing that had hurt us all so deeply. My anger converted to action. I began legal proceedings against the pediatricians who cost us a precious year of development by insisting that nothing was wrong with Joey. I prepared to launch a one man picket line against our medical group whose coverage did not happen to include our problem. Joey and I camped on all the right doorsteps. "No," was a word that did not exist for me at that time.

My persistence payed off. The financial details were taken care of by our medical insurance. Most medical insurance does not cover the expenses involved with pediatric hearing loss. Ours did, but only as a compensation because the insurance doctors were negligent in putting us off.

It is a miracle that he can talk at all.

Anger Into Energy

In retrospect, I guess I vented my anger on a lot of people, anybody whom I thought was delaying or standing in the way of our progress. An unknown side of me emerged and took over for a while. I was obnoxious, persistent, and did not care what people thought of me. I wanted those ear molds and hearing aids *yesterday*. I wanted the best possible care for my baby, and I wanted it immediately. As it turned out, using this anger proved to be a real benefit for my son. I am thankful for whatever gave me the unrelenting energy and singleness of purpose I needed to get things done right.

After the sorrow and anger followed a growing obsession to win out, somehow, over the deafness. Activity became the key for me. As long as I was busy working hard to help Joey, I was able to keep the depression away. I refused to dwell on the depressing aspects of the disability, but I read all the books about deafness anyway to keep myself informed.

I had to know exactly what the score was, just to know what we were up against. It hurt to read the literature on deafness, but as Proust said, "we are healed of suffering only by experiencing it to the full."

Helping Joey

Accepting finally the terms of the struggle before us, I came to consider myself lucky. Life had given me a deaf son, but I also came equipped with what I needed to cope. In a strange way, it was as if I had been preparing for the task of teaching language to my son. I had a degree in English, a solid foundation, and a love of the language.

My job as a youth counselor allowed me four full days a week to work with Joey. I latched on to a monumental need to fight the silence. Although I initially lacked patience, I gave myself a crash course, and was surprised to find a patience I never dreamed I was capable of. And so the work began.

I wanted to share what I have learned due to the dramatic changes in my life. Being the parent of a disabled child is not easy. It has been over two years now, and sometimes I still weep when I am alone. Visions of imagined difficulties my son must deal with get to be too much. On the other hand, I no longer wake up as I used to, with the thought of Joey's deafness crushing my spirit. I like to think that after two years, I am finally getting back to normal, whatever that is.

A New Option

This story has a happy ending. By chance we met an audiologist who told us that even a child with a profound hearing loss can learn to listen and to speak clearly. Her optimistic message was refreshing compared to the grim prognosis given by the audiologist who diagnosed Joey.

Our new audiologist introduced us to a parent named Joan. Joan has a fifteen year old son, Scott, who has a profound hearing loss. When my wife and I met this tall, handsome young man, we wondered why he was wearing hearing aids. We were astonished by his clear, nearly perfect articulation. His speech and his listening were so natural, his responsiveness and attention sharp.

Joan insisted on a demonstration, and Scott groaned, "Do I have to?" She sent him into the next room, and from a distance of fifteen feet began asking him questions in a soft voice. We were invited to do likewise. To our amazement, he answered every question clearly and correctly. And this without being able to see us!

Our new acquaintance told us more about her son. He plays soccer, goes to a regular school, dates girls, enjoys music, even talks on the phone. In other words, he is a "typical" teenage boy. Michele and I were flying high with inspiration. If Joan and Scott could do it, then we could too. Joey's loss was not as bad as Scott's, and Joey was getting an early start. On top of that, we had the advantage of being able to share what Joan and other parents like her had learned.

We enrolled in Scott's program immediately, and have stayed with it. There is an immense amount of work—more than many parents are able or willing to do. For us, it is the only way to go. We can look forward to Joey leading a normal life, and doing pretty much whatever he wants to. Instead of a handicap, the hearing problem will be a mere inconvenience. Joey will not be limited to silence, that world which the diagnosing audiologist had assigned him to.

There is a great deal of controversy in deaf education. It seems that everyone has the blinders on for their particular bias, and unfortunately, confused and hurting parents have to try to make sense of all the conflicting information. What we are doing may not be right for all families, but I feel very strongly that parents should be made aware of all the options available to them. We were very lucky to have found our way, but something this important should not be just a matter of luck.

Hearing Impaired, Not Deaf

Many of our friends cringe at the use of the word, "deaf." Our kids can actually hear with their powerful hearing aids, so we do not consider them to be deaf. Hearing impaired is a more accurate description. We concern ourselves with what our children *can* hear, not what they cannot. We would like our children to be measured by their electronically corrected hearing sensitivity, not by their audiograms. Consider vision: if you wear glasses to drive a car, your corrected vision is what is important to the licensing bureau. A person is not labeled blind simply because he or she has a seeing problem. Similarly, we do not want our children to be called deaf because they have a hearing problem.

The Program

Our involvement in Joey's program has us making weekly 120 mile round trips for speech therapy and parent training. The basic concept of what we are doing is quite simple. As parents, we are trained to be Joey's teachers. Only parents can provide the necessary continuity of care. Children with normal hearing learn much of their early language from their parents. The hearing impaired child's experience should be no different.

Although we use some contrived techniques in order to teach language in therapy situations, we try to keep the child's environment and experience as normal as possible. Joey attends a nursery school with normally hearing children, for example. He loves going, and gets along very well. His playmates accept his "bionic ears" and the explanation that just as some people need glasses to see better, Joey needs his hearing aids to hear better. We have found that kids are generally more accepting than adults.

Today, Joey chatters away all the time. He even talks in his sleep. There are time now when we wish he would just shut up.

Joey's Progress

Joey is actually learning how to listen. What he hears through the powerful hearing aids that he wears on his chest is not the same as what we hear. With the natural linguistic genius that young children seem to be blessed with, however, Joey can learn to make sense of the information he gets through the hearing aids. He must work at listening, and special training is necessary to develop this skill.

Simply putting hearing aids on a hearing impaired child is not enough. Giving crutches to a crippled child and expecting him or her to walk without therapy will not work either.

During Joey's therapy, we cover our mouths and speak in the dark. Techniques like these help to develop his listening ability. Joey reads lips as a way of compensating for his problem, but it is amazing to us what he can actually hear. I can cover my mouth and ask Joey to get me something, and he will be able to do it. When we call him from outside, he comes running.

Many professionals still maintain that these things are not possible in cases of profound hearing loss. I believe that placing preconceived limitations on a hearing impaired child (or any child) will result in a child who lives up to those limitations. If, on the other hand, one expects a miracle and is willing to work very hard for it, one may very well see it come true—as it is in Joey's case.

Of course, one has to be realistic, and realize that there are some limitations. You cannot frustrate a child with unreasonable expectations. We know, for instance, that Joey will probably never conduct a symphony orchestra. However, early childhood development is so dynamic that setting some high expectations may not be unreasonable.

Talking

Today, Joey chatters away all the time. He even talks in his sleep. There are times now when we wish he would just shut up. Joey still has a long way to go. A great deal of his speech is only intelligible to us, his parents. We know, though, that his articulation will improve with time and work, and we finally have a comfortable confidence in knowing that he is well on his way.

It takes the average child five years of listening and speaking to master language. Joey wears his hearing aids every waking moment, except when he takes a bath or goes swimming. He has been "aided" now for a little over two years, so consequently, his "language age" is quite similar to a child at that level.

Joey lost some important early development, and it will take some extra time and work for him to catch up. Because of this, we are probably going to hold him back a year before starting first grade so that he will have reached the level of linguistic competence of his peers.

School

We plan to send Joey to a regular school. The rationale for keeping him out of a "special" program is that once a child is placed in a special environment, it becomes difficult for her or him to function in a setting that is not special. In addition, young children learn a lot of their language from their peers. In a class full of kids who are hearing impaired, there are poor speech models, and deficient speech is perpetuated. My wife and I are delighted to hear Joey now learning language from his classmates at nursery school—"he pushed me," "that's mine," "my turn," or "Daddy a bad boy."

Emotional Support

Michele and I became involved with other parents, a comforting kinship which I would recommend to any parent of a disabled child. We attend regular parent meetings and travel, when we can, to seminars and conferences. I was elected president of a state-wide organization of parents following similar philosophies as we. Sometimes I think I have become a fanatic around this problem, but that is my way of dealing with it. The way I see it, a profound handicap requires a profound effort to overcome.

My growing involvement led me to take up formal studies in the field, and I hoped to get my master's degree in Audiology and Speech/Language Pathology. I wanted to combine my experience and my textbook knowledge to help other parents. Unfortunately, financial problems intervened, and even our modest income disqualified me for financial aid. I thoroughly enjoyed school, and will return again, somehow.

Be Aware

I would like to alert as many parents as possible to their own children's hearing sensitivity. Often, parents and grandparents know instinctively when something is wrong. If you feel that, trust in it and follow it up. It is necessary to challenge pediatricians if you are not satisfied. Insist on testing or getting a second opinion. Two different pediatricians told us that Joey was fine, and that he would be talking in no time.

A simple test that you can perform at home is one that has been and still is used by physicians. While your child is not watching, crinkle onion skin paper behind each ear. After the age of about nine months, the child should turn toward the source of the sound. You can also try jingling keys or lightly snapping your fingers.

Be objective—something that is often hard for parents. Call softly to your child while he or she is not watching. If you think there might be a problem, check it out. Some problems are temporary or minor, and can be corrected medically. An early diagnosis is critical in treating childhood hearing loss.

If your child does have a hearing loss, do not despair. More is being done in this area every day. Miracles like Joey are becoming commonplace.

Parent and Child

Being a parent of a hearing impaired child is a tough job, and a job that none of us asked for. Like many tough jobs, the rewards are very gratifying. A special relationship has developed with my child that might not have developed otherwise. With work and patience, we are winning the battle against the silence.

I have rejoiced over the little triumphs and milestones. I cried when I first heard that little voice calling for "Daddy." Also, I have found a special kinship with parents who share this common bond. This battle has presented a challenge that most people will never have to face in their lifetimes. The satisfactions have been tremendous, though. By struggling to overcome his handicap, my son is growing into a unique individual. ■

With work and patience, we are winning the battle over the silence.

Joseph J. Kulakowski lives in Holly Hill, Florida with his wife, Michele, and their son, Joey. Mr. Kulakowski is the past president (1982–83) of Florida Oral Education for Hearing Impaired, Inc., a state-wide organization for parents and professionals, and currently serves as an information specialist for that organization. He is also employed by the state of Florida as a Group Treatment Homeparent in a residential home for boys.

by Theresa Donar Riniker

The Story of Noah

A Rural Family with a Multi-Handicapped Child

In this article, Theresa Donar Riniker describes the struggles she and her husband faced as they attempted to find the best programs for their disabled son, Noah, one of nine children. With courage, persistence, imagination, and love, the Rinikers have found ways to meet Noah's special needs and to include him as a member of their large family.

I am thirty-six years old. I have had one year of college, and met my husband during that year. At the age of nineteen, we decided we were ready to assume the responsibilities of adulthood, assured in our innocence that all problems were solvable. Not learning from the mistakes of our forefathers and mothers, we seized an opportunity to make a living at farming. Since we are not people who leave a job undone once we have begun, we are still trying to make a living at farming.

With equal determination, we proceeded to produce the large, happy, healthy family fairy tales are made of. I once filled in the line on our income tax form asking for occupation with "pregnancy expert." To be specific, we have had ten children in twelve and a half years. This is no record, but no half-hearted attempt either.

Jacob is 16, Peter is 15, Matthew is 13½, Andrew is 10, Reuben is 9, Benjamin is 8, Samuel is 6½, Elizabeth is 5, and Noah, about whom this story is about is 3½ years old. A daughter, Rebecca, died at 14 months of a rare illness—one of those unsolvable problems.

Noah is another kind of "problem." At first, an unthinkable one, and for a short time, a seemingly unbearable burden. We have since been able to see the problems as frustrating rather than unbearable. I hope the love, joy, and committment we feel for Noah comes through in what I write.

My husband, Lew, and I hope that one thing comes through clearly. It is possible to be undereducated, overworked, underpaid, and undistinguished and yet make a living, raise a family, contribute to your community's enrichment, and parent a child with a disability. You can do it too!

School started this week for eight of our children. Liz, exasperated at 4½ years old, is the only one home. It has been hard to explain to her why Noah, at 3 years of age, is going to school before she is entitled to the honor. She is still not totally convinced that the reason for her staying home is due to her age, and not the fact that she is a girl. All eight attending school from this house are boys.

"Why does Noah get to go?" she pleads with tears in her eyes.

"Because he is handicapped and needs special help."

No matter how we try to explain away the unfairness of the situation, Liz is not sure she likes it.

And it is not fair—to us or to Noah. For that matter, though, what in life is fair? No laws were written up on the day of creation and submitted to

Mother Nature for consideration. We live life as it comes. While we do not have a union to force "fairness" into life's daily flow, we do have each other to help shoulder the load when things go wrong.

People are helping us all the time—in grocery stores, department stores, picnic grounds, doctors' offices, and on the street corner. They ask thoughtful questions, touch Noah's hand, try to establish eye contact with him, and offer suggestions and prayers. It all helps.

But it hurts, too. "That's quite a wheelchair." "Do the hearing aids help?" "Will he walk?" "Can he talk?" "Will he ever be able to sign back to you?" The answer to all the questions is, "Probably not, and he does have quite a wheelchair."

Talking To Friends

Most of our acquaintances have no idea what it means to be severely physically disabled. We say to them, "Noah is a severe, athetoid-spastic, quadripeligic, severely-profoundly deaf, and testing at normal or near normal intelligence—so far."

"What does that mean?"

"He won't walk, talk, feed himself, or write his name the way we do. He can learn at or near the normal level for his age."

"You mean he's not retarded?"

"No, he is retarded—retarded in the sense that he cannot do the things a non-handicapped child his age can do. In fact, he doesn't think the way a normal child does because he cannot see, do, touch, or hear normally. He hasn't had the opportunities to learn what a non-handicapped child experiences."

"But can he learn?"

"Yes."

"Well, that's all that matters!"

Is it all that matters? What about scratching an itchy nose? Or sneaking a cracker out of the kitchen? Or having a secret hiding place for all of one's treasures? How about being able to give the ones you love a hug and a kiss?

And that is not half of it.

Can Vs. Cannot

Noah cannot hear us. He cannot ask us questions to help explain our world. We have to sign everything to him, but he cannot sign back because he has no hand control. We go through lists of things—toys, foods, people, places— trying to find out what it is he wants. Noah watches our hands intently waiting for us to sign the desired object. Sometimes we do not find the right sign, and he gets angry and depressed.

What about emotions? We can sign, "Are you hurt? Sick? Angry? Do you love me?" He answers with his eyes and face. How long will he be able to give full range to his emotions with this limited means of communication? When will he give up and really become retarded?

In the end, what he cannot do is not that important. What counts is what he *can* do. And that is the reason we have fought so hard to get the services he needs. That is why we are willing to sacrifice even his company two days a week to get him into a school where he is part of the crowd, accepted and acceptable.

Finding Programs—A Major Challenge

Sometimes it seems as if all of society is in cahoots against us. We tried, in vain, to get a local program set up for Noah so that he could stay with us. We even tried crossing a state line to a nearby large town to get him into the special programs he needs. Noah is, indeed, too special. He fits nowhere. In a classroom of severely-profoundly retarded children where some beginning signing is used, he is miles ahead. In a mild-moderately retarded classroom, more sign language is used but as a second language back-up. The deaf pre-school classroom did not want him since they are not equipped to handle a physically disabled child. And the classroom for physically disabled children does not use sign language.

We considered a homebound program. For the last two years, I have taken Noah to see specialists three to four times a week—an occupational

---

How long will he be able to give full range to his emotions with this limited means of communication?

therapist, physical therapist, and a teacher of the deaf. Then, he was in a zero to three year old program that saw him once every two weeks. Noah has also been getting four to six hours of training a week under our tutelage. The school could offer five hours a week in a homebound program. The rest would be up to us.

After two years of juggling Noah's schedule, my housework, my other children, my husband, our business workbook, our social life (what's that?), and time for fun with the other kids, I am exhausted. I cannot do it anymore, or at least not as much of it. Someone else has to help with part of the load.

Letting Go
My husband, although he has seen me at my worst, wishes I could do more for the "cause." He is an excellent father and husband. In fact, there is no way Noah would be in our family today if it were not for Lew. He has fed, played, gotten up at night, changed diapers, given baths, and babysat while I was gone with Noah for another session with one of his teachers or therapists.

I once asked a friend who also has a severely disabled child why it seems that parents can give up their disabled children only after they have started to hate them. Is that part of severing the cord? Or is this anger caused by our guilty admission of our failure to meet all of our child's needs? I do not want to have to hate Noah before I can let him go. There has to be another way.

Starting School
So, Noah starts school this week, in a town two hours away by car. I take him to the school and pick him up the next night. That means almost nine hours of driving in two days for me. It is not the school's fault; it is ours. Lew and I could barely bring ourselves to send him away for these thirty-six hours. I feel better about taking him and getting him, for the first month anyway. I know I cannot do all this driving all school year.

It is good for all of us. We get a few hours break from the challenge of caring for Noah. He gets an opportunity at the best education available. Noah is in a multi-handicapped, deaf pre-school classroom. It is not perfect, but it is close.

When I think about it, the Individualized Education Program was the easier of the "must gets" for Noah. Our school system gave us no hassle about the expenses of sending Noah out of our school district. The IEP reads as we wanted it to—all therapies necessary to deal with his cerebral palsy, a total communication/sign language system, and peer interaction. Noah does not have a one-to-one aide, yet. I am working on it. Win the big battles, and sweat out the small ones later.

I wish I could say the same for finding Noah a foster home to stay in one night a week. We looked for six months for a foster family for him with no luck. Finally, Lew and I visited a residential children's home. We liked it, and decided that Noah would be well cared for by those loving people. Although they had never housed a child part-time, they were willing to try.

Little Cooperation
The various agencies we have had to deal with have been much less willing to try. Our local school board agreed to pay the residential costs, but the state school board balked. We would have to be turned down by all other possible financially responsible agencies before our school district could pay.

The Division of Children and Family Services turned us down saying they would pay only if Noah stayed in a foster home. The Department of Mental Health and Developmental Disabilities refused to pay because the placement was for educational reasons only which is the school district's responsibility. It was the state school board who sent us to them. Public Aid said that they would pay if we placed him full-time, permanently. But part-time placement, no way!

I thought the new push with local, state, and federal agencies was to keep these children with their families and in the communities as long as possible. The cost, both financially and in terms of lost human potential, is accelerated when a child is removed from a good family environment. Maybe they want us to keep our handicapped children as families did fifty years ago—in closets, attics, and cellars.

I am angry. There is no reason to put parents through what we have suffered in the past several months. Federal and state law mandates that if a child must leave his or her school district to attend an appropriate classroom, the school district is responsible for residential costs.

We had to drag our marriage license down to the Public Aid office when we applied there for residential payment. Why? Is Noah more or less handicapped if he is illegitimate? Am I a better mother because Lew and I have been married for seventeen years? Our names are on Noah's birth certificate. Our insurance has paid most of his medical bills. He is living with us. What is the definition of "parent" to a government agency?

Our situation seemed so hopeless. We were going in circles. In desperation, we contacted a lawyer and started proceedings to sue the state for non-compliance. The lawyer made a few phone calls to various agencies, and in two days, all hurdles were cleared. *All expenses for Noah's education would be paid by our local school district.*

In the end, what he cannot do is not that important. What counts is what he can do.

Shock set in. I found myself with hours each day to do my work—hours not spent telephoning one official after another, writing letters pleading with various representatives to help us, or in one fruitless meeting after another.

I will never say another bad word about a lawyer.

Foster Care

Ten days before school was to start and one day before Noah's first overnight stay at the residential home, a small miracle occurred. A foster family seemed to materialize by sheer force of will. I had only one thought when I heard—there is a God.

But, we were again back to problem one. Who was responsible for paying for the foster care—the school district or the Division of Children and Family Services? We were able to see the opposite side of the coin with this new development. Everyone wants to be the "good guy." No one was willing to stick out their neck and shake a few bureaucrats out of their comfortable conformity, but once the papers were signed with everything explained in black and white—by our blood, sweat, and tears— everyone wanted to take the credit. Now, all departments wanted to shout proudly, "Look! We did something that no one has ever done in this state before. See, we are flexible."

Frankly, it will not cost anyone a fortune to have Noah stay with them in foster care. We had probably spent more on phone calls in the last three months trying to get approval for this unusual arrangement.

Unwanted Advice and Insensitivity

As parents of a child with disabilities, my husband and I have found that other people often find ways to twist the screw in a little deeper. Why do they feel they have the right to discuss our personal lives with us? My dentist's receptionist wanted to know why the Department of Children and Family Services (DCFS) had taken our poor handicapped baby from us—after all, that agency is the one that removes abused children from their parents. I simply wanted her to fill out a form saying that Noah had seen a dentist in the last six months.

A doctor's assistant nurse refused to consider letting the doctor take Noah as a patient if he should get sick at school or at the foster care home. She said it takes too long to get the money for DCFS children on a green card. I did not even know what a green card was. Our insurance pays for Noah's medical bills to the full extent of the contract, and we pay the rest.

Then there are friends, neighbors, and even relatives who ask us, "How can you send your baby to live with strangers?" or "If you're sending Noah away for two days a week, why not put him in one of those institutions? It would be a lot easier?"

Does anyone out there understand?

Our Lives and Our Children's

We simply want our youngest child to have the opportunity to be the most he can be. We want the same thing for our other eight children as well. Educating our disabled children and helping our families cope as long as possible with what is a stress filled situation produces adults better able to handle society and work, thus rendering needed care less intensive and less expensive.

In the last three years, we have made more enemies and established more friendships than we did in the first thirty years of our lives. I guess that is an indication that we are alive, really alive and willing to risk ego, money, and peace of mind. If I were to give parents one word of advice it would be to know what you can and cannot live with. Do not let anyone tell you that there is only one way to do something—their way. We have the right and ability to make the choices that affect our lives. After all, we are the ones who live with the results. ■

Theresa Donar Riniker lives in Galena, Illinois with her husband, Lewis, and their nine children. She is employed part-time as a counselor-aide at Rainbow Ridge, a group home for physically disabled, mentally alert adults. Mrs. Riniker is active in many organizations, including a support group called, *Parents Make the Difference*, for which she writes the newsletter and organizes meetings.

CHAPTER 31

Selecting and Adapting Toys and Games

Parents, relatives and friends often feel stumped when doing their shopping for youngsters with disabilities. Something happens when we enter the store. The know-how we have acquired in buying for children, the guidelines on the tags and game boxes, the sales people, all seem of little help.

We wonder about what kinds of games or activities can not only interest our children, but what kinds of physical, intellectual or social skills are necessary. Perhaps we forget we are shopping for a child who will enjoy what all children enjoy. A child with a disability is a child first. The child's disability, no matter how severe, is secondary.

There are many new games being sold but more likely they either use new materials or have been renamed. However, those games that were available when we were growing up and have stood the test of time are still the best.

Many toys and games are marked as to the age level of the child for whom they are appropriate. These age guidelines can be very helpful, but they are created on the basis of children who are not disabled. Accordingly, they do not take into account difficulties children may have with intellectual understanding, ability to concentrate for a period of time, and ability to manipulate objects in the world.

You may have had some experience with changing games when you tried playing with your own children. If you have not, a teacher, occupational therapist, or a recreational therapist can help you. The most important guidelines will come from your knowledge of your own youngster.

We are including an article by Barbara Bruno-Goldman and Barbara Coyne Cutler (published originally in THE EXCEPTIONAL PARENT, August 1979) which will describe how to modify board games for your child's enjoyment. The same principles can be used for other activities.

First, here is a shopping list of games and toys that can be adapted for the pleasure of children with disabilities. The age groups—preschool and school-age—are merely guidelines. For some school-aged youngsters, the preschool suggestions may be quite appropriate.

BUILDING

All children like to put things together. Preschool children prefer toys that fit easily and can be put together and taken apart in only one way. Parents may have to help their child to start a project; then the child can continue on his or her own.

Slightly older children like toys where the same pieces can be used to build many different structures. Older grade school children enjoy the challenge of building complex toys and models that include motors or moving parts.

Preschool Children
- Blocks (soft and hard)
- simple put-together toys (popbeads, Lincoln Logs, Tinker Toys and others)
- hammer and pegs
- large blocks/small blocks
- picture dominos

School-age Children
- pegboard and other pattern-making toys
- Lego, two levels
- wood working tools
- beginning models
- complex models: small pieces, may include engines; model planes that fly; visible engines
- erector sets, similar building materials
- large cardboard boxes
- Constructo Straws

ARTS AND CRAFTS

Your child does not have to be talented to enjoy arts and crafts. Paints are popular with children, but they can be messy. Crayons and magic markers are good for drawing and for coloring objects such as doilies. Scrap books are fun. Family pictures or pictures from colorful magazines can be used to make a scrap book. Working with clay is also fun.

Most craft projects—making baskets or mats, for example—are generally successful if the child can see what the finished product will look like before he or she begins work. These materials can all be used to decorate the child's room.

The school-aged child is likely to be interested in several different hobbies. Providing materials the child has already shown interest in will probably be most successful. However, providing new materials in an area of established interest, like giving materials for macrame to a child interested in sewing, can expand a child's fun.

Preschool Children
- scrap books
- Spirograph and Etch-A-Sketch

88

- cooking materials
- finger paints
- easel and paints
- printing sets
- hand or finger puppets
- shoestring sewing
- PlayDoh or clay
- crayons, magic markers
- rub-on pictures
- coloring books, sketch pads
- animal shapes for tracing

School-age children
- candle making
- beginner enameling kits
- embroidering, sewing
- weaving, small looms
- macrame
- mobiles
- pipe cleaner designs
- bead jewelry
- origami (paper folding)
- linoleum blocks for printing
- leather craft
- mosaic tiles
- soap sculpture
- threading materials: macaroni, cheerios, string
- making picture collages
- paper cutting and pasting
- scraps and scrap books
- decorating the room
- papier mache sculptures
- mural painting

IMAGINATIVE PLAY

All children love to pretend. Fantasies and imaginative play are especially important to children whose physical activities are restricted. These activities provide escape from the limits of the bedroom and help to deal with concerns about him or herself. Puppets, dolls, and doctor kits are especially helpful.

Preschool children
- doctor/nurse kits
- hand puppets and finger puppets
- play telephone
- stuffed farm and zoo animals
- dolls and doll house
- large cars and trucks
- toy boats
- cardboard villages and stores
- cars, trucks, wagons, motorcycles, tricycles for riding or pulling
- action figures

School-age Children
- puppets
- stuffed animals and dolls
- simple microscope
- musical instruments
- magnets
- tops
- gyroscopes
- jacks and marbles
- play villages and people
- dolls and doll houses: G.I. Joe, Barbie, action figures, robots, superheroes
- walkie-talkie
- costumes, old clothes for dress-up
- microscope
- binoculars
- telescopes
- yo-yo
- printing press

GAMES

Children enjoy table games. Games for younger children should be short and easily completed. The older child will like adult games like Careers, Clue, or Monopoly.

Table games will often require parents or siblings to play with the child. Some games can be played alone with the child taking the turn of different imaginary players.

Preschool children
- simple card games such as "go-fish"
- easy board games such as Candyland
- puzzles
- marbles
- table games
- games using Nerf ball
- bubble blowing
- bean bag games
- beach ball
- bowling games
- racing track with cars
- board games with simple instructions and rules: Scrabble with fitted or magnetic pieces; checkers; backgammon; Sorry; geo-boards; Yahtzee; bingo

School-age Children
- puzzles—simple to complex
- board games with complex instructions and rules: Clue, Careers, Monopoly
- electric table games: hockey, basketball, football, pool
- dominos

ADDITIONAL PLAY THINGS

Puzzles of under twenty-five pieces are fun for younger children while puzzles with twenty-five to fifty pieces challenge older children. Musical toys and instruments are popular with all age groups.

School-aged children generally are avid collectors. Collections are easy to start, even when a child is relatively confined—stamps, coins, baseball cards, bottle caps, etc. ■

ADDITIONAL PLAY THINGS

Preschool Children
- rattle
- beads
- sorting toys

- books
- magazines
- pop-up toys, such as jack-in-the-box
- music box
- view master
- squeaking toys
- musical instruments and toys
- trucks, cars, boats
- floating toys and objects used in bathtub or sink water play
- aquarium
- plants
- cloth or cardboard picture books
- punching bag

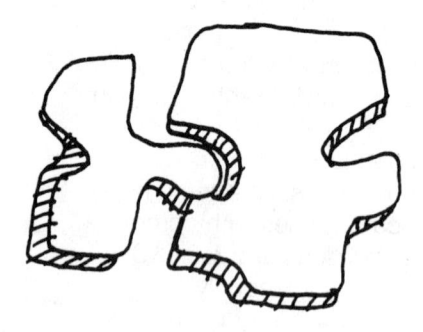

- jump rope (and other toys for large-muscle developement)
- puzzles of under 50 pieces
- mobiles
- brightly colored objects strung across bed (balloons, soft materials, bells)
- photos, pictures, posters- especially family pictures or action pictures
- flashlights

School-age Children
- collections: stamp, coin, picture card, bottle cap, insect, mineral
- membership cards: library, museum, neighborhood centers
- Boy Scout and Girl Scout equipment
- cleaning the house
- water toys (pouring and mixing)
- wood working
- pets

BOARD GAMES

Board games can be enjoyed by the entire family. Often, children with disabilities do not get the opportunity to play board games. Like workbooks, commercially sold games are often too complicated.

They may also involve a variety of difficult skills, such as counting, following directions, or matching items. Sometimes these games require being attentive and waiting turns for longer than a child might find possible. Or, the player may be required to grasp a small object and position it in a small space. This is a difficult feat for a child with coordination impairments.

Parents and teachers (and helpful brothers, sisters and friends) can begin to teach these games by creating "revised" directions to allow a child to take part. With some ingenuity, adults can create "individualized" games that are similar to ones in stores, but are more usable.

The directions involved in playing a board game can be confusing. Some children do not know how to start and how to stop (i.e. "win"). They may not understand what a move is, the number of moves to make, or which direction to move in. Homemade games which take two or three minutes to play can help to reduce confusion and teach these concepts. Here is a color-matching board game which can be used in developing game concepts.

Using the traffic signal colors (green = go, red = stop), make a row of colored squares (red, green, red, green). The child places the marker or playing piece on green. (The size of the squares and the marker can be varied to meet the child's skills.) Then the child draws from a deck of a few colored cards. The deck is "stacked" if necessary—it has no green and only one red card. When the child draws the red card, he or she moves the marker to the square of the same color. The child continues and draws the red card, moves to red (stop) and wins a prize (e.g. star, treat, etc.). The combination of red (stop) and prize signal means that the child is a "winner," the game is over, and perhaps he or she is ready to play again. Soon, the child will learn to take turns. (The teaching of taking turns may require adding other players one at a time.)

If movement on a board game is a problem, create bigger spaces between positions. For example, you can make a town with pictures of stores on separate cards, which you place far apart. This gives the child a larger area for movement. It also illustrates the concept of what a move is. The child can move a toy car from store to store, one, two, etc. spaces after (s)he draws a number from a deck of cards as above, or uses a spinner or dice. Once (s)he learns to move from store to store, you can gradually pull the picture cards closer together.

Once these game concepts are learned, you can continue to build on these skills. Your child can gradually learn to play more complicated games and to take turns with other members of the family.

CHAPTER 32

ENTERING THE WORLD OF WORK

My Daughter is Succeeding

by Ann N. Stearns

The bridge between school and the world of work is a challenge for all young adults. Identifying the specific challenges and tasks to be mastered is often neglected in traditional school programs. Mrs. Stearns illustrates how effective one program was for her daughter.

Like many parents of exceptional children, I had placed so much emphasis on getting Nancy through school that when graduation finally arrived, I was not prepared for what the future would hold. All the years of struggling to obtain valid comprehensive evaluations, correct identification, and appropriate special education services seemed to culminate in that night in June 1981 when my daughter received her high school diploma. The effort had paid off for both of us—she had made it.

Pre-Vocational Training

During her last years in high school, I was employed as a special education supervisor for the local public schools. I had worked closely with colleagues in the field of vocational education and the Department of Rehabilitative Services (DRS) to develop programs in pre-vocational training for our educable mentally retarded students.

An empty building located in the school board complex between the high school and vocational/technical school was renovated and became a model center for transitioning these students from special education classes to specific vocational training. Half-day exploratory programs offered to ninth and tenth graders provided an opportunity to test their aptitude in such skills as carpentry, small engine repair, and horticulture. Job orientation classes developed skills in filling out applications, seeking interviews, and appropriate work habits. By the beginning of eleventh grade, each student was enrolled as a DRS client and a comprehensive, individual vocational assessment was provided in conjunction with a nearby rehabilitation center.

Students who were skilled enough and capable of handling regular high school level vocational programs could begin training at the technical school during the eleventh grade. Students with lesser ability could enter programs at the rehabilitation center. All students had the opportunity for supervised internships or work study during the senior year of high school.

High Hopes and Pride

With no small amount of self satisfaction, I felt that we had designed an exemplary program which would adequately prepare Nancy and others like her to find their place in the world of work. As I watched her walk down the aisle that June evening I felt an enormous sense of pride in this young woman who had struggled so valiantly to complete high school against odds which would have defeated me. She had recently completed an internship in food services at the local hospital, and armed with her diplomas from high school and technical school, was ready to face the world. A part-time job as a kitchen helper awaited her in a small restaurant in town.

Because Nancy had obtained her job through her own initiative, we had little contact with the Department of Rehabilitative Services after graduation. A field counselor visited her once on the job site and then sent a letter stating that her case was closed due to regular employment. In our naivete, we thought that we would no longer need their services.

Six months passed quickly, and for the first time in eighteen years, I began to feel a marvelous sense of relief—Nancy was going to and from work on her own, seemed happy, and demonstrated a degree of self-sufficiency that I had hardly dared to believe would be possible. Then one day after work I watched her crestfallen face, and heard her say, "I've been laid off."

Laid Off

Nancy never saw it coming, and had no idea how it happened. Like many exceptional children with impaired social perception, she had failed to recognize the warning signs. Only months later did she admit that she had been confusing orders, forgetting directions, and having difficulty in getting along with the waitresses.

I remember what happened next as the worst period in our lives. For two long years, Nancy sat at home without a job while I went to work each day worrying about how she would fill her time. You can ignore the vulgarities of TV soap operas until you have a young person sitting at home watching them all day. You run out of suggestions for proper use of leisure time, especially when you live in a small rural community with no organized recreational programs. You tire of helping fill out endless job applications and arranging for transportation to interview sites. You pray, you hope, and finally you despair.

A Rehabilitative Plan

At last we turned to the agency we had previously felt we no longer needed—the Department of Rehabilitative Services. Dealing with a state agency can be a frustrating experience for both the exceptional child and her parents; there are numerous forms to be completed; a physical examination must be arranged; and the waiting period seems interminable. It takes patience and perseverance, but everything in Nancy's life seemed to take extra effort. After eligibility for services was determined, a field counselor developed a rehabilitative plan for Nancy which involved her participation in a work-adjustment program.

Again there seemed to be obstacles because the program was located twelve miles from our home. But the agency quickly arranged to transport Nancy to meet the van, and each afternoon she would walk home from the bus stop.

The work adjustment program run by the Department of Rehabilitative Services served a wide variety of clients—some young people Nancy's age and some adults who were being phased back into community life from the state mental hospital. Some of the young people had been in trouble with the law, and some of the older clients were severely disabled. This did not go unnoticed by Nancy, who has always seemed to be unaware of her own disability. She thought these people were "weird" and wondered what she was doing in the program.

It was certainly not an ideal environment for her, and there were days when she was discouraged and wanted to quit. However, over the nine months that Nancy was in the program she learned not only the appropriate work habits, but also a tolerance for people whose disabilities were greater than hers.

Each day, Nancy worked at repetitive tasks such as sorting objects, clipping wires from used telephone bells, and stuffing envelopes. She saw little relationship to her training in school as a chef's helper, and frequently chafed at the confining routine. Yet, she was learning critical job skills.

Nancy's progress was monitored daily by the staff. She was rated on appearance and grooming, attitude toward peers and supervisors, ability to stay on task, and speed and accuracy. After approximately six months, the staff felt that Nancy was ready for job placement.

At this point, a special job-site coordinator was assigned to Nancy by the Department of Rehabilitative Services. Cindy was an extremely pleasant young woman who quickly won Nancy confidence and became her chief advocate. Funded through a grant from the Joint Partnership Training Act, Cindy's job was to establish contact with prospective employers, arrange for trial placement or internship, and serve as a liaison between Nancy and the employers. In addition, her role was to "job-shadow"—working side by side with Nancy to learn the duties of her job and the employer's expectations for the client.

Cindy contacted employers describing Nancy's training, experience, and limitations. Kitchen work in fast food restaurants was ruled out because of Nancy's inability to perform well under pressure. The search focused on finding a more sheltered environment where Nancy's speed was not a primary factor. Finally, Cindy found a trial placement in the kitchen of a local nursing home. For three months, Nancy's schedule was four days at the nursing home and one day back at the work adjustment program so that the staff could monitor her progress.

The difference between the role of the job-site coordinator and the traditional field counselor became apparent immediately. Cindy learned the mechanics of the job along with Nancy. When Nancy became confused about the number of place settings for each table in the dining room, Cindy drew diagrams for her to follow. If the duties on the early shift differed from those on the late shift, Cindy made lists for Nancy to check. Weekly conferences were held with Nancy and her boss. If an unexpected problem arose, Nancy would call Cindy for an extra meeting.

Through the job-site coordinator, the parent also has a support system. If I saw Nancy was troubled or confused by something that had happened at work, I could call Cindy to request her help without feeling as if I were interfering with Nancy's relationship to her employer.

Another six months have passed and Nancy is now employed by the nursing home. She drives her own car to and from work and banks most of her paycheck. She still lives at home, but comes and goes on her rotating shifts with amazing ease. A letter from the Department of Rehabilitative Services arrived last week—case closed because of regular employment. However, this time we know that the partnership between Nancy and Cindy will still be there if we need it. ■

CHAPTER 33

Related Services and the Supreme Court
A Family's Story

We are happy to name Mary Tatro as the recipient of THE EXCEPTIONAL PARENT Award of 1984 for her efforts and contributions on behalf of her child and all children.

Mrs. Tatro was able to persist more than five years to get the services necessary for her child, although this meant sustaining personal hardship, a prolonged struggle, and an eventual confrontation at the United States Supreme Court. Over the years, she enlisted and collaborated with a variety of agencies and organizations. And she was able to maintain her respect and good will for the educators who were working with her daughter.

The Decision

On July 5, 1984, the United States Supreme Court upheld a 1980 decision by a Texas Federal Appeals Court, that Amber Tatro, a child born with spina bifida, must be provided with clean intermittent catheterization (CIC) by the school district so that she can attend public school in the regular classroom. The Court decided that this service was within the definition of related services under the 1975 Education for All Handicapped Children Act (P.L. 94-142) which guarantees a "free appropriate education to handicapped children."

The school district had argued that the CIC procedure was a medical service that would cause undue financial burden on the school because it would need to be administered by highly trained personnel. The Court ruled "a service that enables a handicapped child to remain at school during the day is an important means of providing the child with the meaningful access to education that Congress envisioned...services like CIC that permit a child to remain at school during the day are no less related to the effort to educate than are services that enable the child to reach, enter, or exit the school."

Accordingly, the Court said that related services were whatever is necessary throughout the school day, as long as such services are not directly provided by a physician.

Mary Tatro was able to maintain her respect and good will for the educators who were working with her daughter.

The Beginning

Amber Tatro was born with spina bifida. During the first year of her life, she had many bladder infections and, as a result, spent a good deal of time in the hospital. When the family was able to utilize catheterization procedures, Amber was much less likely to have bladder infections. The Tatro family lives in an area in Texas in which special education services are provided during the preschool years. As a result, before Amber was three years old, the family approached the special education department of the school district for a school plan.

School personnel and the Tatros agreed on Amber's need for special education services during preschool years and for physical and occupational therapy. Contrary to the opinion of the school system, the Tatros believed that the CIC procedure was a "simple aid to toileting that could be performed by anyone without special medical training." In fact, the procedure is a relatively simple one to perform. Later, when the school officials informed the family that they would not include the clean intermittent catheterization process in Amber's Individualized Educational Plan (IEP), Mrs. Tatro recalls jokingly saying, "I'll see you in Supreme Court."

The Tatros appealed the school's decision, and a due process hearing was held in June, 1979. The officials at the hearing ruled in favor of providing the related service of catheterization. The Commissioner of Education of Texas also supported the ruling. However, the local school board appealed to the Texas Board of Education claiming there were no provisions in P.L. 94-142 for such services. The state board ruled in favor of the school district, overturning the "due process" decision. In October 1979, the Tatros filed suit against the Texas State Board of Education in United States District Court.

An excellent summary of the process from then on appeared in the Journal of Visual Impairment and Blindness in September 1984. With their kind permission, we are excerpting from *Second Thoughts on Educating Handicapped Children: The Supreme Court's Ruling on the Tatro Case* by Barbara D. McGarry which describes the step-by-step process.

"Their suit was based on both the Education of All Handicapped Children Act, and the anti-discrimination provisions (section 504) of the Rehabilitation Act of 1973, as amended. The District Court asserted that CIC was not a 'related service' under P.L. 94-142, and also stated that section 504 of the Rehabilitation Act did not require 'the setting up of governmental health care for people seeking to participate in federally funded programs.

"The Tatros then took their case to the Court of Appeals, which in 1981 reversed the District Court on both counts. CIC is properly a 'related service' under P.L. 94-142, stated the Appeals Court, because without it Amber could not attend classes and benefit from special education. (Ironically, on January 19, 1981, then-Secretary of Education Shirley Hufstedler issued an advisory regulation affirming CIC as a related service for handicapped children, only to have her ruling promptly voided by her successor, T.H. Bell.)

"The Appeals Court also upheld the Tatro's claim that the school's refusal to provide CIC for Amber 'effectively excluded her from a federally funded education program in violation of section 504' of the Rehabilitation Act. Such a finding at the appellate court level automatically means award of attorney's fees to the successful appellant under section 505 of the Rehabilitation Act, and the Texas State Board of Education was therefore ordered to pay the attorney's fees for the Tatros. In 1983, the case was further appealed to the Supreme Court.

"The Supreme Court's decision, while a victory in principle and in substance for handicapped children, could still prove very costly to their parents and advocates. The Tatros spent $27,000 in attorney's fees for the Supreme Court appeal, yet the final paragraph of the Supreme Court's decision, linked to a similar case (Smith v. Robinson), destroyed any hope of reimbursement for costs:

"'...Section 504 is inapplicable when relief is available under the Education of All Handicapped Children Act to remedy a denial of educational services. Respondents [Tatros] are therefore not entitled to relief under Section 504, and we reverse the Court of Appeals holding that respondents are entitled to recover attorney's fees.'"

Amber at School

Mrs. Tatro always took Amber to court hearings because she felt it was important for the judge to see Amber and in that sense "know" the person who was being talked about. Amber's reaction to these proceeding usually was to say that she was "bored."/At times, Amber said that she really did not understand what was going on and would say, "This is boring, let's forget it." At other times, she poignantly would ask, "Did the judge say I could go to school?"

As a result of the proceedings and her medical problems, Amber's school experiences were disrupted a great deal. For the first year, although she had been assigned to a special education class, she did not go to school at all. In the following year, she did not go to school for six months.

Many things happened that seemed to reflect the school board's wish to deny services. For example, at one point, the school bus stopped picking Amber up. For one period of time, the school bus was picking her up later than when school actually began. There were also efforts to change the program that she was in.

At another time, it was suggested that it took Amber too long to get from her bus to the classroom, and therefore, she should not ride the bus. Mrs. Tatro felt that it was important for Amber to participate with the other children on the school bus and in that way get to know the other children going to school.

There was even a time when the school said they would provide the catheterization, but called Mrs. Tatro at 12:00 noon to say they were not going to do the procedure that was scheduled for 12:30. Mrs. Tatro, who is employed 35 minutes away from the school, had to rush there to do the procedure. There were also problems in getting services when Amber was hospitalized or at home recuperating and needed to have home tutoring services.

Mrs. Tatro praised the individuals in the school that Amber attended as wonderful and very helpful to her. The problems Amber had were not because of the school staff working with her but rather problems in reference to decisions made by the school board.

The Effect on the Family

The whole process has been a tremendous drain on Mrs. Tatro and her family. Even Amber's IEP

Journal of Visual Impairment and Blindness & Volume 78, Number 7, Copyright 1984, American Foundation for the Blind, 15 West 16th Street, New York, New York 10011 meetings were a burden. There were as many as thirty people attending. At these meetings, there were endless discussions about the value of the catheterization process and who was qualified to administer it.

Mrs. Tatro reports that the whole process has taken a lot out of her personally as well. She has had problems with her blood pressure which she believes has affected her efforts on her job as well as in her private life. At the present time, the Tatros still owe their attorney $35,000. They have had help paying for some of the fees by organizations. Without the help of groups such as Advocacy Inc., of Austin, Texas, their legal fees probably would have been two hundred thousand dollars. Mrs. Tatro assumes that the school district spent many thousands of dollars in legal fees but she does not know exactly how much.

In the course of this, Mrs. Tatro often found herself becoming, "So mad that I cried." Now that the process is over, she has not felt let down, but rather feels it is time to get to work on other similar issues—to help other children.

Mrs. Tatro says that her husband was a constant source of strength. He has claimed that all he does is "pay the bills," but according to Mary Tatro, he "hung in there, came with me, and was always supportive."

A number of organizations joined in and were very helpful, in particular the Spina Bifida Association of America. The local Dallas chapter of SBAA helped with attorney's fees and also helped by lending some money to the family. In addition to the Spina Bifida Association of America, the National Epilepsy Foundation, the United Cerebral Palsy Association, the Association for Retarded Citizens, and the Down Syndrome Congress all joined in filing a brief with the Supreme Court supportive of the Tatros. In contrast, the National School Board Association and several other groups representing public school administrators supported the school district's appeal.

At times, the Tatros considered giving up and sending Amber to private school. However, they found that private schools were not geared to a child of average intelligence who was physically handicapped. Private schools that they were able to find which were equipped for children with disabilities were established for children with learning problems or who were mentally retarded. They were unable to find a school that would "fit" Amber.

Amber is now in the third grade in a regular class. She reads and spells very well. Overall, she does well in school and enjoys it a great deal. Amber has missed school from time to time because she has had four operations since the beginning of school.

Mrs. Tatro has served as president of the Spina Bifida Association of Dallas. She has found that being involved in this organization has been especially helpful to her because she was able to find a group of supportive people who really understood what she was talking about.

Mrs. Mary Tatro's determination and persistence are lifelong traits. "My mother and my grandmother always said I was stubborn." Her battlecry is, "Just don't give up. Don't stop. If you stop, we all lose."

Unfinished Business

A major issue remains unresolved for the Tatro family. That is, while the Supreme Court ruled in favor of Amber's catheterization (unanimously, in the opinion delivered by Chief Justice Warren E. Burger) as part of her Individualized Educational Plan, the Court ruled against the Tatro's in their efforts to recover their legal fees, with two judges supporting recovery of fees.

Legislation has been filed by Senator Lowell Weicker (R-CT.), Chairman of the Senate Subcommittee on the Handicapped, to reimburse parents. In a similar case on which the Supreme Court also ruled on July 5, 1984, the court ruled against a family in Rhode Island who had attempted to collect attorney's fees under Section 504 of the Rehabilitation Act.

The dilemma for all parents as a result of this is that, at the present time, it is uncertain whether they can be assured of collecting their attorney's fees when they win a case of this kind. ∎

—S.D.K.—

The following are excerpts from Senator Lowell Weiker's (R-CT.) statement regarding the bill he has introduced to amend P.L. 94-142 to "authorize the award of reasonable attorney's fees to certain prevailing parties, and to clarify the effect of the Education of the Handicapped Act on rights, procedures, and remedies under other laws relating to the prohibition of discrimination."

"The court's rationale [in denying the Tatro's payment of attorney's fees] was that the comprehensiveness and detail with which the Education of the Handicapped Act addresses the provision of schooling to handicapped children implies that Congress intended to generally limit remedies to those explicitly provided in P.L. 94-142. The court argued that plaintives could not circumvent or enlarge P.L. 94-142 remedies by resorting to other statutes, in this case by providing for attorney's fees.

"Unfortunately, the court has not only misinterpreted the congressional intent underlying the Education of the Handicapped Act, but it has also frustrated Congress' intent in enacting Sections 504 and 1983 which I and many members of this body assumed protected the civil rights claims of handicapped children...

"...the intent was to close gaps in our civil rights laws whereby awards of fees were not explicitly available. It is clear to this Senator that it was not the intent of Congress to leave the constitutional claims of handicapped children seeking a free appropriate public education unprotected.

"Similarly, when Congress approved section 505 (b) of the Rehabilitation Act and addressed the need for attorneys' fees, referring to the rights Section 504 extended to handicapped individuals, there was no exception made for handicapped children seeking an education. The 1978 Senate and House reports accompanying Section 505 (b) explain that disabled individuals were one of the very few, if only, minority groups in this country who had not been specifically authorized by Congress to seek attorney's fees. The purpose of this provision was 'to correct this ommission and thereby assist handicapped individuals in securing the legal protection guaranteed them under Title V of the Rehabilitation Act.' It certainly was not the intent of Congress to exclude from the coverage of Section 505 (b) the claims of handicapped children seeking a free appropriate public education...

"My amendments to P.L. 94-142 are for the limited purpose of clarifying what I believe to be and has always been the intent of Congress; that attorneys' fees be available to parents, guardians, or other representatives of handicapped children who prevail in an action to enforce their child's right to education.

"The proposed amendment is not in any way unique. At present, there are at least ninety separate attorneys' fees provisions to promote enforcement of over ninety different federal laws. This amendment should correct any doubts the court may have had and make clear Congress' intent to afford full protection for the educational rights of handicapped children..."

Senators Stafford, Mathias, Kennedy, Randolf, and Eagleton all joined Senator Weicker in introducing this bill which they have cited as the "Handicapped Children's Protection Act of 1984." ■

It is clear to this Senator that it was not the intent of Congress to leave the constitutional claims of handicapped children seeking a free appropriate public education unprotected.

CHAPTER 34

PARENT ADVOCACY NETWORK

by Dianne L. Ferguson

Dianne Ferguson describes a parent-run program which can help other parents work effectively with educators and other school officials.

Parents of children with disabilities, like all parents, want a good education for their children. My husband, Phil, and I have spent twelve years struggling to secure an education for our severely disabled son so that he can learn what he needs to know. In many ways, our current struggle is a victory. Twenty, even ten years ago, Ian would not have received an education. Earlier battles fought and won by parents groups established both Ian's right to go to school, and our right to struggle for the "good education" he needs.

The lessons of the past have led us many times to combine our efforts for Ian with those of other parents. Most recently, we have joined a group to develop a network of parents who want to obtain decent educations for their children. In the process, the group hopes to improve the overall quality of education for *all* children who are disabled.

The Parent Advocacy Network (PAN) began in March, 1980. Five parents and a professor of special education at Syracuse University held a series of meetings for parents who wanted to become advocates for their own children and for other parents who needed help. Our group has made an effort to define the challenge for parents, to understand the people we encounter in schools, and to explain the strategies we choose to employ.

The Information Gap

As the group began to talk about our experiences with schools, we were struck by the similarity of our stories. As parents, we approach school personnel with a large informational disadvantage. We do not know how the system works, what to expect, what we need to say, or even how to say it. No matter how well we might know our own children, we are not prepared to talk to teachers, principals, psychologists or counselors, much less participate in the educational decision making process.

Although parents do have a lot of information, it is not the "right" kind. When we go to speak to administrators at school we hear about IEP's, MA's, criteria, auditory processing, regulations, and sometimes, due process. At first, there seems to be no correspondence between what we know and what the people in schools are talking about.

"The first time I didn't know anything at all. We weren't prepared."

"I was mum all the way for years. I just kept signing papers and believed everything was fine."

Only one parent was able to say that she and her husband had a very good experience with their Committee on the Handicapped, but said that they had been "coached to the hilt."

Difficult initial experiences can cause some parents to stay silent. Others begin to search out information, and eventually learn to speak the language of the schools. One of our members suggested, "If you say 'perseveration' instead of 'he does it again and again and again and again,' it makes it sound as though you know what you are talking about."

Still, other parents seem traumatized. One woman described seeing parents come out of meetings "simply vibrating" with anger and frustration. Others talked of being humiliated, intimidated, overwhelmed or, maybe at best, ignored. While parents may feel similarly discounted with other professionals (doctors, for instance), school experiences seem different and even more troublesome. Perhaps this comes from knowing that we will have to maintain an on-going relationship with these school professionals, day after day, year after year.

Self Confidence

The feelings created by the information gap lead to the need most often mentioned by the group: self-confidence. One woman explained that she had been afraid to ask questions, sure that she would sound "dumb." But as she listened to others, she discovered differently.

"The questions others asked were no different than the ones I might ask. And the answers they got could easily have been an answer that I might have given if someone asked me. I guess I really knew a lot more than I thought I did."

As members of the group talked together, we realized that one of the most important things we could learn was how to speak up with confidence, instead of being afraid of "sounding stupid." Changing one's perceptions of oneself is not a novel idea—countless self-help groups have sprung up in the last ten years with just that objective. But for parents, the effort is complicated by our own insecurity in the face of an overwhelming responsibility. There is so much at stake in trying to assure that one's child receives a fair and decent education. Having to deal with school officials in this capacity can make parents feel as if we are students ourselves. As one woman put it, "Whenever I send in minutes of the Home and School Association for typing, I always feel like they're going to come back with a B minus on the top."

Knowing what to do, knowing that you have legal rights, and being able to use words like "perseveration" and "auditory processing" are not enough. Whether it is called self-confidence, courage, or belief in ourselves, somehow parents need to develop it.

Parental Perspectives on Schools

The way parents act with school officials is not solely a matter of our own knowledge and confidence. The people in schools have their own perceptions and expectations of parents that contribute to our view of ourselves and how we behave. In the discussion, our network group described our perception of school people in three ways.

As well-intentioned but inept

Some of our members described people in schools as awkward and inept with parents, but genuinely well-intentioned. They are perceived as amiable people who really *do* want to educate disabled children and work with their parents. Quite unintentionally, in their manner, style, and use of jargon, they give parents a wrong impression. Many parents make an attempt to understand their difficulty. "It isn't that they don't care," one woman said, "After all, they have problems, too. They have a lot of other children to provide services for. There are budgets, bosses, class sizes, and all the rest of it." With support for their efforts, it may be possible to turn ineffective intentions of school people into action.

As threatened and defensive

Others perceived some people in schools as afraid of parents, afraid that they might learn something, suggest something, or ask a question. This view was explained.

"They've lived in their own little world for so long, doing things the way they want to have them done. They really don't want anyone to come in and disrupt it. It is set up so well! Why would they want anybody to come in and blow it?"

The group's understanding of this is that school people see the status quo as preferable, and change as threatening. To be asked to change implies to them that they have not been doing their jobs well enough. Accordingly, these professionals do not tell anything to parents that they do not feel is necessary. They cover the bases legally, though; they rush through a meeting, get the parent's signature, and breathe a sigh of relief as they go on to the next "case." While they might not intentionally mislead a parent, they will withhold important information because it is safer and easier.

As rejecting

This perspective was described most succinctly: "They just don't want to serve children with disabilities." Having disabled children in schools can cause problems for them. As one parent said,

"If a school system really does not want to provide services, they can easily find ways to talk parents out of it. They act as if the parent doesn't know what they are talking about, and is trying to get something for his or her child that the child doesn't really deserve, or isn't capable of doing anyway. Their attitude is that the parent is too protective or over-involved, and just wants an unreasonable amount for the child."

"Maybe they are at a loss about what to do," one parent hypothesized, "but surely there are enough professionals around nowadays that know all about the law and about different programs. They just don't want to deal with us or our children."

The "Power Gap"

Regardless of the different perspectives parents had experienced, the common theme was the power gap. One parent noted, "One group has power and the other doesn't. I think the ultimate lack of power is to have a child who needs."

There was a contradiction present when we discussed the power gap.

"As a parent, I provide a child which makes their job in school possible. I am also a taxpayer who makes their paycheck possible. They have to answer to me. I'm in charge here. I'm the employer now."

How can a parent both "be in charge" and lack power?

"Schools ultimately own the door that opens to get various programs. But you have a legal right to have the appropriate door opened. The real strength of the situation, however, is on the other side simply because they have the services you want."

Is there any way to equalize the situation? Can the power gap ever be closed? One parent pointed out that if he took his child out of school because it was not providing adequate care or programs, it would not be hurting the school. If the school decided to send his child away, though, it would be very painful.

By the nature of the situation, it always seems that the school has a certain amount of residual power. And for parents, there is always a degree of insecurity.

Two Strategies for Relating to Schools

After getting prepared, figuring out the school, and appreciating the inevitability of a power gap,

CHAPTER 35

Unthinkable Thoughts

by James J. Gallagher

For many years, James J. Gallagher has shaped the field of special education. First as the Assistant Commissioner of Education at the U.S. Office of Education, and then as director of the Frank Porter Graham Child Development Center, he has taken us all to the forefront of knowledge and practice. His unique abilities are reflected in this article.

The following statement is excerpted from Dr. Gallagher's presentation at the twenty-first annual meeting of the Association for Children and Adults with Learning Disabilities. These excerpts have been published previously in the ACLD Newsbrief, *May/June 1984. A further perspective on these issues will appear in the* Journal of Learning Disabilities *in the fall.*

Dr. Gallagher's "Unthinkable Thoughts" questions the assumptions of everyday practice, and not only improves our ability to work, but to determine the new horizons as well.

What is an unthinkable thought? It is a projection of a present problem into the future with the implication behind it so disturbing that most of us do not want to think about it. The point of unthinkable thoughts is that once they are stated—once they are put on the table—then there is a press and a drive and a need to deal with the issue. So the trick is whether we can state relevant issues with such clarity and force that they demand some kind of action.

In 1955, if we had been asked what would have been our heart's desire, we might have said, "Here is what we want: research to generate new ideas and thoughts; personnel training to provide a well trained cadre of professionals and teachers; demonstration projects to illustrate exemplary practices; technical assistance, in-service training, and dissemination to aid the professional already on the job; and a guarantee that no disabled child would go without an appropriate special education program."

And what do you think? In the 1980's, we have all of those things that we dreamed about, and now we find that paradise is less exotic than it appeared from a distance. Many of our educational colleagues who used to be supportive have turned cold, if not downright hostile.

What happened? Well, we need not be bashful about our contributions from exceptional children to the educational field in general. Our special problems have yielded many contributions, not just for the children with whom we deal but for all children. We in special education are the United States Marines of American education. The really difficult jobs are sent to us, and out of these difficult jobs come very important contributions. I will remind you of only a few.

1) The development of measures of aptitude and ability—these were developed because we needed them.

2) Diagnostic tests and procedures to pinpoint specific developmental and academic problems.

3) The IEP specifying measurable objectives.

4) Parent participation in the program, not just on parents' night, but all year round.

5) The development of self-monitoring and sequential learning techniques.

6) The understanding of information processing and that tricky business of the executive function.

It is clear to many observers that we are in a transition phase in designing special education for children with learning disabilities. What we will be doing ten years from now will probably not resemble in many respects what we are doing now. For those who doubt that statement, let me remind you of one particular issue that cries out for some action: what about the prevalance figures for learning disabilities?

There are either eight hundred thousand or eight million children with learning disabilities in the United States. They are either clearly identified by an unusual developmental pattern or they are just not doing well in school. Clearly, the vagueness by which we identify the target group, the uncertainty with which the educational program or treatment is provided tells us that we cannot passively pass such uncertain procedures and methods to the next generation of professionals.

One of the puzzling observations that we can make by people standing somewhat apart from the situation is how easily we have fallen into one of the clearest logical fallacies. If I said to you, "All our group considered two possible strategies: being a mediator, or being an advocate.

Being a mediator

This style was the first choice of our group. Words and phrases like "assertive but not pushy," "being firm but nice," "Presenting yourself not as an adversary but as an assistant," and "being cooperative," characterized the mediator style. It was our feeling that calm and pleasant behavior would demonstrate trust and willingness to listen. At the same time, information and persistence serve to set the limits beyond which one is not willing to negotiate or compromise. For example, one parent explained her strategy.

"The building principal knows that I know. And he knows that if I'm not happy with what is going on, I will go right to the director of pupil personnel and the assistant superintendent. He knows I don't make much noise, threaten people or throw things about, but I don't go away either."

Sometimes people noted a distinct note of manipulation and connivance about this style. Parents are putting on a kind of false front. "By your manner, by your style, by your information, and by the way you negotiate and play things, you can perhaps trick them into thinking they don't have quite as much power as they think they do. They can share a little of it with you. You sort of benignly trick them into thinking that they have made a good decision. [It's] kind of sneaky."

Parents who preferred this style also recognized that school-parent relationships *can* be confrontational or adversarial. But they concluded that more can be accomplished if confrontations and stand-offs can be avoided.

Being an advocate

Several of the parents explained that being an advocate "puts people's backs up." That is why being a mediator is better.

One parent objected to the advocacy style because it suggested courtroom procedure. She said the style is "loaded" by the notion that there is a situation in which there are two opposing views that will be fought out. A resolution comes in which one side is seen as clearly winning and the other as clearly losing. She described parents as put in the position of "preparing a case" and "bringing a brief" with them to present to the school.

Another parent said advocates are usually thought of as being over-bearing and very demanding, even militant. School people get "turned off" by having someone "pounding on the table" in order to be noticed, or heard, or to get something done. Unfortunately, the "run of the mill parent" thinks of advocates this way, and concludes that they cannot be one. Yet they are discouraged because they may think that they cannot work with schools to get a good education for their child any other way.

Even though the group indicated a clear preference for a "mediator" style, several talked specifically about the need and usefulness of the "advocacy" style in some cases. In particular situations, for an individual child, "indirect" methods may allow an inadequate situation to drag on for years and years. Sometimes parents have to draw the line and demand what they know is right. The trick is to know when to draw the line.

One parent wanted to "hold back" the advocacy style for the "really big ones"—the test cases.

"There are times when you've got to take all your parents on the bus and go to Capital City. You have to know [when] you have reached the end of all the negotiating procedures and you simply have to change the rules of the game and start applying different kinds of pressure."

The group voiced two cautions about using the advocacy style. First, be *sure* about the issues because you do not want to create any backlash that will hurt your child. Second, remember that there is a risk that you will change or even destroy your relationship with your school. And you still have to go back next year.

Our Network is starting to grow. Parents call us. We will be beginning another series of meetings soon. Maybe someday parents will not have to struggle anymore. But for now, there are still parents who

- really want to be involved in their child's school program.
- eagerly seek information about schools, but distrust the information schools offer.
- are convinced their partnership with schools will always be unequal.
- know that each year brings another problem, another struggle. But most of all, who
- continue to try—for themselves and in support of others—in spite of fears, frustrations and fatigue. ∎

cats are animals. Therefore, all animals are cats," you would feel sorry for me and say I have been working too hard. But if I said to you, "All children with learning disabilities have trouble in school. Therefore, all children who have trouble in school are learning disabled," then we find a significant proportion of the professional community who seem to accept that proposition in their actions if not in their words.

More Unthinkable Thoughts

I first voiced unthinkable thoughts in 1967. Now, seventeen years later, here are some additional unthinkable thoughts.

(1) *Is there really a viable category called "learning disabilities" in the first place?* We should be clear that until we can agree about whom it is that we are talking about, no discussion of treatment programs, professional training, project costs or program evaluation makes very much sense.

A number of observers have pointed out that the key element in populations of children with learning disabilities is not their commonality but their diversity—not their diversity from other groups of children but their diversity from one another. There is an ugly and somewhat justified suspicion that the learning disabled child of 1965 is not the learning disabled child of 1980. They are different groups and different kids.

(2) *Do children with learning disabilities belong in special education?* The answer to this question depends to a large degree on how we define the condition in the first place. In particular, special education was designed to provide special services for children who could not be handled in the regular program effectively. One can have considerable sympathy for the local education administrator who has a variety of youngsters under his or her responsibility who are not performing well in school and who tries to use the learning disabled category to slip them in so they can get some special help.

The temptation is strong to want to call all these youngsters learning disabled. The inability to resist that temptation has resulted in a moving boundary line of special education and prevalance figures to an uncertain ceiling, with no reasonable demarcation line in evidence. It is the issue of the profession itself today, and those advocates who value the gains we have already made need to address this issue with some better solution than we have previously provided.

(3) Another unthinkable thought is the resource room treatment strategy. *Is the "pull-out" strategy really useful in helping learning disabled children?* The results of current studies certainly raise the issue of the usefulness of resource room strategy to remediate the academic and behavioral problems of students with learning disabilities. Research suggests that much more intensive and comprehensive services may be necessary before meaningful modification can be made in the developmental patterns of such children.

The unthinkable thought here is that the resource room is an easier and more comfortable pattern for the local school system to follow. It will keep at bay the potential harassment from the federal government over the issue of the least restrictive environment. But the limited special education contact provided may not be of the intensity necessary to do the job. It may also deny the intensive special education intervention to those youngsters who really need intensive work in dealing with their developmental problems. Many studies need to be conducted to deal with this proposition. The burden of proof, however, rests with those who would say that the resource room "pull-out" strategy provides positive educational experiences.

(4) A final unthinkable thought: *Are the secondary programs for learning disabled students merely an extension of the elementary programs or should they really be something quite different in the services required?* In North Carolina, we have discovered an astonishing diversity of program and service delivery in the secondary schools for children with learning disabilities. In some schools, they did not even know which students were supposed to be learning disabled. They were being mainstreamed, you see. In other areas of exceptional children, we have had similar attempts to graft elementary programs onto the secondary schools with little success.

Strategies to Address These Issues

It should be clear by now that if these issues could be solved by half-day meetings at a convention or a long distance conference call or a round robin correspondence, they would have been solved a long time ago. It is likely that whatever pattern is to be followed, it will be a long and painful journey. But three strategies suggest themselves—research, policy analysis, and demonstration. These are organizational solutions that require careful planning and sustained support by state and federal government.

Research: It is unfortunate that five LD institutes that were funded by OSERS are no longer receiving major support since what is needed is sustained programmatic investigations. One possible strategy to help our definitional problems is to use sophisticated statistical methods to try to sort out identifiable sub-categories of learning disabled children. The basis for the investigation of the sub-category is that we can separate groups of children on the basis of how similarly or differently they score on a variety of instruments or measures of development or adjustment.

Through complex statistical procedures we can then cluster children together and try to identify what it is that makes them similar to other children in the sub-group of identified children with learning disabilities. In this way, we can obtain three, four, or five separate sub-categories of LD children and perhaps eventually provide differential educational programming for them.

Policy Analysis: There is obviously a large number of children or clusters of currently identified children with learning disabilities who require special schooling. So how do we find a better model than the service delivery system that the schools have now? We would propose a joint planning effort that involves leaders from regular and special education to join together in a search for a more effective policy to cope with the total group of children that we are now talking about—the children at the margin, at the boundary line between special and regular education, and to learn how school systems can organizationally meet their responsibilities to all of these children.

One approach would be a historical revision. We have a lot of literature from the regular education area. As you know, some of these children in one school system will be placed in a special education program. In another system they will be placed in a program for the disadvantaged, and, in a third, they may be placed in a remedial reading program. A synthesis of the available information from all of these areas is required.

Another approach would be a working conference bringing together equal numbers of special educators and regular educators along with some groups of policy analysts and economists—with parents there to keep the whole group on task. The job of this conference would be to explore the range of options. We would then design a policy analysis that would list the alternative strategies on one side and the criteria that allows us to choose which strategies on the other. The criteria would involve things like cost, political feasibility, past evidence of effectiveness, and vertical equity (the unequal treatment of unequals in order to make them more equal).

Vertical equity is a fundamental value system at the heart of American society that supports our programs for the handicapped, the disadvantaged, and other people low on the socio-economic scale. The results of these steps would be disseminated through associations and conventions and made available to policy makers, state legislators, governors' offices, etc.

Demonstration: We need program demonstrations of alternative ways to deliver effective services to LD children. Funds from state and federal sources could be established that would illustrate various approaches and models. Each of these models would specify in detail how they selected the learning disabled children, document the manner of service delivered, and provide assessments of the effectiveness of the program. They would be chosen for their diversity so we would have secondary programs, preschool programs, programs that would stress intensive periods of service delivery on one side and mainstreaming perhaps on the other. From this collection of carefully assessed programs would then come some different ideas for the next generation of programs in our field.

The Future

Secure in the knowledge that the future will be different no matter what we do, we need to influence that future by staring the problems right in the eye and finding viable alternatives to current practices. We need the state and federal government to support the research, innovation, demonstration, and curriculum development that will allow these issues to be met and, hopefully, solved.

I will look forward to coming back to this organization seventeen years from now to give you another set of unthinkable thoughts. ■

Dr. James Gallagher is the director of the Frank Porter Graham Child Development Center at the University of North Carolina. He is the president of the World Council of Gifted and Talented Children, and serves on the board of a number of educational associations.

CHAPTER 36

Helping the Visually Impaired Child Succeed in School

by Patricia Anne Davis

Participating in school involves the learning of academic and social skills. The visually impaired child can have difficulty since a great deal of learning is acquired through vision. Nevertheless, many can participate successfully in regular public school. Parents of a young visually impaired child can help make success in school possible.

During Infancy
Contact your local school district.

Do this as soon as the visual impairment has been diagnosed. Find out at what age special education programs begin. If the school officials offer to send a vision teacher, accept. The vision teacher will be an invaluable resource to you throughout your child's school career.

If they offer another type of parent/infant program, try it. If you find that it is inappropriate, you can discontinue it.

Contact your local school district even if you do not intend to send your child to public school. They may have an early intervention program that no private source could provide.

Help your baby be aware of the environment.

If your baby has any vision at all, try to teach him or her to use it. Use light and brightly colored objects to attract the baby's attention. Hold them close and move them around. Some children who seem totally blind as infants, actually have usable vision and can learn to see fairly well.

Attract your baby's attention to sounds, showing the source of the sound whenever possible. Teach the child to get information through touch.

When Your Child is Preschooler
Provide special experiences.

Even though it takes a little extra time, take your child with you as much as you can. When you go to the supermarket or the hardware store, take the child along. Explain how things are arranged.

Point out the source of various smells and sounds. Let the child join you to observe and assist when you cook or work with tools. Remember that activities and objects which are casually observed by a person with normal vision must be pointed out and explained to a visually impaired child.

Encourage physical activity.

Visually impaired children are less motivated to move around than are those with normal vision. They are not attracted to objects in the environment, and may be fearful of moving in unfamiliar places. Still, they need to develop their motor skills like all young children.

Encourage your child to run and jump and to ride a tricycle. Provide protection from any obvious or serious hazards—as you would for any child—but do not be overly concerned about minor bumps. All children get their share of these; the visually impaired child is no exception. If you do not take minor bumps too seriously, your child will not either.

Encourage sensory development.

If your child has usable vision, use coloring books, blocks, large-piece jigsaw puzzles and similar items. Point out details in the environment and in pictures. Encourage the child to find hidden objects and identify the source of sounds.

Make these activities fun, so that both of you enjoy them. For example, when the telephone or doorbell rings, ask the child what is making the sound. Allow the child to answer the telephone as soon as he or she is mature enough to do so responsibly.

Teach getting along with other children.

It is difficult for visually impaired children to watch the behavior of others in order to learn what is socially acceptable. By observing your child playing with others, you can determine whether the child seems to be behaving like his or her peers. Visually impaired children need to learn social skills such as sharing and taking turns just like other children.

Nursery school can be very helpful. A visually impaired child with no other handicapping condition does not need a special nursery school. A regular program can be very suitable and may not require much modification. The child can learn to behave like non-handicapped children and have the experience of doing what other children do.

School Age
Take part in the placement decision.

Since the passage of Public Law 94-142, parents

have the right and responsibility to be actively involved in all educational decisions affecting their child. There are several options available for educating a visually impaired child. Investigate them carefully, and decide which seem best for your child. Although the decision may not be entirely yours, be certain that your opinion is heard. The following suggestions apply mainly to children in regular public school.

Have a talk with the child's teacher.

The regular classroom teacher is the most important person in your child's educational life. You will want to get in touch with each new teacher as early in the school year as possible. Offer to copy any papers that your child cannot see. If the child is a braille reader, it is helpful—and not very difficult—to learn braille.

Keep in touch with the vision teacher.

Most school districts provide the services of a teacher for the visually impaired who will maintain contact with your child all the way through school. This teacher is likely to have the following responsibilities:

a) To provide special materials and equipment, such as large-type or braille books, braille writers, tape recorders and typewriters for the child to use in school;

b) To teach the child special skills, such as typing, braille, listening and study skills;

c) To consult with other teachers about the child's educational needs;

d) To counsel parents and students about the problems of visual impairment;

e) To attend all meetings concerning the child and to serve as the child's advocate in school matters.

The vision teacher is a main source of information of value to you and your child. Although the teacher will probably call you several times a year, he or she will not know when you have a specific problem or a question. Vision teachers are there to help and guide the parents. Do not feel hesitant about calling them.

Help in matters of everyday life.

All children get teased. Children get teased about any characteristic that other children consider different and undesirable. To tease a child about being blind may be similar to teasing a child about being fat, thin, clumsy, red-headed, etc. It may benefit your child to understand that teasing is an unfortunate part of growing up in order to help him or her deal with it accordingly.

Help your child develop social skills.

Visually impaired children are at a social disadvantage. It is difficult for them to recognize persons that they may know quite well. A visually impaired child may sometimes be considered a "snob" because he or she does not reply to waves or smiles. Teach your child to respond to the greetings of other children even when he or she may not be quite sure who they are.

It will help you child's popularity—especially when starting a new school—if your home is a place where children want to come. Give a party. Have your child invite friends home after school.

If your child is invited to a party, it will be socially beneficial to wear the right clothes. A visually impaired child may not know exactly what everyone else is wearing. Check with another child or the parents of another child, so that your child will know the proper thing to wear. Wearing the right clothes eliminates one source of teasing.

Use your own judgement.

You will receive many suggestions from various sources as your child grows up. Consider each suggestion carefully because it may be something that would be helpful. If, however, after considering it, you feel that a specific suggestion is not appropriate for your child, do not hesitate to say so. You do not need to feel that professionals always know best.

On the other hand do not reject a suggestion just because the child does not want to do it. Sometimes visually impaired children in regular programs will refuse mobility instruction or special equipment because they do not want to be different. Parents and professional need to deal with this resistance together since it can lead to greater dependency in the long run. A visually impaired person can best achieve independence by understanding his or her disability, and using all compensatory skills and equipment to the greatest extent possible.

A visually impaired child is a special child. Raising a special child requires a special effort. However, there are also special rewards. You can help your disabled child grow into a happy, confident and competent adult. ∎

Patricia Anne Davis teaches visually impaired children—infants through high school—at the Baltimore County Public Schools. She has earned a master's degree from the University of Virginia in teaching the visually impaired, and a Ph.D. from the University of Pennsylvania in Russian language.

CHAPTER 37

"I'm not going to high school if you don't take me the way I am."
Mainstreaming in the High School

The Browns came because their daughter Cheryl's placement in high school was in question. Cheryl wanted to be placed in a regular classroom, but the teachers were concerned about how her behavior problems would affect the other youngsters.

"**My daughter says** she will not go to school if she is placed in a special class at the high school." Mrs. Brown, a short, slender, dark-haired women in her early forties sat back in her chair and spoke barely above a whisper.

"Cheryl is fifteen and she will be entering high school in the fall. She was born with spina bifida. It was a long, hard pregnancy compared to that of my other three children. The labor and the delivery seemed to go on forever and at the end they had to assist the baby coming out. Even though the doctors disagree, I think that's where the injury took place.

"The school problem goes back to Cheryl's very first days in kindergarten. She had a fair amount of surgery when she was three and four to try and correct the physical problems. It was a terrible period in our lives. My husband, Jack, and I were constantly discussing what needed to be done. We were very preoccupied with decisions about Cheryl's surgery. Cheryl was inconsolable as a youngster. She never stopped crying. We had little time to think about whether she was learning very much or could learn a great deal.

"When she was three and we first approached the nursery school our other kids had attended, they weren't sure they wanted to take her. She wasn't going to be there for the entire year because of her schedule for surgery. The school finally agreed to let her enter on a part-time basis.

"The public school was reluctant to discuss her entry into kindergarten when she was five and a half years old. They suggested that on the basis of what they had heard about Cheryl's behavior in the nursery school she wasn't ready to enter kindergarten.

"We had to decide whether or not to accept their judgement. We spent many evenings talking and trying to figure out what was in the best interest of our child. The school personnel pointed out that she was eligible for the special classroom because of her physical disabilities. They also thought she would have learning problems because of her difficulty in sticking to anything for any length of time.

"Cheryl always wanted to be like her older brothers and sister. She wanted to go to a regular school and a regular class. It always seemed to be just beyond her reach. When she was in elementary school, she had difficulty leaving our house and getting to school. She was sick an awful lot and it seemed that she never really had a decent, continuous year where she spent most of her life in school until she was almost in the fifth grade.

"Cheryl has always been a very sensitive or emotional child. She wanted to learn like her brothers and sister and was always watching them bring their papers home. They were all very successful in school.

"When Cheryl had difficulty doing something in school, like an arithmetic problem, she began to have temper tantrums. She would shout for the teacher's help and cry if she didn't come right away. The school had her in an unstructured classroom so that the teacher could wander from the kids doing regular work to Cheryl. The principal told us that if Cheryl could learn more and bring her work up to grade level, she could spend more time with the other kids. Those were their expectations. But when she began not only to meet grade level but go somewhat ahead of it, they seemed to change their expectations. That is almost the story of my life and why I am here.

"From the beginning I didn't know what to expect from Cheryl. I spent a lot of time talking to the various physicians about what we should expect. Were we expecting too much or too little?

"Her classroom behavior got worse when Cheryl

entered junior high school. She wanted to be with the other kids and move around from class to class. First the school people said that because of her difficulty in getting around physically the special classroom on the first floor where all the subjects were taught and where the students got individual attention would be best for her. Cheryl said it was a place for dummies. By ninth grade she was helping them with their work. The school people said that as she settled down and got along better with other kids, they would move her into appropriate classroom settings.

"Her learning has continued in an excellent fashion. Cheryl still does best when she is alone with a teacher. She almost learns as much in an hour alone as she does when she is able to spend two or three hours in a regular classroom. Nevertheless, this is what Cheryl's ambition is and mine—I think it's my husband's too although he seems to be more skeptical.

"The school people kept saying 'if she would behave' Cheryl could be placed in the regular classroom. That seemed to be so vague and so general that it was too much of a burden. Was she supposed to behave for an hour, a day, a week, a month? I kept pushing them to be more specific. They would come back and point out how frustrated she was, how she talked too loud and couldn't modulate her voice.

"So then we began to work on voice modulation. I took her to a singing teacher and the teacher worked well with Cheryl. Still, when she gets excited, she sometimes forgets that she doesn't have to shout or speak loud and that people will still understand her. If she could learn to whisper she would be better off.

"The reason we came is because a week ago we met with the school team as well as the principal to make the decision about Cheryl's high school placement. They obviously met in advance. We knew that by what they said. The principal started by saying that he disagreed with the rest of the team. He felt that Cheryl was ready to make an effort and should be able to profit from attending regular high school classes. The various members of the team had questions as to whether this was too much stress, whether we had unrealistic expectations and whether Cheryl herself had unrealistic expectations that were doomed to failure.

"The principal also made it clear that his decision would stand, but he wanted to let us know that Cheryl would still be in jeopardy. If things did not work out Cheryl would have to go to a special classroom where she would be instructed in her various subjects.

"I talked to Cheryl about this and she seems to feel that it's unfair. She feels that what they're saying is a threat and threats really don't work. I think she feels like she is being punished for something, only she doesn't understand what she's being punished for.

"When she was having difficulty in junior high school, she began to see Mrs. Kennedy, the school psychologist. Cheryl has seen her now regularly for three years. We're not sure where that's going or whether they will continue in high school. Mrs. Kennedy tells us that Cheryl is doing very well and yet I wish I could see that translate itself into behavior.

"**I'm the reason** we have come here." Mr. Brown, a short, heavy set man in his late forties spoke bruskly. "I got sick and tired of the annual negotiations between the school and my wife about Cheryl's program. Sometimes, you have to tell people what you want and let them worry about your expectations rather than the other way around.

"Cheryl told us that everybody has promised to have her in regular classes for years, and we should insist upon it. The law, as I understand it, is on our side. Every year, for the last six or seven years, we meet with a whole group of people and they tell us

---

I think she feels like she is being punished for something, only she doesn't understand what she's being punished for.

---

what the proposed plan for next year is and technically they can't do anything without my wife and I signing the plan.

"I'm not sure what's right in this situation. I know my expectations are also a problem. Our older three children had no difficulty at all. I know we were blessed. I didn't know it before Cheryl was born. They were great kids—terrific in school, in everything they did.

"When Cheryl was born, my wife took on all the responsibilities for her survival, and then her growing up. I'm not sure I could have changed what I did even if I wanted to. At the time, it never occurred to me. My wife's time with Cheryl became so extensive that, pretty soon, I began to get involved in caring for our older kids and spent little time with my wife and Cheryl.

"It seems to me that we've allowed Cheryl to dominate our lives. Cheryl has seen a psychologist for about three years now. This began when Cheryl was entering the seventh grade because even then it became evident that she could learn but she couldn't behave.

"We would see it at the dinner table. I was

I'm sick and tired of other people's expectations. When are we going to live with Cheryl's expectations and our own for her?

brought up to believe that the oldest children talked first and that sooner or later the younger ones got their chance. Mainly, this would happen when the older ones went off to school.

"Cheryl never let that happen. She always interrupted others, wouldn't let them finish sentences. The other kids began to skip meals and not bring friends home. It became chaotic. This only seemed evident on weekends because our other kids were so involved in sports and school activities and sometimes I worked so late that we weren't together that often as a family during the week. We were never able to say to her, 'Behave or you leave the table,' which we would have done with the other kids.

"Mrs. Kennedy gives us explanations of Cheryl's behavior. More and more they seem like excuses to me. If Cheryl and she understand so much, why doesn't Cheryl stop? I get vague generalities from my daughter's psychologist—discussions between Cheryl and Mrs. Kennedy are confidential. My expectations are if you hire a professional, they should get something done. And if they don't get something done, get another one or another opinion.

"This is why I wanted to talk to you. Somehow, whatever we're doing as a family or as parents isn't working. We've got to approach the high school program with the same questions. I want to know what would they allow *us* to do for Cheryl rather than asking what are *they* going to do for Cheryl.

"**A**t elementary school, they said I could do things if I was toilet trained. After I was trained they said I was learning so much in a special situation why move me?" Cheryl Brown sat forward in her chair and spoke excitedly.

"When I was in grade school they thought I was a dummy so that when I started junior high school they said that between my having to get around and my problems in learning maybe I should be in this special classroom. Even then I knew I could learn. It's just that I used to get so upset whenever anybody called on me.

"They got me to see Mrs. Kennedy and we've been together for almost three years now. She keeps promising me, too, that the more I understand about my problems in growing up and how I behave, the more acceptable I will be. But I figure if I don't call a halt, pretty soon I will graduate from high school and I'll never have a chance to be friends with regular kids.

"They tell me when I 'misbehave,' but I don't seem to know how to stop it. When I'm with other kids I talk loud. They say I want to be the center of attention. But how are you ever going to learn how to behave when they say you can't be with them because they say you don't know how to behave?

"I don't know how to end this vicious cycle without saying I'm not going to go to high school if you don't take me the way I am and the way I want to be."

"**I** was sticking my neck out by trying to be honest with the Browns." Mr. Richards, a tall slender man in his mid-thirties spoke softly. "It's a situation in which I could have hidden behind the legalism and not given the Browns any sense of how the decision was made and protect everybody. But that's a legal business. I really felt that if we all knew in advance what kind of concerns we all had and what the reservations were, then things might work better. What happened was that what I said made things worse—not only for Cheryl and her parents, but for my teachers. They looked at Cheryl's school record and there were some very interesting issues there.

"First of all, she is an exceptionally bright girl, so that she is eligible for the advanced classes. But the advanced classes are much more task-oriented; these are serious kids who really want to do their work. The advanced placement teachers are worried that Cheryl will behave like she did in junior high school. She would have a temper tantrum or talk too loud when she had the chance to be with other kids. This would be unfair to everybody. If she were an average student it would be less of a concern. We have plenty of kids who are disruptive in other classes; they seem to be the average kids in the average classes, nothing special.

"She also is going to have trouble with our physical set up. In high school, the classes are all over the building and you don't have the same kids in all your classes. In junior high school at least the same kids move together from class to class so somebody could help Cheryl get from one room to another if it were necessary. I know that that is not insurmountable. There is no reason that I can't, with a little imagination, change a few classrooms. We could find some way of helping her when it was time for her to go to her classes. That's not a big deal.

"Because I am a new principal, the teachers are trying to figure out how much authority I am going to exercise on this. After all the criticism, I wonder where am I going to get any support in any of this?

"I think Cheryl can make it. I've seen kids like

her make it and yet I would not be too upset if she tried it and it didn't work. All I'm trying to do is to get the best possible situation so she would have the best possible chance to succeed.

The Browns came because their fifteen year old daughter, Cheryl, who has spina bifida, threatened not to go to school if she was placed in a special classroom when she entered high school in the fall. For all of her school career, Cheryl spent most of the day in a special classroom, away from the regular students' room because of her disruptive behavior.

Over the course of Cheryl's school life, Mrs. Brown had made major efforts to help her daughter and the school manage to work with each other. Each year, Mrs. Brown would attempt to identify the school's expectations and then worked with Cheryl throughout the year so that she could meet them. This had helped Cheryl achieve academically, but never socially.

Mrs. Brown found herself having to negotiate with a whole new social system—that of the high school. Cheryl was finally comfortable in the junior high school. Now, she was going to have to manage the vastly different intellectual, social, and physical challenges of the high school. Mrs. Brown was upset by Cheryl's threat because she felt she had let her down after promising her for so many years that Cheryl would be with the other students in school.

Mr. Brown thought that his wife had not made adequate demands on either the school or Cheryl. He believed that his wife was so dependent on the expectations of others that she could not make very realistic demands of her own. He had not played a significant role in his daughter's life. At the same time, Mr. Brown felt that his wife had spent so much time and energy with Cheryl and her problems in growing up, that he had to take responsibility for their other youngsters.

The principal of the high school was ready to accept Cheryl and give her a fresh start. Mr. Richards was not ready to accept the judgement made by the junior high school. He felt he had to make clear to the Browns that his own teachers were very skeptical. He hoped doing this would help the Browns prepare Cheryl. However, he found himself upsetting, not only the family, but his teachers as well. The Browns wanted a commitment to Cheryl for the whole year—the teachers felt Mr. Richards had overturned their considered recommendation.

As children get older, the tasks they have to master and the ways they have to negotiate them keep changing. Children's patterns of dependency change as the parents try to help establish them as independent, self-sufficient young adults. Social, psychological and biological challenges change over the course of a child's growing up. The school's pattern of organization also changes to meet the changing issues of the child.

The Browns had ignored the social and sexual part of Cheryl as they focused on the problems of physical and intellectual development.

Elementary school tends to be highly organized—the children spend most of the day with one teacher. Even when there are multiple teachers, there is a central teacher to whom the child has to relate. This helps the child make the transition from the parental influence at home to accepting an adult substitute at school.

In entering junior high school, the child is beginning the emancipation from the family and looking to adults for support as well as to peers. In junior high school, the youngsters generally are in classes with the same children all day but with changing teachers and changing classrooms.

High school begins the process of preparing the youngster for the ultimate separation from school and family. Everyone is moving—the students and the teachers. They are dealing with the end of childhood friendships and developing new adolescent ties. Some of this stems from the emerging new sexual identity. Some comes from meeting students from the broader community and changing interests. Giving up old loyalties and establishing new ones is always a painful process.

Anticipation is a problem for the youngster with a disability and their families. Both parents and professionals lack the experience and knowledge that helps to predict how a specific disability will affect a youngster's school and vocational adjustment and how to help them.

The lack of certainty and of guidelines made Mrs. Brown dependent on school experts as she tried to identify ways of helping her daughter. She helped Cheryl during these early years as she managed many of the issues of growing up. However, Cheryl had difficulty in sharing attention with other youngsters. This was as true at the dinner table at home as it was in the classroom.

The school system's expectations were such that if the child did not meet them, she was excluded. The social progress that Cheryl and her parents had wanted for her was placed in this double jeopardy. Since she could not meet the challenges of staying in an ordinary classroom, she was excluded from it. The result of this was minimal experience in meeting the challenges of an ordinary classroom.

When a child enters high school, he or she is faced ordinarily with the social and psychological issues of adolescence. The youngster whose problems makes them concerned about their own bodily integrity from the time they are born have difficulty when these issues are particularly aroused and emphasized during adolescence.

Cheryl was able to discuss some of these issues with her own psychotherapist. She needed to make some demands for independence. However, she made the demands in her typical way—which was to call a halt by threatening not to participate at all. What Cheryl was asking for was a right to represent herself. But she was doing it in a way that made her parents more skeptical about her.

The Browns had ignored the social and sexual part of Cheryl as they focused on the problems of physical and intellectual development. The Browns understood their need to reassess Cheryl as an adolescent rather than a disabled child. When I met with Cheryl and her parents, everyone agreed that Cheryl should be given the opportunity to speak for herself about her school plans, and that she needed to take more responsibility for her behavior. We agreed to meet regularly during the next school year.

The principal was willing to have Cheryl attend the meeting that was set to plan her schedule. It was also the first time the teachers had the opportunity to hear Cheryl present her own concerns and her own expectations of herself.

Cheryl's social year was uneven. It had ups and downs. Cheryl made an effort to join several social groups within the school. She was accepted in the theater club, and was helpful in assisting people learn their roles and helping doing the coordination of the scripts.

She learned a great deal, including some of the pleasures of friendships. At the same time, she found herself believing that she was rejected from the cast parties. Cheryl had one episode in math class when she was frustrated late in the spring, but everyone was able to use this to share with her how much growth and progress she had made. ■

—M.J.S.

This case has been selected from private practice and consultation files. The names and situations have been changed to preserve confidentiality.

CHAPTER 38

Have we pushed too hard?
An Adolescent in High School

Everything seems to have gone wrong since the very first days of high school.

"I'm glad you could see us on such short notice." Mrs. Travis, a short somewhat strong grey haired woman in her early fifties spoke softly. "It's about Doreen. She is fifteen now. The last time you saw her I think she was eight.

"Let me begin with last week. Doreen's guidance counselor called me and said that Doreen has warning slips in three subjects. That means that there is a chance that she will fail her English, math and French for this marking period. Miss Jones had talked to Doreen's teachers. Doreen doesn't say much in class, does not finish her exams, and she has been late with all of her homework. That's part of the problem that Doreen and I seem to have at this time.

"Let me see if I can fill you in on the years since you saw Doreen. Doreen did a lot better in school than any of us imagined she could. You saw her when she was in the first grade and having difficulty in learning just to read and write. At that time, we knew Doreen had some kind of a brain problem but it wasn't clear how much.

"You helped us understand Doreen's style of learning. Doreen had to be absolutely sure before she would try anything new. That was whether she was learning to ride a bike or to play on the swings or to do anything. She really had to size up things very carefully before she was sure enough to take any risks.

"Talking to the teachers helped them understand her style and work with her. You saw her again when she was in the second grade. After that, things went so well we never saw the need to call you again. From time to time, I meant to call you to tell you how much better Doreen was doing than anybody would have guessed.

"Doreen worked very hard and the whole family helped her. Sometimes it was her older sisters, but most of the time it was me. We made sure that we went over her homework with her. Somebody always was reading to her. One of her sisters, either Jean or Paula, tried to teach her how to play the games that kids her age were playing. Slowly but surely, Doreen progressed.

"By the time she was in the fifth grade she really was a popular youngster. In fact, in many ways, he was the leader in games. Everybody always respected her fairness.

"She was in a small private school. Because she had done so well in the sixth grade, the school placed her with the best students when she started her junior high program. And again she did very well. She had a little trouble in the seventh grade because she didn't know all the kids and the teachers didn't know her. We were able to explain her style of needing to be sure about herself. We said we were confident that when she got accustomed to them and they got to know her, everything would work out.

"Again, I did some work with her almost every night on her homework. One of her sisters would pitch in subjects areas like algebra where I wasn't helpful at all.

"Even though this is a competitive program, her grades again improved. By the ninth grade, whe was in the top twenty percent of her class.

"We thought a lot about the best high school program. We debated that one but Doreen wanted to go to the public high school where her sisters had gone. She had spent a lot of time going with them to the football games and some of the social events.

"Although my husband and I were apprehensive, I thought she would do well. The high school people did too because they put her into an advanced program. Everything seems to have gone wrong since the very first day of high school.

"Since elementary school, I used to drive Doreen every day. Now, Doreen wanted to go by school bus like everyone else. I guess I was disappointed because the high school is about two blocks from where I work part-time as a secretary so I thought it would be much simpler for everybody if I just took her myself. We got into an argument that was really unnecesary. My husband suggested to me afterwards that I hadn't realized how disappointed I was that she wanted to go off by herself.

"Doreen is the last child at home. Our other two daughters are away at college and doing very well. There is no question that we all miss them. I guess I understood how much my husband and I would miss them but I hadn't appreciated how much Doreen misses them too. She was on the phone to one or another of them almost every other night. I felt like asking them to tell Doreen to talk to us. I thought Doreen was having trouble in her classes. I could tell because she didn't want to talk over anything with me. She used to be glad to come home and tell me what went on in school. We would talk about her various assignments and, as I said, I always helped her whenever I could. We would sit together while she studied. The day she started high school, she didn't seem to want me to know what was going on at school. She told me it was time for her to do her homework herself. Now that she's doing so poorly, I think it's my fault. I should have been able to do something about it.

I think she's actually been getting good marks because they like her.

"**I am sorry that** Doreen is in so much trouble in school." Mr. Travis, a tall, somewhat heavy-set man in his mid-fifties, spoke quietly.

"I am also troubled that my wife is so upset. I have been worried for a long time that everybody in the family has been so involved in helping Doreen that they hve not been able to figure out what she could really do and what she really couldn't do. I was against her going to the public high school from the beginning. She had been doing reasonably well in a small, very helpful place.

"It takes a long time to understand what Doreen says. Sometimes, I think she's actually been getting good marks because they like her.

"My wife has spent more time with Doreen than she has spent with anyone else in the family. During the school year, she used to be so preoccupied with making sure the homework got done that she had little time for either her other daughters or myself. I know it may sound like sour grapes but we all pitched in and helped as much as we could.

"Doreen's idea has been to be just like her sisters. But she can't be. She has a problem in walking and talking which means that she can never compete the way they do. And I'm not sure it's been fair the way everyone has encouraged her.

"If I say let's be realistic about what Doreen can do, everybody gets mad at me. Yet, she has done so much more than I ever believed possible. I'm not sure what realistic means anymore.

"My feeling is that we ought to get her back into the school that she came from. Then I'm sure, sooner or later, she'll catch up. What we still would be faced with is what to do after high school. There, it seems to me we have to find some way of figuring out what she really is capable of doing. I've been trying to say this more directly for years but it seems to me that I've been just ignored.

"**I know I have** everyone upset." Doreen Travis sat slouched in her chair. At first, it was hard to understand her speech but as she became more comfortable her articulation improved. By the end of the interview, it was relatively easy to understand her.

"I know my mother and father came to see you last week and my sister Judy called me from college. I'm glad that you could talk to me before you talked to anyone at my school. It's been harder to get started in high school than I expected it to be.

"On the other hand, as far as the academic work goes, even though most of my teachers are worried, I know I can do the work. And I really do understand the material. I guess I had not appreciated how big the school was and how hard it really would be to go from one class to another.

"Sometimes, changing classes has gotten me in trouble for exams. I have trouble working quickly anyhow. Once, I came to my math class five minutes after the exam started. Not only didn't I get the usual number of problems correct, I didn't have time to finish the last question or check my work like I should.

"I knew that it was going to be hard adjusting to the kids. I only knew a couple from church and I really still am an outsider. I know that it's not easy to get to know me or to like me because of the way I look and the way I talk. But I had hoped that I'd get to know some of the kids in my class. I've been more afraid to talk in class than I thought I would be.

"I keep forgetting that in my old school, I'd been there for so long that everybody knew me. I always figured that sooner or later they would understand me or try to understand me. But now when I look around in the room and the teacher calls on me, by the time I get up enough courage to speak, they often assume I don't know anything and go on.

"I also haven't been able to talk to the teachers even though they have invited me. I would like to tell them about the amount of time it takes me to take tests, that I'm always slow. I think if they let me finish I could show them what I could do. You know, on some of the exams that I have taken, I have only completed half of the test before time was up. But, the work I've done is right.

"Mom is also upset with me. We used to talk a lot but right now I don't want to. She used to spend a lot of time with me after school helping me do my work. But now I would like to do it by myself. I think I can do it by myself but I'll never find out if she is always there helping me.

"The other thing is that she's always wanting to know about how I'm getting along with the other kids. Well, I'm not getting along well and I don't think it helps her if I say that because she gets very upset. I can't talk to my father because I don't think he thinks I can do anything. Since I started school, it was my sisters and my mother who encouraged me and helped me when I needed to be helped.

I know that it's not easy to get to know me or to like me because of the way I look and the way I talk.

Now, I'm the only one at home and my father still doesn't ask me about how things are going at school. Usually he waits until I leave the room to whisper to my mother.

"I want to stick it out. I don't know how to make better arrangements with everybody but I think I could figure it out. I don't have much time with the guidance counselor at the high school because it's so big and I figure maybe that's the kind of thing you can help me with.

"I guess you could say I'm really worried. I see my sisters at college doing all kinds of things. I wonder what will happen to me.

"For example, I have trouble getting to my next class in high school. Where my sister goes to college, classes are all over the place, in different buildings.

"I wonder about boys too. I wish I could talk about this with my mother, or my sisters, but I'm afraid to bring it up. I sure think about it a lot."

The energy that it required to get to school, to get to classes, as well as get to know other people, was more than Doreen had anticipated.

Doreen, a fifteen year old girl with cerebral palsy, was having difficulty in her school work in high school. She had spent her educational life in a small private school where she had done well academically. Although her parents, as well as the private school, encouraged her to continue there, she wanted to go to a local public high school where her sisters had attended. In the discussions about class placement, she was placed in advance courses. Her previous academic work seemed to justify this; however, the guidance counselor at the high school was unsure whether she would be able to compete. After a month, several teachers had sent home warning slips, indicating that she might fail their classes.

Mrs. Travis was upset because her daughter did not want to discuss this matter with her. She merely indicated that she would take care of it herself. Mrs. Travis felt that she had supported her daughter's desire despite her own concerns and her husband's objections. She was very troubled by this most dramatic change in her relationship with her daughter. In previous years, she had spent a great deal of time with Doreen reviewing homework as well as other school assignments.

From the time she entered high school, Doreen was reluctant to discuss anything with her mother, whether it was school or her relationships with the other youngsters. This made her mother even more upset when the unexpected warning notices arrived.

Mr. Travis was as concerned about his wife's reaction as he was about his daughter's school performance. He believed it was time that they really find out what Doreen could do on her own. He felt that any realistic plan about her life should be based on understanding her ability to achieve. He felt that she had been too much by his wife and by her sisters. But, he really couldn't tell what Doreen was capable of accomplishing. He also thought that his wife had spent so much time with their daughter, that she had neglected his other daughters as well as himself. He believed that it was time for her to allow Doreen to do more things on her own.

Doreen was still relatively certain that she was

capable of mastering the academic work. She was surprised at how hard the work of participating in the high school had been. The energy that it required to get to school, to get to classes, as well as get to know other people, was more than Doreen had anticipated. She felt her problem was related to her inability to talk to her teachers about her special style of working and learning. She had never had difficulty of this kind before and was surprised that she was uncomfortable about asking for any help or advise. She was also troubled by her inability to get other students to get to know her. She recognized her father's doubts about her and wished there was some way that he could respect what she had intended to do.

All adolescents face the challenge in making the transition to high school. Life in high school is often a clear indication of what the future for the child will be. Academic programs and achievement will indicate the kinds of vocational careers they are likely to undertake. Adolescents are also moving usually from a smaller school to one in which they are meeting large numbers of new youngsters for the first time. Not only does it give them the opportunity for expanding their lives, but increases their possibilities of rejection. It is also a time when they are turning more to their friends as they are beginning to emancipate themselves from their parents. It is a common time for parents to feel their children are less willing to communicate to them about their personal experiences.

Meeting these challenges was complicated for Doreen by the dilemmas that stemmed from her disability. It was harder for people to accept her and understand her on first meetings. Her style of working was based on the ability to master things, but not master them quickly. To the extent that school tests require accomplishing things within a certain space of time, she was likely to be penalized. To appreciate her achievements, making arrangements so that she could demonstrate what she could do at her own pace, was going to be very helpful.

Since she had attended a small, private school, Doreen had not been in the mainstream of her own community. This meant that she did not have any experience with most of the youngsters who made up her public school environment. She had also had little experience in approaching teachers who were occupied with a larger number of students than she had experienced in her private school.

Doreen's concern about upsetting her mother and her wish for greater approval from her father, led all three to agree monthly meetings with me to discuss their mutual concerns. Not only could this make it easier for them to live together, but would make it easier for them to support Doreen's efforts to master the social and academic challenges of the high school.

At the same time, Mrs. Travis was encouraged by her husband and her daughter to go to a career counselor. They felt that Mrs. Travis had been a very able and active woman who needed some way to harness her energy and intelligence. She agreed to explore a program that helped women to make a transition from taking care of their families to careers.

Mr. Travis was encouraged to take a more active interest in his daughter's school work. She wanted his interest in her various courses, especially her history class. Mr. Travis indicated that he had felt excluded and was not sure how well he would be able to discuss the academic work with his daughter, but was willing to try.

I met with Doreen and her high school guidance teacher in order to help her begin to make the kinds of connections at school that were going to be necessary. Although her guidance counselor was initially skeptical about Doreen's ability to achieve, she had a clear understanding of what work she and Doreen were going to have to do to facilitate her academic and social achievements. ■

—M.J.S.

This case has been selected from private practice and consultation files. The names and situations have been changed to preserve confidentiality.

CHAPTER 39

Vocational Training and Employment Guidelines for Parents

by M. Sherril Moon and Andrew V. Beale

As the first generation of students with handicaps served by Public Law 94-142 leave school, these citizens, as well as their families and professionals who have worked with them, and are increasingly dismayed with the lack of opportunities and appropriate vocational services. Families who have grown accustomed to services under a legally mandated and federally coordinated service system learn that adult services such as vocational rehabilitation do not operate under entitlement. This is particularly true in terms of the provision of remunerative work, the expected outcome of school preparation. Parents, teachers, and school officials are often shocked to find that students with adequate job skills and appropriate social skills graduate and then sit at home for years. On the other hand, rehabilitation service agencies may not know the vocational potential of certain graduates when formal transition planning has not been initiated by the school system. "The bottom line is that 50% to 75% of all persons with disabilities are unemployed" (U.S. Commission on Civil Rights, 1983), and the more severe the handicap, the less the likelihood that the person affected will ever be employed.

In fact, students who are severely developmentally disabled or those who may have been labeled as moderately, severely, or profoundly retarded, autistic, multiply handicapped, or severely physically handicapped, have typically not been placed on the caseloads of vocational rehabilitation agencies which traditionally have provided vocational services for less disabled individuals (Office of Special Education and Rehabilitative Services, 1984). The result is that most severely handicapped citizens usually end up in day activity programs which often does not provide paid employment opportunities, or they remain at home without any programming. This is both unfortunate and unnecessary since research has repeatedly shown that persons with severe handicaps can work when an appropriate on-going, or supported employment training program is provided.

In the late 1970's and 1980's a number of model vocational training and job placement and training programs demonstrated the ability of the adolescent and adult with severe handicaps to work in nonsheltered jobs. Wehman and his colleagues at Virginia Commonwealth University and Rusch and his colleagues in Illinois, have shown the ability of citizens with moderate and severe handicaps to hold competitive jobs. Bellamy and his associates in Oregon have shown that even profoundly retarded persons can work in a specialized industrial setting which pays a decent wage and allows the worker to have regular contact with nonhandicapped persons. Other work alternatives such as mobile work crews and work stations in industry have also been used to successfully employ citizens with severe handicaps. As a parent of a child with severe developmental disabilities, you no longer need to settle for placement of your child into an adult day program or a sheltered workshop that pays no wage or a very small sum of money paid only on a piece-rate basis.

Guidelines for Elementary School Level

Vocational training for elementary-age pupils who are developementally disabled focuses on assisting them to develop: (1) self-care and daily living skills; (2) positive human relationships and good social skills at home and at school; (3) awareness of vocational opportunities at the upper grade levels and beyond.

For Your Child

1. *Familiarize yourself with your state's regulations dealing with the education of handicapped children.* Write to your representative in Congress and in your state legislature encouraging their commitment to legislation that will enhance the vocational training and employment opportunities for all students. Find out about the policies of your local and state rehabilitation and developmental disabilities agencies regarding employment for the developmentally disabled. On a national level, employment has just recently become a priority for these agencies and there are now several government initiatives.

2. *Work with your local schools to insure that vocational training and, in some cases, job placement is an integral part of your child's schooling.* "Be sure your

child's current individual Educational Program (IEP) specifically addresses employment training." Make sure that the IEP addresses any self-care skills such as eating, toileting, dressing, and grooming that your child does not have. These should be taught in the early school years so that middle and high school programs can lend more time to specific job training. Talk with school officials about employment training opportunities available in the upper grades and make sure that your child's teacher is preparing for the transition into these programs. See that students in special education programs are included in vocational education classes and special vocational-technical education training centers that many school systems now have.

3. *Assign specific jobs/duties to your child around the home.* Pay your child a small allowance based upon the successful completion of assigned tasks and insist that s/he perform his/her duties completely and on time. Encourage your child to manage his/her money and discuss how planning is essential to good money management. Encourage your child to make independent decisions and accept their consequences. Do not compare your child's efforts with the accomplishments of brothers, sisters, or friends, but rather have him or her continually improve upon his/her own performance.

4. *Find out about successful school and adult training programs and the variety of employment options that are now opening up for even profoundly handicapped citizens around the country.* Do not settle for the notion that your child cannot work!

With Your Child
1. *Create opportunities for your child to learn about workers and what they do.* Point out workers to your child when you go out in the community. Discuss what the worker is doing and encourage your child to think about what jobs s/he might like or not like. Share books, magazines, and pictures which introduce workers to your child. Be realistic about the types of jobs a retarded adult is likely to be successful in performing. Some jobs which have proved to be particularly good for disabled workers, including those who are severely handicapped, include: maid, orderly, janitor, auto mechanic helper, food service worker, porter, hand packer, laundry worker, farm laborer, and assembly line worker. Talk about the jobs performed by family members and friends. Discuss the reward of working other than money, e.g. personal satisfaction, friendships, and independence.

2. *Emphasize personal appearance, physical fitness, and good social and communication skills.* Provide opportunities for daily physical exercise or activities so that your child will develop coordination, stamina, strength, and dexterity. Give your child the opportunity to practice independent eating, dressing, toileting, and grooming skills, and try to avoid doing these things for the child. Encourage your child to develop acceptable social skills by having him/her interact with a wide range of friends, relatives, peers who are not handicapped, and members of the community. It is essential that your son or daughter exhibit socially desirable behaviors and be able to relate with other people if s/he is to hold a job.

Middle School Level
When a student who is severely developmentally disabled reaches the age of twelve or thirteen, a large portion of his or her school day should be devoted to specific vocational training on a variety of jobs in community-based settings. At this point, parents need to make sure that schools are providing community-based vocational training for at least several hours each day.

For Your Child
1. *Actively support the teacher's efforts to provide job training in community-based sites.* Help the school identify training sites that are directly related to potential real jobs in the community. Such sites can be hotels, cafeterias, hospitals, and businesses in which family members or friends may work. At the very least, lobby for training in various school sites such as the grounds (grounds maintenance), cafeteria (food service worker), office (messenger), and overall building (janitor). Remember that training in a traditional classroom is the least desirable for students who are severely handicapped.

2. *See that your child's IEP addresses specific vocational training in a variety of potential jobs.* Do not settle for the notion of "prevocational" or "readiness" training that is supposedly related to specific job training. "The only way your child will learn a real job is to practice these job skills in a real job setting."

3. *Make sure that you know what job training is available for your child in the high school program.* High school programs should include at least a half-day of job training and inclusion of some actual job placement and paid employment for students nearing graduation. There should be a formal liaison between high school teachers and your local rehabilitative services agency. Find out whether this is occurring, and if not, insist that planning for transition from school to work begin to take place.

4. *Get in touch with your local rehabilitation agency to find out about the training services and job possibilities available for your child.* If the situation looks bleak in your community, insist that changes be made. Agencies have been mandated by federal governing bodies to increase services to citizens with severe handicaps.

5. *Find work outside the home for your child to do*

during the summer, weekends, and after school. At this point, volunteer work is okay, for the essential factor is to get your child used to working. Having to follow a schedule, get to places punctually, and interact with people other than family members can never be practiced too much!

With Your Child

1. *Continue to work with your child on improving his/her appearance and physical fitness.* Disabled citizens are often turned down or let go from jobs because of their sloppy or dirty appearance or because of their supposed lack of initiative or laziness. Require your child to dress and maintain grooming habits like everyone else. Make sure that exercise is a regular part of each day to build strength and help control weight.

2. *Require your child to complete household chores on a regular basis and provide an allowance only on the basis of correctly completing allotted chores.* The value and importance of work can be reinforced at home by showing your child that everyone has certain important jobs to do, and that payment is based on doing the jobs correctly and on time. As a child gets older, you can assign more tasks and require that they be done in increasingly shorter periods of time. Complying with instructions, working at a fast pace, and increasing work complexity are all important aspects of holding a job.

3. *Get your child into the community for leisure activities.* Go to restaurants, movies, and community events. Take him or her to the grocery store to help with shopping and let your child help choose his or her own clothes. "It is important that a person be able to behave properly in all settings, and exposure is the best way to learn." Exposure is also necessary in terms of the general public accepting the handicapped citizen as an equal.

High School Level

By the time a child reaches high school or is between ages fifteen and sixteen, a major part of his or her school day should be devoted to vocational training. By graduation time, a specific job or an adult training program should have been identified for him/her by a team of professionals and family members. As a parent, you may have to see that educators and adults service providers are formally planning the transition of your child from school to work.

For Your Child

1. *See that vocational training in specific jobs is built into your child's IEP.* Teachers should have in mind specific potential jobs based on both sheltered and competitive jobs available in the community for your child. Insist that training for these jobs be conducted in community job settings as part of your child's IEP goals and objectives.

2. *See that a transition team composed of yourself, the teacher, and a rehabilitation agency representative is formed to make plans for your child's employment after graduating.* Advance planning in the form of written goals and objectives similar to an IEP is the best way to assure services for your child after graduation. Remember that adult services are not mandated by law as are school special education programs.

3. *Encourage school personnel to find, place, and train your child in a job, full or part-time, that pays a wage while he/she is still in school.* Because of the lack of mandated employment services for the severely handicapped and overload of clients on rehabilitation case managers, you should support job placement during the school years. It is easier for adult service providers to provide support services for someone already working than to have to start at the beginning.

4. *Find out about all adult programs in your community and make plans before graduation to have your child enter one where some sort of employment is offered if earlier employment cannot be secured.* Of course, the most desirable option for your child is employment in a regular job that pays at or above minimum wage and decent benefits. If this is not attainable while your child is in school, see that he or she gets into a sheltered facility or adult program where the potential for employment exists. Such programs that offer a variety of employment options are the best. Many facilities are starting competitive work programs, work crews (groups of workers who are always supervised) or special industrial programs that pay some kind of wage an enable workers to spend time with nonhandicapped people.

With Your Child

Continue to do all the things that you began while your child was in middle school. Promote exercise, good grooming, wise handling of money, and the completion of household chores. Allow your child to be as independent as possible and give him or her ample opportunities to get out into the community. ■

M. Sherril Moon, Ed.D., and Andrew V. Beale, Ed.D., are colleagues at Virginia Commonwealth University in Richmond. Dr. Moon is Director of Training at the Rehabilitation Research and Training Center; Dr. Beale is Professor at the School of Education.

CHAPTER 40

Understanding the Whole Child

The Key to Coordinating Services

by Irene M. Lester

He has been force-fed, starved, and tokened in a series of recommended behavior-modification programs, none of which cured anything.

A child with a disability will often require the services of many different health and education specialists as they grow up. Coordinating and interpreting this mass of sometimes conflicting information is the central task for developing a comprehensive program for the youngster. Irene Lester describes this dilemma and its consequences. She illustrates the value of a coordinated approach in giving care to her "whole" child.

Like all parents, my husband and I consider each of our three children exceptional.

Our oldest son, Lamar, has completed his freshman year at the University of Georgia where he maintained a B average, survived the rigors of joining a fraternity, worked during after school hours for the university and, in general, made a good adjustment to his first year away from home. Identified as gifted, he has been a member of the Beta Club and National Honor Society, and a sports enthusiast, he has filled our home with ribbons, medals, trophies, and friends since the day he arrived.

Our daughter, Laura, also bears the "gifted" label. A high school senior, she is active in sports, dancing, piano-playing, and is an officer of her sorority and her class. She fills non-school hours with social events, work at Wendy's, and shopping trips to the mall. Laura is a social butterfly with comb in one hand, telephone in the other, and her checkbook handy at all times.

Billy

The most exceptional of our children is our third child, Billy—a thirteen year old boy. He is not as easy to describe as the other two, for he does not fit easily into any category, other than "exceptional." His life has been a circuitous path through a frustrating maze of tears and illness, low-grade fevers, delayed motor development, super-short stature, and infected tonsils and adenoids with accompanying surgery. He has also suffered from hernias, allergies, copious vomiting, difficulty chewing and swallowing meat, hyperactivity, learning disabilities, severe and extended temper tantrums, physical and social immaturity, and facial features growing more Down syndrome-like daily.

The path has led us through the offices of pediatricians, gastro-enterologists, endocrinologists, geneticists, orthodontists, neurologists, clinics for the mentally retarded, a developmental analysis center, radiologists, a hospital in our home state, and finally, a teaching hospital in a neighboring state.

Over the years, Billy has taken a variety of medications in an effort to stabilize his behavior and lessen hyperactivity. He has been force-fed, starved, and tokened in a series of recommended behavior-modification programs, none of which cured anything. However, they gave us the feeling that we were doing "something" and got us through another day of suffering, searching for answers, and wondering what the real, underlying problems were.

Diagnoses ranging from Minimal Brain Dysfunction to parental mismanagement to Noonan's syndrome simply did not stack up when compared with the symptoms. We were beginning to feel that our child was, in the words of my husband, "beyond medicine."

A Program and Diagnoses

One positive program for our son during this time was the public school learning disabilities resource room. Billy was tested before starting kindergarten and was found to have the necessary discrepancies in ability to qualify for the program. He was immediately placed in the program in first grade and has remained there ever since, receiving well-planned instruction and loving attention from the specialists in each school he attends. While this did not address the various causes of his condition, it certainly helped in ameliorating the symptoms

> *All too often, parents are left to coordinate their child's programs by themselves.*

and continues to be the happiest time of his day.

Last year, around the time of his twelfth birthday, our son was hospitalized for a week. Working in teams, the doctors began to uncover the underlying conditions that were causing such grief. The first discovery was spike and slow-wave discharges in the temporal lobe of his brain, a condition similar to epilepsy, with psychomotor seizures a possible explanation for his lengthy and severe tantrums, hyperactivity, and difficulty in concentration.

The gastro-enterology clinic found that he had an "incompetent" sphincter between his esophagus and stomach, explaining the copious vomiting that has plagued him since birth, as well as eating problems and stomach cramps. The lower five centimeters of his esophagus were damaged by the stomach acids backing up into this organ, injuring the lining and causing pain and indigestion.

Medication was prescribed for both conditions and we returned for further testing in January, at which time medications were altered and a third constellation of abnormalities was detected. An afternoon in the cranio-facial clinic revealed several problems involving an open-bite, a spastic and protuberant tongue, problems with his palate, a hyperactive gag reflex and thickened vocal chords. This clinical team's recommendations included an orthosurgery evaluation, cineflouroscopy to study his swallowing mechanisms, a cartilage graft; and orthodontics, a wonderfully normal sounding word!

We are anticipating a return trip to the hospital early this summer for further evaluation of his anticonvulsant and exophagitis medications, as well as an in-depth cranio-facial evaluation. While this does not necessarily sound like an ideal vacation trip, it does represent a real breakthrough. We have some facts we can deal with, as well as treatable conditions. We see a light, however dim, at the end of the tunnel and have hope for our son's eventual "normalcy," knowing full well that we have a long way to go.

Considering the Whole Child

Billy's story dramatically illustrates that the treatment of an exceptional child can be like the blind men describing an elephant. Each professional—and in our case they were all medical doctors—looked at his or her area of specialty and diagnosed accordingly. Tunnel vision appeared to be the order of the day. Until we got to the teaching hospital in Florida, no one seemed to consider the whole child, except those who were certain that he was the unwitting victim of emotional problems, incompetent parents or some obscure syndrome.

We believe that the most urgent need of the exceptional child is a coordinated approach to the diagnosis and treatment of his or her condition. We are grateful that there are groups that attend to this need. It would have been so helpful to us to have had a central agency to whom we could have appealed for assistance.

Most of us are not well-prepared for parenthood. None of us, I would venture to guess, is prepared to parent an "abnormal" child. When you realize, with certainty, that your child is not normal, you enter a condition of shock and a period of grieving in which you travel through the stages of denial, anger, depression, and finally, hopefully, acceptance. It is a lonely experience and you need help coping with your feelings, your child, and your family.

Frequently, the medical profession is the first and only source of aid to the exceptional child and his or her parents during the pre-school years. Most doctors are geared to treat and to cure. They busily rush through their days dispensing antibiotics and aspirin, handling crises and critically ill children, operating and making patients well. Chronic conditions, like Billy's, do not respond to this approach, and so for us the system was ineffectual.

All too often, parents are left to coordinate their child's program by themselves. Because they are not trained nor aware of available facilities, they may not do well. Besides, most of us have our hands full with day-to-day survival as we live with our exceptional child.

I have a dear friend with whom I have talked frequently over the years. She is a widow, in delicate health, raising a teenage son on a meager education and limited income. I will always remember her words of wisdom: "The Lord has promised that He will never send more than you and He can handle together, but, sometimes, He comes mighty close!" And, I might add, all help is gratefully accepted. ■

Irene M. Lester lives in Savannah, Georgia with her husband, Lamar, and their three children, Lamar, Jr., Laura, and William. She has a degree in elementary education, and is now working part-time as a substitute teacher and tutor for children with learning disabilities.

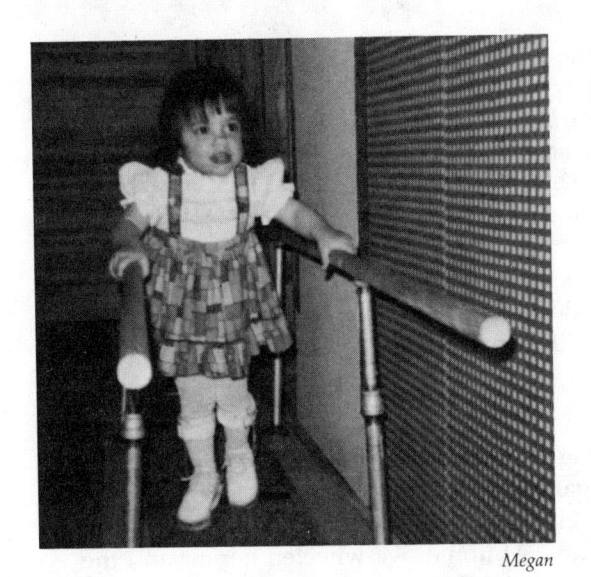

Learning From Megan
Adapting to Orthopedic Surgery

by Rita Spillane

Megan

> *I remembered from my days in nurse's training to look for the "wellness" in a person rather than to dwell on the "illness."*

It is no secret that parents of physically challenged children often have an extra burden to bear. Children with physical disabilities may require repeated surgeries. This frequently means that parents must participate in the extensive physical therapy for their children. It can be both an emotional and physical strain for parents to watch their children struggling, working hard, getting frustrated, or experiencing physical discomfort.

Rita Spillane describes her daughter Megan's progress following corrective orthopedic surgery, and the strength she gained from watching Megan's fortitude and determination.

As the elevator doors snapped shut, I tried to swallow the big lump in my throat and hold back the flood of tears rushing to my eyes. I had a mental image of the gentle orderly dressed in scrubs standing alongside my little Megan, sleepy now from her pre-operation medication, and clutching her Baby Dreams doll. The compassionate operating room staff allowed children to bring their favorite doll or stuffed animal to the operating room with them.

I had spent the night on a cot next to Megan's bed, and was able to wash up and grab a bite to eat while Megan was being operated on. Doctor R.'s words kept coming to mind: "You'll have to work extra hard after surgery. If we do more than one orthopedic correction, Megan will need extensive physical therapy. You will have to be firm and consistent." Partly because of my insistence and promise to work harder than ever, Dr. R. did three procedures at once.

The Beginning

As I sipped on some hot coffee, my mind wandered back to the beginning of all this. Megan was a year old when our pediatrician first used the words "cerebral palsy" to explain why Megan was unable to walk. She would stand next to the furniture, but always on her tippy-toes with her legs held tightly together. She lacked balance and had to grip tightly to protect herself from an inevitable fall should she let go.

Fortunately, our pediatrician referred us to an early intervention program for infants and toddlers with cerebral palsy. Every Tuesday morning, rain or shine, snow or sleet, Megan, Maureen (her older sister), and I drove to the neighboring town for Megan's therapy. One of the best therapists and friends we were ever to meet was in charge of this program. Each child was her special challenge, her success or her failure. Her approach to parents was up-beat. She could rejoice about and praise what seemed to me the smallest twinge of progress.

Megan screamed at the sight of the building as we approached it. I was prepared to learn as much as I could—to do whatever it would take to help my little girl's legs work. I remembered from my days in nurse's training to look for the "wellness" in a person rather than to dwell on the "illness." Megan could hear, see, laugh, speak, think, and had good use of her upper extremities. She was blessed with a sense of humor and a double dose of determination and fortitude. Megan was diagnosed as a spastic diplegic.

Two exercises that were a must in the beginning were stretching her heel cords and abducting her legs. The stretching was very uncomfortable and Megan cried during the procedure. Abduction of the legs was easier to be religious about. I simply had Megan straddle my hip whenever I carried her from place to place to keep her legs apart.

It was a treat to see Megan's feet flat on the floor for the first time in four years.

Surgery

So much has passed since those early days of stretching, straightening, balancing, shaking, and even bracing Megan's tiny legs, all in preparation for this day.

Megan was four years old when we agreed that the time was right for surgical intervention. I had bought her a ring with her birthstone as a gift for after surgery. I quickened my step back to Megan's room to finish waiting for her to return from the operating room. Suddenly, Megan arrived. The nurse said, "She wanted to see her mommy so we didn't really spend time in the recovery room. She is awake and doing fine."

Megan's cheeks were flushed and her lips cherry red. Her legs were spread broad eagle in a cast with a bar stretching from knee to knee. She looked so uncomfortable "stuck" in this unbending apparatus. Once safely positioned in her bed, she asked the usual, "Are you o.k., Mommy?" I showed her the ring I had bought her. She slipped it on wondering when I was able to get it for her since she had not seen it the night before. "I'm so hungry I could burst," she said. When lunch came, she seemed more enthusiastic about the containers the food came in than the actual food itself.

During the night, Megan had spasms in her legs and required pain medication as well as frequent turning from back to belly. Each time I turned her, I rubbed her back with lotion which seemed to relax her.

The morning after surgery, Megan was propped on my lap as I read a story to her. The doctors came in on rounds. Megan's brow was wrinkled and the corners of her mouth turned down.

"How are you, Megan? Is there anything I can do for you?" the doctors asked.

"I want to go home," she said in her low voice.

"O.K. then, we'll check with Dr. R. If it's all right with him and with your mom, you can go."

Now the big smile—big enough for everyone in the room that morning.

"Daddy and Maureen won't believe this," she said with a grin and a devilish twinkle in her eyes.

Coming Home, Back to School

Megan did not complain as she layed sprawled out in the back of our station wagon like a piece of furniture. At home, we wheeled her around the house in a carriage converted into a stroller. This arrangement enabled her to join us at the table during mealtimes.

Megan slept on a pull-out sofa which was sufficiently wide enough to allow us to make our 180 degree turns. Neither Megan nor I got much sleep at night during these first few weeks at home. Spasms required baby aspirin, re-positioning, and reassurance every hour during the night. Each time Megan needed me she would say, "Sorry to wake you, Mommy, but I can't help it," and "Thank you." While I would get situated on the sofa across from her, she would drift off to sleep again.

Megan knew nursery school was in session and was anxious to go back to school. There was only one problem: "I can't wear slacks, Mommy, and if I wear a dress, what will I do for underwear?"

By evening, I had a plan. When Megan's daddy arrived home from work, I took off for the shopping center and bought six new pairs of underpants for Megan and several yards of velcro. The next morning, I cut the side seams of her panties and sewed velcro strips on the sides. "Now let's put on a dress today and try our new invention," I said.

Megan beamed. "Now I'll be able to go back to school!" She seemed undaunted. We talked about the kid's reactions to her casts. Megan thought she could handle the questions and stares, neither of which were foreign to her. Who was I to "chicken out?"

We passed the afternoon painting pictures on the leg casts. They began to look less foreboding, even cute, with Big Bird, Kermit, and other characters on them.

I could not wait to pick Megan up after her first day back at school.

"Well, how did it go?"

"Oh, fine," Megan answered in her offhand manner, "The kids wanted to know all about my casts—Jason even wanted to smell it! Gross! So Mommy, what are you worried about again?"

Rehabilitation

Six weeks past surgery, Megan's casts were removed. She was extremely fearful of having them taken off, and was reluctant to cooperate. Dr. R.'s most successful method for dealing with Megan at times like these was to say something like, "Megan, the casts have to come off. I will be back when you are ready to cooperate with me." He rarely got more than one foot out the door when she would call him back and let him proceed.

Now our work was cut out for us. Physical therapy was of the utmost importance. It was a treat to see Megan's feet flat on the floor for the first time in four years. Our plan revolved around two major goals—to reduce spasticity and to establish a sense of balance. Megan's brain damage caused both muscle groups in her legs to contract and her balance center was greatly affected.

Because Megan resisted her exercise sessions, we decided to set the alarm clock so she would know when exercise time was over. Her anticipation of the clock ringing seemed to distract her from the discomfort. We also sang songs to accompany certain exercises. "Row, row, row your boat..." matched the one where we sat facing each other on the floor with my legs on top of hers to keep her knees straight and her legs abducted. We would join hands and lie down and sit up singing as we stretched. When we bicycled her legs, we chorused, "You'll look sweet upon the seat of a bicycle built for two."

My husband constructed parallel bars for Megan to walk through—plumbing pipes, 2 x 2's and dowels did the trick.

For practice with balance, we tipped a round hassock on its side; Megan straddled it and rocked from side to side tapping the floor with her foot. At first, I held her hands. Gradually, she could balance without my intervention.

When her brain-leg coordination improved, we thought riding a tricycle would be of benefit both physically and socially. It was almost impossible for her to keep her feet in contact with a pedal. We overcame this by sawing the wheels off of a pair of roller skates and attaching the foot pieces to the bike pedals. We slipped Megan's feet into the foot pieces, strapped them in, and off she rode with the other kids. Naturally, she was unable to get off of the tricycle by herself, but her sister or another child would open the straps and free her feet.

Megan progressed to a walker, concentrating on her gait—right, left, right, left. I would walk behind her using one of my knees to guide her steps.

Crutch-walking was made easy and fun. We tied bright yarn bows on Megan's shoes to match the bows we tied to the crutches and taught a four-point method. "Pink crutch, pink shoe," "green crutch, green shoe." Before long, Megan began "zooming" around on her crutches.

A Day to Remember

I will never forget "that marvelous day." I was preparing supper and bustling around the kitchen. Megan came in to chat. On one of my hurried turns from the refrigerator to the stove, I stopped dead in my tracks and stared. "Megan, you are standing all by yourself right in the middle of the kitchen!"

"Yeah, I know," she said with her usual I-told-you-so grin. "It's a miracle," I said. And I repeat it every time I see Megan walking to the mailbox to bring in our mail all by herself ■

Rita Spillane lives in Gainesville, Florida. She is a registered nurse and an advocate for children and the elderly. She and her husband, Leonard, have six children, Maureen, Megan, Michael, Margaret, Melanie, and Martin.

CHAPTER 42

Coordinating Medical Services—An Eternal Problem

Finding a professional with whom one can have this long-term relationship has always been a problem.

When a youngster has a disability, quite often, more than one part of his or her bodily system is affected. In addition, a disability can affect more than one area of a person's life. It may affect mobility and intellectual ability, as well as social skills. As a result, the family and the child will ordinarily seek help and guidance from more than one expert at any given time. Complicating this is the fact that as the child grows older and has changing needs, the family may need to seek out new experts.

In the past decade, we have seen an incredible explosion in the availability of new information—some verified and some unverified. Much of this new information is tentative, ambiguous, and not necessarily proven. Parents as consumers are always on the spot of evaluating how much of new knowledge may be enthusiasm of the researcher and how much of it is applicable. Parents need some professional with whom they can maintain a long-term relationship to help evaluate and coordinate the range of information that is going to be necessary for the fullest understanding of the whole child.

In *Understanding the Whole Child—The Key to Coordinating Services*, Irene Lester describes the problem of finding some coordinator so that her child will not have to repeat the same tests endlessly, nor will the information gathered be so fragmented that it is not used on behalf of her child.

Finding a professional with whom one can have this long-term relationship has always been a problem. In earlier days, it was only teaching and research centers that had the range of expertise or interest in the child with a disability. They were the ones that provided theories and methods of coordination. Now that the information is more available and many people are aware of the need for more than one professional opinion, there is a greater need for a professional as a coordinator.

The person with the intellectual and technical ability may not be willing to serve as a coordinator because he or she cannot devote the amount of time necessary or find this role either emotionally or financially satisfying. Parents are often on the spot of trying to sell themselves and their child as worthwhile of the interest and attention. Once a coordinator begins, parents are reluctant to leave the professional even when it is clear that he/she has a lack of interest and energy.

Even when one finds the appropriate expert, we are a nation on the move. It is difficult enough to tap into the network of families who might be able to give you information in your community about professionals who are interested. But moving and having to re-establish roots and ties, which happens to many people each year, further complicates the problem of finding the appropriate coordinator.

Finally, the methods of providing and funding health services have changed dramatically. For example, the particular kind of insurance plan that your family is participating in may have more to determine the group of professionals that are available to you than any single factor. Secondly, the new forms of group professional practices (health maintenance organizations, emergency medical centers, professional provider organizations, etc.) have styles of their own that need to be understood and evaluated if the family is to find some kind of ongoing, consistent care.

In 1985, we will be describing the impact of new technologies and new methods of providing service on the health care issues for families with a disabled child. We would like to have ideas for dealing with today's health care. ■

—M.J.S., S.D.K.—

CHAPTER 43

Surgery for the Adolescent
The Impact on the Family

Mrs. White did not know what to do when her thirteen year old refused corrective surgery. She confronted the family with the need to examine its pattern of getting along with each other and resolving problems.

"We've come to discuss our daughter, Judy." Mrs. White, a tall, slender, attractive woman in her late thirties spoke rapidly. "It might be more accurate to say that we came because we can't manage to discuss our daughter's problems together. At least that's my view.

"Judy was born with cerebral palsy. In order to help her walk better, she had some corrective surgery when she was very young. She is now thirteen. For a few years, there's been a plan that she have some more corrective surgery at this time.

"At the last meeting with the orthopedist, Judy said that she was not going to allow this to happen to her. She was in tears and almost hysterical. I have been trying to talk to her about this at home for several months. But she would only start crying and go to her room.

"When she and I discussed the topic with the doctor, the floodgates really opened. She proceeded to blame me for everything she could think of, but mainly the wish to have surgery. She accused me of being more interested in how she looks because of the kind of person I am, rather than whether it's going to be any good for her.

"Judy can't walk very well now. Nobody's going to promise her that she'll be able to walk any better later. So what's the use?

"She has been asking me about my own growing up for the last couple of years. She's been looking through my old scrapbooks and talking to my mother and father. I was an attractive, socially active teenager. There are a lot of pictures from what I now would look back at as very happy times.

"She has wondered about whether she would

Judy has begun to ask me about sex, menstruation, and dating. It is true that I've found this very upsetting.

ever get married. She's been very laudatory about how nice I looked and what a nice person I must have been. She is very curious about my friendships and she has begun to say that she could never be like that. And in the outburst, Judy accused me of wanting to live through her again. I don't know where she gets such ideas.

"I am very worried about what is going to happen to her. Judy is very bright. I knew this from the beginning even when other people weren't sure. I realized that she caught on quickly and she was alert even though it didn't seem so. She's done well in school, and has always been in the advanced section of her classes.

"The other thing that I think has been very fortunate is that she has been part of her school's activities. Of course, we've had the money to send her to a small, private girls' school. Nevertheless, it's been remarkable to me how friendly the girls have been to her and how they have accepted her. She's been invited to their parties, and occasionally now sleeps over.

"We've known these families for a long time—for as long as the girls have been in school. They don't ask the same kinds of questions or have the same kinds of worries as they did when Judy was young as to whether they could manage to have her with them. I also know that in junior high school with the parties and the social life starting that Judy may find herself more shut out than she has been up to this point.

Judy changed our marriage in ways that I never expected.

"Judy has begun to ask me about sex, menstruation, and dating. It is true that I've found this very upsetting. I think she has been talking to other youngsters and I don't know quite what she thinks or has learned.

"Judy is our oldest child. My husband and I had been married a couple of years and we both had independent and full lives at the time. My husband already was considered a promising young banker, and we were able to start with our own home. We were looking forward to having children and I was delighted when I became pregnant.

"It was a long, hard labor. I thought it would never end. Finally, I had to have a cesaerean section. I remember waking up and my husband and the pediatrician coming into the room looking awful. I was frightened.

"At first, I thought that the baby had died. Then they told me that something had happened during the delivery and that she had brain damage of some kind. The doctor said she was going to be very difficult to live with. Those are my words. I have gone back and talked to the pediatrician and he says that's not quite what he said.

"I think any child changes a marriage. But I think Judy changed our marriage in ways that I never expected. Until Judy came along, my husband made all the decisions that had to be made, and I was delighted to have someone so smart to take care of everything.

"It seems that since Judy has been born, I'm expected to make all of the decisions. If I try to involve John, he always just says, 'You know what's best.' I almost feel this is a terrible putdown—as if matters about Judy aren't worth discussing.

"Five years ago, we had a second child, John Jr. This time, thank God, everything has gone well. My husband loves him and as little time as he has spent with Judy, he's made up for it by spending it with John.

"When Judy was young, I was going from one specialist to another, from one therapeutic program to another. It just seems like an endless span of time. If I didn't have it written down or if it wasn't in my pediatrician's records, I don't think I would remember it at all—who did what and when.

"When Judy was about three, we went to a hospital where she had surgery and I was able to live-in. I was frightened myself. That is, I didn't like being away from my own home. I didn't like the hospital environment, and found it very unsettling to be with so many desperately sick children. In some ways, I was grateful that Judy was as healthy as she was. At the same time, I was afraid of what horrible disease I was going to see next in the hospital ward.

"It was a long recovery period. Judy didn't fully understand how she was going to have to cooperate. She was cranky and whiny for the next six months. It almost took me two years to recover my own sense of well-being after that. John would keep reassuring me that I was doing a terrific job. It seems to me that he was always suggesting we go off on one kind of vacation or another.

"John is a meticulous person and I think he's always found it difficult to have Judy at the table with us. As much as she tries, she is often very clumsy. Certainly when she was younger, it seemed like I was always cleaning up one mess after another. I felt trapped. My husband's behavior showed me that he was not happy, and my daughter was crying because she knew she was upsetting everybody.

"When Judy refused the surgery, I really didn't know what to do. I talked with the orthopedist. He felt, although he couldn't promise dramatic changes, there would be enough gain to make it worthwhile.

"Then I went to talk to my husband. I've been trying to get him more involved in this process and all he keeps saying is, 'Whatever is all right with you.' I asked him whether he would sit and talk to Judy with me.

"At that point, he said to me that that was a mother's job. Mothers should talk to daughters and fathers should talk to sons. Then he accused me of wanting to make more trouble than what was necessary. I demanded that he participate. First of all, whatever decision is made is going to be an important one in my life and our family's life. I would at least like to feel that we had really talked about it.

"I need to talk to somebody about my doubts about this. I know how upsetting surgery was in the past to me and in some ways I wonder if that is what Judy is responding to. At the same time, it seems to me that John should be doing more with Judy. He's delighted with her grades, but he doesn't seem to be happy with her."

"**I'm not sure** what my wife is talking about." John White sat apart from his wife and spoke softly, barely looking at her. "I've always praised Ann. I think she has doubts about herself that she shouldn't have. She's done a magnificent job of taking care of Judy and helping her grow up.

"Judy has done far better than I ever expected. It is true that sometimes I find Judy's behavior upsetting. But that's true of anybody who would be in that spot. She isn't attractive and I do wonder about whether she is going to succeed, no matter how smart she is. I ask myself, 'Would any business hire her no matter what school she graduated from?'

"I've admired my wife's persistence in making sure that Judy gets everything she can possibly get. I've never interfered with any decisions she's wanted to make. Judy is not happy about the thought of surgery. Maybe she's right. On the other hand, I'm not sure anyone should let a child make that decision. That's a decision that should be made by adults.

"My wife has friends who talk all the time—they're on the phone all the time discussing things and sometimes discussion makes things worse. What it makes you look at are things that you really can't settle.

"When I was growing up, I had a cousin who was retarded. It destroyed my aunt and her marriage. She was on the phone all the time with my mom trying to understand, discuss, find miracles. I always knew when my mom was on the phone with my aunt because she would be sort of short tempered with all of us. I felt there were some things better not discussed."

"**My parents expect** you to talk me into having the operation." Judy, a wiry looking, blond haired thirteen year old struggled into the room with her crutches, settled cautiously onto the chair, and appeared tentative and anxious. "Whenever I don't want to do something, my mother talks me into it and then she says to me, 'You see, it wasn't as hard as you thought.' But not this time.

"Can you understand me? Sometimes when I am upset people who don't know me can't understand what I am saying."

"Everybody seems to want me to have this operation, but I don't want it. The doctor tells me he thinks it will help me, but how much? My mother expects me to do what the doctors say. She always tells me that I have to like myself the way I am, and that if I don't like myself, then who will? Well, if I'm supposed to like myself the way I am, why is everybody always trying to change me and why do they want me to have this operation?

"We always discuss that my friends have to accept me the way I am, but I'm not sure that makes any sense either. Don't friends have to try to change for each other? I don't like everything about

---

Whatever decision is made is going to be an important one in my life and our family's life.

If I'm supposed to like myself the way I am, why is everybody always trying to change me and why do they want me to have this operation?

---

all of my friends, and I'm sure they don't like everything about me. But you know, they can change and I don't think I can. We always talk about how perfect you have to be to do all the things that everybody wants to do. If you have to be perfect, that certainly leaves me out."

"I've just started junior high school. I have so much to do, and it is so hard to get around that at the end of the day, I'm just exhausted. I look at my friends and I see how much energy they have. They're already making friends with the eighth and ninth graders; I wish I could. Even though it's a small school, I find it difficult to make new friends. And I'm afraid of losing the friends that I have. I have to ask myself everyday, 'Is it worth it?'

"My friends are already talking about parties and boys. I'm interested in parties and boys but I'm not pretty and I know I make people uncomfortable—even my father. My father spends all of his time with my brother. He has taken him to places that he would never take me to. Whenever he comes home, he always asks how his day's been, what's he doing, what's he done. I don't remember that he's ever asked me that three times. When I get my report cards—and I am a good student—I can't wait for him to get home so I can show him. But he never seems to be interested. My mother is always enthusiastic and she always says, 'He's just too busy, but he really loves you.' Well, if he really loves me, why doesn't he show it?

"The operation really scares me. I can remember when I was a little girl in the hospital. Even though my mother was there, I was scared to fall asleep. I used to think that if I shut my eyes, I would never wake up again. When I talked to my doctor, he said I'd have to miss almost the rest of the school year. I'm not sure if I do that how I'm going to keep up with my school work, and that's the only thing I do well. If I do what they're asking me, maybe I'll walk a little bit better. But maybe I will never catch up with my classmates.

"Are you just going to try and make me do what my mother says or what?"

The Whites had come to discuss their predicament with their thirteen year old daughter, Judy. An orthopedic surgeon had recommended that Judy, who has cerebral palsy, have some corrective surgery to help with her gait. While surgery had been discussed over a number of years, Doctor Green felt that now was the time before Judy got much older.

Judy had become adamant about not having surgery, and absolutely refused to discuss this with her mother or father.

Mrs. White felt she was helpless to continue acting on the doctor's recommendation without the help of her husband. After Judy had been born, Mr. White had left the major responsibility for the care and nurture of his daughter to his wife. Mrs. White had undertaken not only to make sure that her daughter had the best care and education possible, but at the same time, had unwittingly allowed her husband to do little with Judy. Mr. White found Judy's behavior upsetting, especially eating at the table with her. Despite Judy's success in school, he also remained pessimistic about her future. Mr. White's behavior with Judy was dramatically different than his behavior toward his younger son.

Mr. and Mrs. White had never actively debated or argued about these issues before. As a result, Mrs. White always felt that she was the parent who had to bear the blame if any decision that was reached was a problem.

All adolescents struggle with the problems of becoming. They are faced with beginning to emancipate themselves from their parents, finding some career opportunities for themselves, and struggling with the newer issues of relationships with members of both sexes. Underpinning these social concerns are the biological changes that are taking place. All adolescents must deal with concerns about body growth and body integrity. Resolving these concerns is more difficult when one's body actually does not function as well as other youngsters.

Judy not only had to deal with these emerging concerns, but to discuss "the assault" upon her already imperfect body. Judy had a very good relationship with her mother who constantly supported her and encouraged her. This helped Judy have good friendships at school with girls, and facilitated her intellectual growth.

Adolescence stirs up questions that daughters often have about their mothers. Judy, in her effort to find out how her mother negotiated her own adolescence, learned about her mother's popularity as a teenager. Mrs. White seemed to have achieved in the areas that Judy felt that she would surely fail. Finally, a young woman's relationships with men are strongly influenced by her relationship with her father. Judy's uncertainty about herself in relation to boys was reinforced by the difficult relationship between Judy and her father.

Mr. White felt that discussion only created conflict, and that conflict only led to making things worse. As a result, in the White family, many things were never resolved.

Judy's refusal to have surgery made Mrs. White question her good relationship with her daughter. It also forced her to look at her husband's relationship with her daughter and herself. She felt that his seeming lack of interest made both she and her daughter feel very uncertain about Judy's adolescence.

In a meeting to review the situation, Mr. White was able to acknowledge the impact he made on his wife and daughter. Both parents recognized the wish to avoid controversy meant that ordinary as well as difficult matters were not fully understood or resolved. They understood they needed counseling if they were to change the family's typical ways of living together. Judy asked for an opportunity to work with a psychotherapist for herself.

Mr. and Mrs. White and Judy agreed to postpone any decision about surgery until they had a chance to resolve some of these difficulties. ■

—M.J.S.—

This case has been selected from private practice and consultation files. The names and situations have been changed to preserve confidentiality.

CHAPTER 44

Help for Drooling

I always read, with great interest, the *Parents Contacting Parents* section as soon as I open my EXCEPTIONAL PARENT magazine. It is so helpful to know other parents of children with special needs and it is so essential to give and receive new ideas; to "keep the boat afloat" so to speak since we are all in it. A letter in that section inspired me to share our experience.

My son, David, is a bright and happy ten year old boy who happens to have both a physical and mental handicap. We had a great problem with drooling. He was a "SIX BIB A DAY" kid. Our first solution: we made specially colored bibs designed and tailored to match his clothes. We reasoned they were not so terribly noticeable as he passed the age when bibs were totally inappropriate.

Voila! In January 1981 a physiotherapist at Ontario Crippled Childrens Center in Toronto mentioned a new experimental kind of surgery that might alleviate some of David's drooling. An Ear, Nose and Throat specialist had just "invented" it. I said "it sounds like a magic wand and it certainly made sense." The drooling was driving everybody crazy including David. Who wants to have a wet chin constantly? He was a little boy who enjoyed finger painting without a "Drool Drip" design.

The next year, on our annual visit to have David's wheelchair re-evaluated and a communication assessment performed, we met a speech therapist. She asked, what I thought at the time, was a DUMB question. She inquired if David's drooling bothered him or us. Well, I gave her this look like.....what a dumb question! We all disliked it immensely. She said we could arrange for an appointment with the team of doctors at the Drooling Control Clinic. (That name was chosen by toss-up over Salivation Control Clinic the dentist informed me later. What options!)

We went to the Drooling Control Clinic the next day. They were friendly and very helpful. They said David was a prime candidate for this type of surgery. It involved small salivary gland ducts, (tubes) which drain in the front of his mouth, to the area where tonsils are. The tonsils would have to be removed, as a prerequisite, at least two or three months in advance of this surgery. Our decision would have to be made within six months otherwise a new assessment would have to be performed. This made my decision a little easier because it gave me a time limit. Surgery is always risky especially for children with cerebral palsy; like David has.

David and I returned to Windsor with great anticipation. I told my husband, Paul, about the specialist's plans. What a breakthrough we thought! Was this worth the risk? We consulted with our dentist and doctor. They thought it would have definite benefits for David. We asked, "Could it stop all the drooling?" No, we discovered, but it certainly would alleviate 75% of the problem. We decided, "Let's go for it!"

Our family doctor referred us to a great Ear, Nose, and Throat specialist in Windsor who would perform the tonsilectomy. When we went to discuss this surgery with him, he was very receptive and scheduled the tonsilectomy as soon as possible to allow the necessary time span needed between surgeries. David certainly did not want to be laid up during the Sailing Season. This initial phase to the process went very smoothly. David enjoyed being with other children who were experiencing the same "tonsil" feelings. We answered ALL the usual questions for his hospital roommates: "Why is he in that chair?" "Does David talk?" "Has he got tonsils just like me?" David returned home the next day with the regular sore throat and the ice cream-jello diet for the next few days.

The next phase followed three months later. The date for the duct surgery arrived and there we were with David, a little apprehensive as any child would be, in this Hospital for Sick Children, 300 miles away from home. The next morning, about two hours after the surgery began, it was over and we all sat together again waiting for David to fully awaken. The next few days were spent in the hospital swallowing slowly, first liquids then more liquids; then on to the ice cream-jello diet again. David has no problem with the ice cream but the jello is always so slippery. We used the old "open the hangar-door" routine during the next few days. Finally it was time to go home and even on the long late drive David laughed with my friend Judy who accompanied us home from Toronto.

Back at home Kirk, Jessica, and Dad anxiously awaited his return. Welcome banners greeted us and David knew he had made another new step to his development.

It has been almost two years since David's surgery. It was very successful and the majority of his drooling has been alleviated. He feels much better and so do we. People are more accepting and treat him as a little boy first, his handicap second. He is still a bright happy boy who happens to be handicapped. Although, his friends say he looks older now. Why I asked.....cause he doesn't wear bibs any more! ■

Alison Ouellette
Windsor, Ontario

An Advisory Board Member Responds

We continuously use our advisory board to assist us in areas in which we have little or no expertise. Dr Gans, in reviewing Mrs. Ouellette's letter, emphasizes the need for parents to know the range of options in dealing with drooling before they take any action.

Thank you for the paper to review the question of surgery for drooling.

[Mrs. Ouellette] presents one particular technique that is not widely used to my knowledge. Nevertheless, the identification of drooling as a functional problem that is worth some degree of surgical intervention is a common component of my practice because so many physicians and parents are not aware of the fact that intervention is feasible.

In general, we approach the drooling problem first by considering an optimized positioning, head control, and oral motor therapy. Secondly, we consider the possibility of medications, including Probanthine and other drugs that reduce salivation, and thirdly consider surgical interventions. The surgical interventions that we have our Ear, Nose and Throat specialists consider fall into the categories of denervation and restriction of procedure that denervates the posterior salivary glands and markedly reduces their production of saliva without effecting the quality of saliva.

Our Ear, Nose, and Throat surgeon prefers to perform this procedure in addition to a ductal ligation, which further diminishes the flow of salivation. I think that there are several other procedures that are performed in some areas, although my experience shows that they are less well tolerated and have greater incidences of side effects and other complications.

In summary, there are a number of procedures available for drooling control, as well as medical and therapeutic management techniques. If this paper were published only with this one particular therapeutic option, it would be an unwisely restrictive article. I would recommend that you get additional input, probably from either our Ear, Nose, and Throat specialist or one of the other physicians around the country who is enthusiastic about this type of surgery so that a more balanced review could be made.

Bruce M. Gans, M.D.
Chairman
Department of Rehabilitation Medicine
New England Medical Center, Tufts University
Member, EXCEPTIONAL PARENT Advisory Board

CHAPTER 45

The Right to Live
Disability is Not a Crime

by Lisa Blumberg

I cannot describe the horror I felt when one day three summers ago during a lull at work, I found myself reading a newspaper article putting forth the proposition that it was acceptable for doctors and parents to decide to end the life of an infant with an obvious handicap. Since I have a very noticeable physical disability resulting from a neurological injury occurring at birth, I had firsthand knowledge of society's prejudice toward people with disabilities.

However, I had never imagined that anyone would even consider allowing the killing of disabled children. The article haunted me day and night for nine months. Yet I clung to the hope that it had been written by an extremist and did not represent the views of even the minority of the American public.

Since then I have read reports of infants with physical or mental disabilities being denied basic medical care, or starved or drugged to death. These have not involved situations where doctors and parents have allowed a terminally ill child or a child with little brain activity to die a natural death by not using extraordinary means to prolong his life. Rather, these have been situations where persons have deliberately caused the death of a child who would otherwise live with a permanent disability.

While it is tragic that babies may needlessly die, what is appalling to me is that so many people now seem to feel that a parent should be able to choose death for a baby if doctors have reason to think that the child has a substantial disability.

The rationale usually given for allowing parents and doctors to end life of an infant with a noticeable physical or mental disability is that the child may not have a life worth living. However, the people who hold such views are invariably not disabled themselves. They only assume that it is better to be dead than handicapped, with no consideration of whether people who go through life with a disability share their views.

The disabled adults whom I know believe that a viable infant with a permanent disability has the same human right to live as any other infant. Our views as disabled persons are not identical to those of right-to-life proponents. We do not think that people must be sustained indefinitely or respirators, or that major surgery must be performed to prolong a vegetative existence. Like the rest of society, we are divided on our feelings toward abortion. However, we see no difference between denying a child routine medical care or food because of his sex, race, or religion. There is nothing morally wrong with being born lacking the use of one's legs, or without arms, or with impaired coordination, or without the capacity to read. Yet denying a child with a disability the care that any normal child needs to survive is the same as treating the disability as a crime to be punished by death.

Disabled people are not breathing medical problems or nature's mistakes. They are individuals who, like others, have varying interests and talents. They differ from the average person only in that in one or more areas they have noticeable limitations that others do not have. Since my walk is a slow stumble and my speech is slurred, I cannot compete with ordinary people when it comes to running or singing. However, my disability does not imply anything about my personality, earning capacity, or sexuality.

It is far from true that most disabled children must face a life oriented around treatment. Many people have physical handicaps that have little or no impact on their general health. Indeed, studies have shown that, on the average, disabled employees have less job absenteeism than nondisabled employees.

Of the many children with disabilities born each year, only a small number will have devastating limitations. Most will have slight to moderate impairments which will have some impact on their lives and the lives of those who raise them, but which will not prevent them from attending schools and day care centers, or eventually participating in the adult world.

There are thousands of Americans with disabilities who are leading satisfying lives. Disabled people are husbands, wives, and stamp collectors. They are members of virtually every profession. Time and time again, disabled individuals have proven that anatomy is not destiny. Many people believe that doctors are specially qualified to determine whether a child should live or die. Yet doctors are frequently wrong about the severity of an infant's disability. There are many people walking today whose parents were told they would never walk. There are many people with college degrees who were initially labeled mentally retarded because they had a physical impairment such as spina bifida, which can sometimes be accompanied by mental handicap, and there are people who were once categorized as vegetables who are only slightly retarded.

Even when doctors can accurately diagnose the physical effect of a condition, they cannot predict what kind of person a child will become or how he will compensate for his disability. Some physicians do have unconscious prejudices toward the disabled; a medical degree does not render a person wiser or more moral than others. I have met many doctors whom I would not trust to advise me on where to spend my vacation much less on whether my life or the life of a child had any worth.

It has actually been argued that it is humane to let a disabled baby die because he may not be accepted by others. However, few if any people meet with universal acceptance. Moreover, negative attitudes that the nondisabled may have toward the disabled are open to change. As a result of the modest strides disabled Americans have made during the last decade in achieving equal opportunity in employment and education, more and more of the nondisabled are meeting disabled individuals in everyday situations and coming to view them as people with whom they share common ground. Similarly, many parents who at the outset think they cannot cope with disability derive much joy from the child after bonding occurs and they become aware of the child's personhood.

It is ironic that debate over whether a disabled infant's life can be ended for so-called quality-of-life reasons should be occurring at a time when technology can do so much to minimize the effect of even the most severe disability. Artificial limbs are more lifelike in function and appearance than ever before. Wheelchairs can now be operated by a person's breath. Computers that simulate human speech enable people incapable of articulating their thoughts to converse. Such devices may be expensive, but so are cars, and they are uniformly used by the nondisabled as well as the disabled to increase independence and mobility.

A multitude of factors play a role in shaping the type of life that a child will have. Many severely disabled people achieve much in life while some able-bodied people, like some disabled people, have lives that are less than rewarding. It is totally arbitrary to use the presence of a disability to prejudge the quality of another's life.

Civil rights organizations for the disabled have taken the position that the government has a legitimate role to play in safeguarding the lives of disabled infants. Certainly there can be reasonable differences of opinion as to the form this role should take. Government intervention in the much publicized Baby Doe case was probably unwarranted, since the baby girl apparently had been given good basic care—although her parents have opted against the spinal surgery that might extend her life span. Yet government does have the obligation to make sure that disabled children are given the same protections to life and limb that other children are routinely given under the child abuse laws.

Not one of us is perfect. Every child born will be a person with a mix of abilities and disabilites, talents and shortcomings. Some disabilites, like some abilities, are just more obvious than others. All persons have the same human right to be free from persecution, to live, to love, and to be masters of their own fate. Disability is a natural part of being human. It should not be punished as a crime.

This fall, federal legislation was passed to protect disabled babies from being starved to death or denied basic medical care in hospitals. Yet as happy as disabled people are with the new law, we know that there will continue to be cases where disabled infants are killed unless society as a whole begins to see disabled children as having the same value as other children.

Parents of disabled children have both the right and the obligation to become involved in the fight to protect the lives of infants with disabilities. Like the disabled themselves, parents who are succesfully raising disabled children are experts in disability and can distinguish between fact and fiction regarding disability better than the general public can. Parents have credibility when they say that a disabled child and nondisabled children can grow up together in the same family with no one being harmed by it. Parents have credibility when they say that a career and raising a disabled child can be combined. Parents know and can explain to others that a child with a disability is not a child who is forever ill but simply a child with a limitation. Parents know and can explain to others that doctors do not always know best, they do not always treat a child or their families with respect or compassion. Above all, parents have been there. They experience the panic and desperation that is natural for someone to feel upon being told that one's baby has a permanent problem. Loving parents can say and indeed they must say that no one must be allowed to make the mistake that they themselves might make if given the opportunity.

I am an adult, a career person and a taxpayer. Yet what the press called the "Baby Doe" issue has shaken my sense of self worth to the core. I simply can not imagine what must be going on in the mind of a disabled child or teenager who is aware of the issue. One of the ways that a parent can reassure a child that he is indeed loved and wanted is by supporting efforts to protect all children. ■

CHAPTER 46

Sex Education and the Disabled—
Teaching Adult Responsibilities

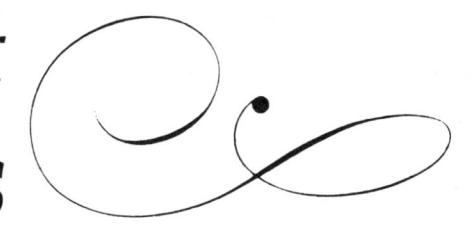

by Theresa Varnet

All parents have to educate and inform their children about issues related to sexuality. This process presents special difficulties for parents with a disabled child.

Theresa Varnet, in discussing the process of communicating information about sexuality to her adolescent daughter who is mentally retarded, offers useful guidelines that may be helpful to all parents.

Sex education is a topic which brings about a number of mixed emotions among families with retarded children. We have many burning questions and concerns that we need to talk about. Yet, sometimes we would prefer not even to think about our children facing the sexual realities of life. Often, unless we are forced to think about it, we put the issues on a back burner, and continue to try and convince ourselves that our children are not interested in *that*. This denial—trying to believe that our retarded children do not need to know about sexual matters—is a dangerous pitfall for us.

I could have very easily fallen into this trap myself. Fortunately, I learned from my experience working with a small group of adults who had moved from an institution to a community group home in 1974. These people were "making it" in the community in all areas, except that they were involved repeatedly in minor sex offenses such as urinating in public, touching themselves or others, and acting inappropriately with strangers.

The solution seemed relatively straightforward. We had to give these adults the information they needed so that they would not keep making the same naive mistakes. The big question was how and what to tell them. None of us had ever taught a sex education course for retarded persons.

In 1974, since there was little information to guide us, we tackled it from a common sense approach. We began by asking ourselves, "What information do persons with mental retardation need to know to make it in the community?"

The course was a growing experience for all of us. To this day, I am grateful for all that I learned since it has enabled me to help my own retarded daughter tremendously.

Jennifer

My daughter, Jennifer, was only six years old in 1974. My concerns about puberty and sexual matters for her were far in the future.

My contact with the group home residents made me aware of how some of my habits could cause problems for Jenny when she was older. For example, when Jenny was six, she was just beginning to be toilet trained. I would sit her on

131

the toilet, and leave the bathroom door opened. I seldom pulled the shade when I changed her clothes, and I would change her in the living room even when others were present.

I did not realize that I was teaching Jenny bad habits which would be hard to change when she entered puberty. It would no longer be acceptable for her to be semi-dressed in the living room or to sit in the bathroom with the door open. I was not teaching Jenny the difference between public and private behaviors. I realized that teaching appropriate social/sexual behavior can begin early so that our children do not have to unlearn socially unacceptable habits.

We would rather not even think about our children having to deal with the sexual realities of life.

Sex Education

When Jennifer was nine, I began to think about how I was going to prepare her for her menstrual period. I spoke to Jenny's teacher and to her pediatrician. It was obvious that they were both uncomfortable with the subject, and took the approach, "we'll deal with it when we have to."

From what I had learned from my group home experience, I knew that menstruation could be a particularly stressful experience for retarded women because they probably would not understand it, and might think they had done something terribly wrong. Several women I knew in the institution thought they had been sent away because of their period. In one respect, they were not wrong—puberty is the second most common time that a retarded person is placed.

I began preparing myself to deal with Jenny's eventual sexual development, and asked that a health or sex education program be added to her Individual Education Plan (IEP). Jenny needed to know that soon she would be developing into a young woman. Information about body changes and menstruation needed to be introduced to her. This process is done for "normal" children in the schools. Retarded children deserve the same rights to information about their bodies.

I was told by the school that they would teach Jennifer how to use a sanitary napkin when she started her period, but that any other details about sexual development were the parents' responsibility. The school had been wonderful in teaching Jenny all of her other self-help skills. I felt

I wanted Jennifer to have information so she would not be exploited, and also so she would feel good about herself and act as our society expects an adult to behave.

that this was just another basic self-help skill.

If teaching a retarded child about appropriate sexual behavior is the parents' role, then who is going to teach the parents? I wanted the information introduced in Jenny's IEP, and reinforced by my husband and me at home.

Many people opposed my desire to make sure that my daughter was given a responsible sex education. Her pediatrician felt that this was information Jenny did not need to know because she was never going to have sex. The principal at Jenny's school suggested that I may want to consider having Jenny institutionalized if I were afraid she might get pregnant.

It upset me that many people thought I wanted sex education for Jennifer just so she would not get pregnant. That was but one of my concerns. More importantly, I wanted her to understand what was happening to her body. As a young woman, there were many things she had to know. I wanted Jennifer to have information so she would not be exploited, and also so she would feel good about herself and act as our society expects an adult to behave.

I felt that this information belonged in Jenny's IEP, and challenged the school's decision not to include it. I appealed on the basis that information on sexual/social development was basic self-help information that Jenny needed to know in order to survive. The school finally agreed, and to their credit, Jenny received an excellent program.

Sterilization Is Not The Answer

There are some people who still feel retarded girls cannot learn to take care of their menstrual hygiene needs. In the community which I am now living, many retarded girls have hysterectomies between their tenth and thirteenth birthday because their parents feel they will be unable to care for their period. Will a hysterectomy keep these girls from being sexually exploited? Will it enable them to behave in a manner that is sexually/socially appropriate in public? Will it help them to understand the changes going on in their bodies? Of course not!

A hysterectomy is not a solution for our children living independently in the community. All it does is remove the problem of unplanned pregnancy and the menstrual period. This situation demonstrates the need for more community awareness and education about the abilities of girls with developmental disabilities to care for their menstrual hygiene needs. It is a serious problem when many doctors, parents, and teachers make the assumption that retarded girls cannot care for themselves, and, therefore, prematurely opt for a radical procedure like a hysterectomy.

As parents and teachers, we need to ask ourselves whether we are sterilizing our daughters or students for their convenience or for ours. There has not been any research done on the long term physical or mental health effects of early sterilization. The operation is not without its risks.

It would be healthier and less dehumanizing to develop a curriculum to help parents and special educators deal with menstrual and other puberty related needs of young people with disabilities. As parents and teachers, we need to work together to make our children informed and self-reliant.

The Value of Information

Many people are uncomfortable talking about human sexuality. I know I am. My heart starts beating fast and my palms get sweaty whenever I have to discuss this subject with Jenny. I am still afraid of saying the wrong thing. In one sense, It might have been easier for me to have kept Jenny "innocent," but that would not have been in her best interest. By ignoring this area of our children's development, we have to ask ourselves whether or not we are contributing to society's perceptions about the limitations of the retarded by keeping them uninformed.

Theresa Varnet has worked as the coordinator of the Green River Area Service Cooperative, and as a member of the Kentucky Special Education Advisory Panel. She is currently living in Muscat, Sultanate of Oman and is employed as a social worker by the Oman Women's Association.

The following resources were provided by Katherine Simpson, director of the Planned Parenthood Disability Program, Walnut Creek, California.

An Easy Guide For Caring Parents, Sexuality and Socialization: A Book for Parents of People With Mental Handicaps, Lyn McKee and Virginia Blacklidge, M.D., Planned Parenthood of Contra Costa, 1291 Oakland Boulevard, Walnut Creek, California 94596. $5.95 plus $1.50 postage and handling.

Toward Intimacy: Family Planning and Sexuality Concerns of Physically Disabled Women, Task Force on Concerns of Physically Disabled Women, Human Sciences Press, 72 5th Avenue, New York, New York 10011. $3.95 plus postage and handling.

Sexuality and Physical Disability: Personal Perspectives, David G. Bullard and Susan E. Knight ed., C.V. Mosby Company, 11830 Westline Industrial Drive, St. Louis, Missouri 63141. $19.95 plus postage and handling.

ies
Sex Education
A Commentary From the Advisory Board

by Betty Pendler

Parents, too, have to recognize that our children are sexual as well as human.

Sex education is a topic that concerns all parents. In our June 84 issue, Theresa Varnet spoke on the importance of sex education in the lives of children with disabilities. Betty Pendler, a member of THE EXCEPTIONAL PARENT Advisory Board, elaborates on this important subject.

Congratulations to Theresa Varnet on her excellent article, Sex Education—Teaching Adult Responsibilities.

I especially want to commend her for her courage in insisting that sex education be included in her daughter's Individualized Education Plan. It is interesting and troublesome to see how so many people are afraid to touch the subject, and use all kinds of excuses to stay away from it. It may be a subtle message from society that people with disabilities are not sexual beings. As Sol Gordon once said, "It has taken us years to convince people that most parents and professionals can handle the human part, but not the sexual."

Beginning Early
Parents have to recognize that all our children are sexual as well as human. A child's self-image becomes a basic part of his or her sexuality. As Robert Perske wrote, all human beings have sexual development, being held close in a mother's arms, being fed, tickled, bounced on a knee, hugged and shoved by siblings, and discovering feelings one's own hands can produce.

Much is written about how a healthy personality depends on an early positive self-image—that includes a happy self-awareness of one's body, and pleasurable experiences. That seems to me to be a good way to begin. If your child—through self-discovery and self-stimulation—discovers that his or her body feels good, then it is easy to go on and encourage the youngster later about proper grooming, and a good feeling about him or herself.

Self-Stimulation
Many professionals in the field of human sexuality write that masturbation is now considered quite appropriate. Masturbation allows a child to get a feeling of self-sufficiency and bodily pleasure. Parents must look to their own attitudes and realize that masturbation can be a healthy activity. It can contribute to the physical and emotional well being of their child, and does not hurt anyone.

With a non-judging attitude on our part, I am sure that masturbation would not increase a child's desire to do it more often. If anything, it would take away the feeling of guilt, and make it easier for us to give the message that it is all right, but that it should be done in private.

Teaching Our Children
Teaching daughters about menstruation is a subject that haunts most parents. We assume that our daughters who are disabled are not going to understand us. It is very important for both girls and boys to be told in advance as they approach puberty about what will be occurring to their bodies. I used the idea that these changes would occur because my daughter was *growing up* and stayed away from the words that something will *be happening* to her.

Long before my daughter Lisa was ready, I began to talk to her about menstruation. I showed her what she would see when the time came when she "growed up." As I was showing Lisa the sanitary napkin, her younger brother, Paul, passed by the bathroom and looked in, so he got a lesson too. (That was not part of my plan.) One morning, Paul walked into the kitchen and said to me, "You know the thing you showed us; I think it happened." And Lisa, who is mentally retarded, followed him and said to me, "Mommy, I growed up today." It was that easy!

In fact, she was so proud that she began to tell everyone whenever she got her period, that she "growed up." Like everything else, I had to tell her over and over again that this was private and that she should only tell me. Eventually, she got that message too. I tried to explain menstrual pains and told her that sometimes when she eats ice cream and pickles she gets a stomach ache and that it goes away. After a while, these pains go away too.

Parents' Concerns
It is understandable that parents feel uncomfortable discussing this subject. We are beset with the fear that a basic knowledge of sexual matters will foster experimentation and stimulate sexual behavior. Experts believe that lack of knowledge can be more injurious. It is important

for us to enlarge our narrowly focused view of sexuality regarding the person who is disabled. We need to view him or her—even an individual who is retarded intellectually—as having sexual needs and characteristics common to the non-disabled population.

This is not easy, for most of us tend to vacillate from one extreme to the other. We may point out our children's deviation and lack of judgement, instead of looking at their common human needs. We see sex as dangerous and adding to their already anxious lives.

Parents as well as professionals sometimes stick to the belief that sex is private, so let's not talk about it. Our concerns are constantly, "Will our child be able to control impulses so she or he will not embarrass us socially, be exploited, or get into trouble?"

The truth is that the more comfortable children are with their sexuality, the better they can deal with their feelings. How can we ask our sons and daughters to be responsible for their behavior—sexual or otherwise—if we allow, and almost guarantee their ignorance by continuing to resist telling them the truth about themselves? We must not believe the myth that people who are handicapped are asexual or uncontrollable, and that their sexual feelings must be ignored or confined.

In our effort to convince the schools that this subject should be taught, we could use the term "social sexual training" instead of "sex education." The distinction is more than just a semantic one because the ultimate goal is to help the person who is disabled to fit into society and feel confident about him or herself. Sex education in today's society can deal not only with sex per se, but with social relationships and emotional fulfillment.

The question should not be whether our child should have sex information, but when, how and by whom? Sex education includes learning about relationships, body feelings, stimulation, control, male and female roles, etc.

Sex education does not breed experimentation, nor stimulate the student to sexual activity. Rather knowledge can act as a deterrent, for it teaches control. It cannot begin too early. Children learn only what they are capable of comprehending—but it can be too late if we wait too long. ■

> Betty Pendler lives in New York City. She has a son and a daughter, both of whom are living independently. She received a masters degree in community health from Hunter College. Ms. Pendler is a member of the New York State Developmental Disabilities Planning Council.

CHAPTER 48

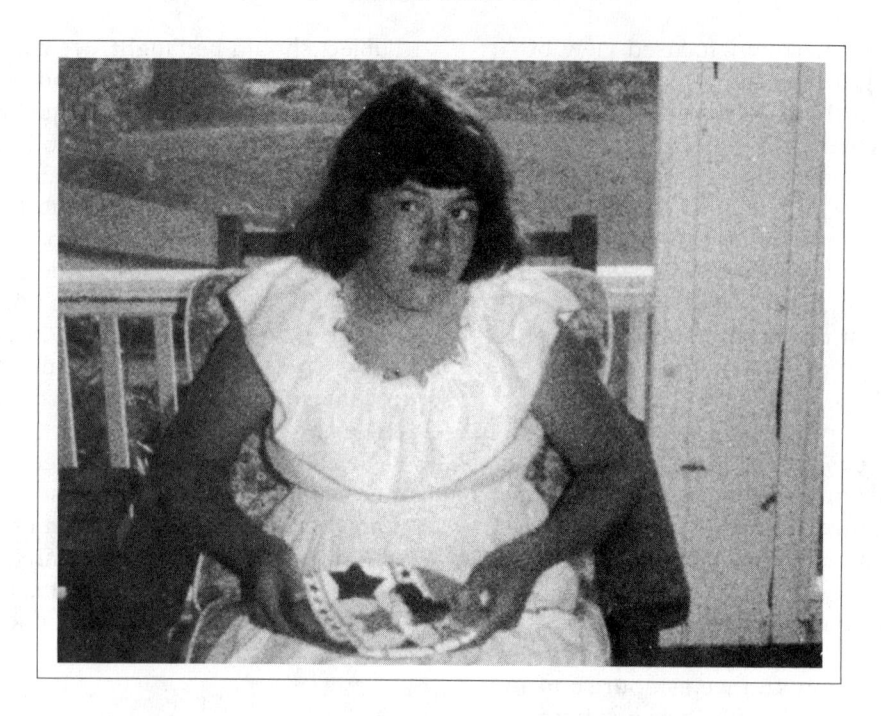

Sex Education
LET'S NOT PRETEND

by Katherine Barnes

It is easier to focus on the "child" part of their teen and pretend the physical body and its feelings do not exist.

Our sixteen year old daughter, Katherine, will sometimes climb into bed at 8 p.m. and call out, "Daddy, come say good night to me." She has one thing on her mind, to be physically close to him.

Is this surprising? No, not if we understand the hormonal changes that occur in her body monthly and the sexual arousal accompanying them.

How does Katherine know the correct words of endearment and body movements? Many of her favorite T.V. shows (e.g. Dallas) portray loving couples in bed. My husband sits on a chair beside her bed and rubs her back, telling her a story. When he leaves he makes sure she has her teddy bear to hug. This bear sleeps between her legs many nights.

For parents of teenagers and adults who are mentally retarded, the sex drive is confusing and upsetting them. Their teen may act developmentally like a six year old who wants "Baby Sit Up" for her birthday, (or toy trucks if he's a boy). Yet she has a woman's body with breasts, pubic hair and the menstrual cycle and its hormonal demands.

Let's Talk About It

Most parents do not talk about their retarded teen's sexuality. It is taboo. It scares and embarrasses them. It is easier to focus on the "child" part of their teen and pretend the physical body and its feelings do not exist. By not talking about it, parents are missing valuable information and help.

Most teachers of retarded adolescents have to deal with students who "play with themselves." Do they ever talk to the parent about it? Rarely. It is taboo. They sometimes talk to fellow teachers. How helpful it would be, if parents and teachers could communicate about the teen's behavior and use similar methods at home and school to help the retarded young adult.

I would like to describe how Katherine's sexuality evolved and our response to it. In two previous articles, (THE EXCEPTIONAL PARENT, Dec. 1982; THE EXCEPTIONAL PARENT, Feb. 1982), I described my talks with her, using well-illustrated books showing the physical changes in her body

She knows her body now and wants to handle it herself. I am glad I gave her the infomration early.

and a boy's, how sexual organs work, the feelings associated with their bodies, and how to handle them responsibly.

My experience shows me that the time to talk about these physiological changes is when the teen is beginning to develop. Do not put it off.

You will need to go over diagrams and explanations many times. The prepuberty years will be the time your teen will listen most attentively. Their body changes really fascinate them. Once the changes take place and they are used to their breasts and pubic hair (for boys, their penises) and have explored ways to bring themselves pleasure through touching and stroking, they will not want to listen to you talk about their bodies. Modesty springs up.

Katherine surprised me a month ago, when I told her that it was natural and O.K. to stroke herself; it feels good. She responded, "Mommy, don't talk about that," and pushed me away. She closed the door on that conversation and yet a year earlier she listened carefully. She knows her body now and wants to handle it herself. I am glad I gave her the information early.

What do we talk about now? Appropriate ways to act around the boys at school. I try to help her build an image of what she will be like when she is twenty-one and living in a group home away from me and her dad. We talk about her needing to know how to cook, shop, clean her room, do her laundry and we build these self-help skills. We build leisure skills such as bike riding, making puzzles, playing the piano, listening to records. We also talk about the job she will be doing when she leaves home. (We hope she can help in a day care center. She helps two afternoons a week now in a center for disabled children. She gets paid by Mom, not the agency.)

These dreams of Katherine living away from home and doing things for herself may be just dreams, but they help all of us build for the future. They motivate her and us to keep growing. Last week, she packed her suitcase and said, "I'm going to live with my cousin in Oklahoma. Will you miss me?" I answered, "Yes. Couldn't you just visit for two weeks this summer and come back?" She responded, "I have my own life to lead, Mom. I have to get started." Wow! That sounded grown up for her!

As parents of a sixteen year old, sexually mature teenage daughter, my husband and I do not consider sex talk taboo. We have found it necessary to acknowledge her sexuality and talk about it together and with other parents.

We recognize at certain times of the month her sex drive will surface very strongly. Those are the nights she takes longer baths, sleeps without her nightgown and takes all her stuffed animals to bed with her. We also help her channel her energy into building leisure, self-help, and social skills.

The sex drive is strong. It influences us, our handicapped, and non-handicapped teenagers. Making it a taboo subject does not make it disappear. Encouraging Katherine to express it in her bedroom appropriately and channeling her energy into building life skills has helped her mature into an independent retarded young woman. ■

Katherine Barnes is a doctoral candidate in Child and Family Development at the University of Georgia. She resides in Augusta, Georgia with her husband, Travis, and their children, Cristina, Katherine, and Edward. Mrs. Barnes received the 1984 Outstanding Volunteer in Community Services Award from the Georgia Association for Retarded Citizens.

CHAPTER 49

Abuse of Children with Disabilities— Time to Stop Pretending

> *In recent months, the reports of the sexual abuse of children have received national attention in all of the media—television, radio, and newspapers.*

We can no longer deny that children with disabilities are victims of physical and sexual abuse. We must open our eyes and confront the upsetting reality in a constructive fashion.

The extent of child abuse—physical and sexual—has reached crisis proportions. In the past decade, society became aware of the extent to which children were being abused by a variety of people—family members, school and recreation personnel—as well as strangers. In recent months, the reports of the sexual abuse of children have received national attention in all of the media—television, radio, and newspapers. And again, the "abusers" are mainly people who are involved in the everyday lives of the youngsters.

When society became aware of physical abuse as a serious problem, action was taken. Laws were instituted that required physicians and other health and educational professionals to report cases in which there was either the suspicion or evidence of abuse. These laws contain legal protection for the people who are required to report so they cannot be involved in expensive legal suits or costs.

Diagnostic and treatment centers, community hotlines, and public awareness programs were developed and instituted throughout the country. Over the course of the past decade, we have begun to learn how to recognize, prevent, and mobilize community resources on behalf of the abused child and the family. The experience gained from these programs involving physical abuse will be of great benefit in developing sex abuse treatment and prevention programs.

Taking action has required paying attention to what was happening to children and what they were telling us. Believing that children can be physically or sexually abused is so intolerable that we had often ignored those clues that would have informed us as to what was happening.

Children with disabilities are more likely to be abused than other children. One reason for this is that caring for children with disabilities and helping them grow usually increases stress—not only on the family, but on every social organization (school, health, community) that lives or works with them. Children with disabilities usually require more time, energy, and interest than their siblings or their peers. It can be very frustrating to slowly learn how to understand their needs and have to modify both the environments and parental behavior. When children have difficulties in growing it is harder for parents and others to experience a sense of developing mastery or satisfaction in their efforts to help the child grow. This adds to the stress involved.

Challenges in life require that we mobilize our energy for taking the actions necessary for coping. Dealing with challenges that are prolonged or not resolved—like parenting a child with problems—often is a continuous drain on the energy necessary for managing other areas of our lives.

We all know that when there are extensive problems at work, we may find ourselves taking out our frustrations and our decreasing sense of control on members of our families. We have all

> *Believing that children can be physically or sexually abused is so intolerable that we had often ignored those clues that would have informed us as to what was happening.*

seen the aspirin commercials on television which so vividly portray the mother taking out her frustrations by shouting at her children. Studies of the effects of unemployment clearly illustrate how stress on one family member can disrupt the social and physical functioning of all family members.

There are many impulses—both sexual and aggressive—that we have learned to manage over the course of our lives. When we are fatigued, any of us may lose control of these impulses and direct them against the people—both adults and children—that we love and care for. Afterward, people often feel so guilty and ashamed that the problems are often never discussed or resolved. Over many years, the new and difficult challenges become the chronic stress that depletes the energies that parents need for everyday living. Depleted of energy, we can understand why these families are more vulnerable to doing inappropriate things to their children. As a result, these families need to be aware of these dangers and methods of helping them must be developed and made available.

Another reason for the incidence of abuse is that many of us have denied the possibility that children with disabilities do grow up, can live in the world, and even be interested in sex. This makes them more vulnerable to abuse—both sexual and physical. We have developed ways of preparing "ordinary" children to cope with moving out from the family, going to school in the surrounding community, and dealing with new difficulties they may encounter.

Children with disabilities have less preparation and may need more help than other children in coping with the unseen emergencies of everyday living.

We at THE EXCEPTIONAL PARENT have not been immune from the wish to overlook the most difficult things. Our articles have often described the intolerable and upsetting thoughts and feelings of members of the family and community. We have hoped to reassure people that thoughts and feelings do not have to lead to action when people understand them. At the same time, we have not directly presented articles about abuse, helping people understand the problem, and describing programs for prevention and rehabilitation.

We are taking that step in this issue with the article, *Talking About the Best Kept Secret* by Janice Daar Watson. We will continue to present emerging programs that have proven effective so that you, our readers, can be better informed and the children that we all care for will be better served. ■

—M.J.S., S.D.K.—

CHAPTER 50

Talking About the Best Kept Secret
Sexual Abuse and Children with Disabilities

by Janice Daar Watson

Janice Daar Watson describes how to recognize when children may be in a sexually abusing environment. She also provides a practical guide for understanding and preventing abuse.

Among the large number of children, both girls and boys, who are victims each year of sexual abuse—rape, incest, molestation, child pornography, or other unwanted sexual activity—there are many who are physically or mentally disabled.

A recent two year study in Seattle (the Seattle Rape Relief Developmental Disabilities Project) estimated that there may be up to five hundred mentally and physically disabled children and adults victimized by sexual abuse each year in the Seattle area alone. These numbers stand in startling contrast to the belief that people with disabilities are somehow "immune" from sexual abuse because offenders would "feel sorry for them" or see them as "undesirable."

Like many other myths that often cloud discussions of sexual abuse, this belief has kept a real problem hidden for far too long. There are, in fact, a number of reasons why many children and adults with disabilities may be particularly vulnerable to sexual abuse.

Vulnerability of Children with Disabilities

Offenses such as rape and incest are less a result of sexual urge than they are an offender's need for power and control over another. Children with disabilities are likely to be more dependent on adults for their physical and psychological needs than are other children. And both children and adults with disabilities are often encouraged to be compliant and passive towards those who provide them with personal care and assistance, particularly in institutional settings.

Children and adults with disabilities may therefore be seen as "easy targets." Some offenders have been known to seek out victims deliberately who have specific disabilities such as blindness or limb amputation. Threats by offenders ("Don't tell them or I'll have to go away and leave you all alone") can inspire greater fear. More subtle forms of coercion ("Come on, you know I take good care of you, don't I?") may go unchallenged by the victim. Some children with disabilities lack

> *Most disabled victims are abused by someone known to the child.*

good social skills and judgement, making it easier for offenders to trick them into dangerous situations ("Your mommy told me to take you to my house").

Poor social judgement combined with a lack of experience about appropriate sexual behavior can leave a child unable to recognize deviant behavior when it occurs. She or he may be more easily misled by offenders who misrepresent moral standards. For example, someone may actually teach a child that sexual activity with him is normal.

Social behaviors considered inappropriate for other children, such as excessive displays of affection, are sometimes condoned in the exceptional child—hugging visitors in the classroom, for instance. These may be used as an "excuse" (certainly an invalid one) for sexual exploitation.

The more restricted environments of many children with disabilities—the special schools or classes, special transportation, a lack of independent mobility—do not offer protection from sexual abuse. Most disabled victims—99% in the Seattle study—are abused, not by a stranger lurking in some dark alley, but by someone known to the child and trusted by the family, even a family member himself.

Signs of Sexual Abuse

In the Seattle project, it was estimated that only 20% of all sexual abuse cases involving disabled people are ever reported. Feelings of confusion, shame, guilt, and fear promote silence. Many disabled victims may not know how to seek help; others may not be understood because of poor verbal ability. Still others may not even realize that they are being abused—that they have any right to be in control of their own bodies.

Public misconceptions about the vulnerability of disabled children to sexual abuse also mean that when children do tell someone about an incident of sexual abuse, they frequently are not believed. Myths about children's expressions of sexual fantasies persist, despite the fact that there is no evidence to support the idea that children falsely report sexual abuse. Even if it is not immediately dismissed as a fabrication, a child's version of an incident is still usually considered less credible than that of an adult. A disabled child's report of abuse may be given even less credence, particularly if she or he has been labeled as mentally retarded or emotionally disturbed, or is unable to identify an offender by sight.

While children with disabilities may be physically or psychologically unable to report an experience of sexual abuse, they may display symptoms that should alert parents and teachers. These can include:

- Suddenly avoiding or showing fear of a particular person or place.
- Sleep disturbances (nightmares, insomnia).
- Suddenly behaving like a younger child.
- Appetite disturbances.
- Unusual demands for affection or attention, or unusual withdrawal.
- Any other sudden and unusual changes in behavior or habits.
- Knowledge of sexual behavior far too advanced for her/his age and education.
- Difficulty sitting or unusual walking problems.
- Pain, swelling, or itching in the genital area.
- Pain in urination.
- Vaginal or penile discharge.
- Bruises or bleeding in the genital or anal areas.

Some victims will show no symptoms and may not give any indication of trauma. Some severely disabled children may not even identify the abuse as anything bad, although this does not mean that it should be ignored. Some emotional problems can, of course, be indicative of things that have nothing to do with sexual assault. But all warrant further investigation and perhaps professional assistance.

Responding to Actual or Suspected Abuse

The thought of being confronted with signs indicating a child has been sexually abused is a parent's nightmare, especially if, as in the cases of so many disabled victims, it appears that the abuser is a family member or acquaintance. However painful, action must be taken to help the child and protect her or him from further abuse.

Some things to keep in mind:

1. *Do not prematurely dismiss the possibility of sexual abuse.* It is important to follow up on any warning signs through observation of the child and careful questioning. Keep in mind that sexual offenders—and their victims—come from all walks of life, all racial and ethnic backgrounds, and all types of family situations.

2. *Ask increasingly focused questions.* "You seem angry at Uncle Harry or Mr. Jones, or Daddy." "Did he do something that bothered you?" "Did he touch you?" "Can you point to where he touched you?"

3. *Use language appropriate to the child.* Children may not know the correct terms for body parts or actions. Let them point and use slang terms. Try to be sure you are getting the whole story.

4. *Believe a disclosure.* Children frequently disclose incidents of sexual abuse in unusual times and places, sometimes without seeming the least bit upset. These responses suggest the kind of confusion often felt by abused children, but does not mean that the abuse was any less traumatic.

5. *Remain neutral in your reaction.* The most helpful response to a child victim is one that is supportive and calm, e.g., "I can see why that upset you." Letting them know that other children have been in the same situation can also be helpful. Showing shock or disgust will only increase the child's anxiety.

6. *Affirm and reassure.* Perhaps the most important response is to let the child know that she or he has done the right thing in telling you what has happened and is not to blame for the abuse.

7. *Avoid making judgements.* Avoid "why" questions ("Why did you talk to that stranger?" "Why didn't you tell me before?") No matter how "responsible" you feel the child is, remember that she or he is still the victim, not the offender.

8. *Report the abuse.* You do not need to have every detail or absolute proof of sexual abuse to report it to the police or the appropriate social services agency in your community—a strong suspicion is enough. After a report is made, the child will be questioned in detail—often more than once—by police and social workers. Make sure the child understands that it is all right to talk to these people. Also be sure that these interviewers are aware of the child's communicative ability, level of understanding, or other special needs.

Myths about children's expressions of sexual fantasies persist despite the fact that there is no evidence to support the idea that children falsely report sexual abuse.

Many communities now have rape crisis centers, rape hotlines, or community mental health facilities. Trained counselors and volunteers are often available at these agencies to answer questions about sexual abuse and provide support for the victim and the family.

Preventing Sexual Abuse

It may seem almost impossible to try to lessen the vulnerability of exceptional children to sexual abuse without making them unnecessarily fearful of all adults or distrustful of all affection.

Often adults give warnings with little discussion and few details. For example, it is common to warn children not to take rides or candy from strangers—and then just hope for the best. Sometimes this is done without even explaining what a "stranger" is. Many children become either overly anxious or not anxious enough, depending on their interpretation of the message. Warnings rarely include information about what a child can *do* if she or he is bothered by someone, especially if that someone is the babysitter, Uncle Harry, or even Daddy.

Fortunately, there are some specific skills and concepts that most exceptional children (and non-exceptional children) can learn. These skills will better prepare them to recognize and avoid potential abuse and to increase the likelihood that they will seek immediate help if actual abuse should occur. The basic concepts include:

1. *An understanding that there are different kinds of touch.* All children need to know that touch can be good or comfortable, and also confusing, uncomfortable or hurtful. They need to be aware of the body parts that are more "private" than others and the limited circumstances (e.g. health or hygiene) under which private parts should be touched by older persons. They also need to differentiate between strangers, acquaintances, friends, and relatives, and the kinds of touching behavior appropriate for each.

Information about touch can be conveyed informally in a variety of ways. Children should be encouraged to share their feelings about the kinds of touching that they like and the kinds of touching that make them feel uncomfortable or bad. Their feelings about touching behavior like tickling, wrestling, or even the way they are carried or assisted with physical needs should be respected.

Explaining that private parts are those covered by bathing trunks for boys and two piece bathing suits for girls can illustrate the concept for children with limited understanding. Playing with dolls and puppets is another way to introduce the idea that every person has private parts that should only be touched in special circumstances.

Pictures in magazines and photo albums can be used to help children classify people into the categories of strangers, acquaintances, friends, and relatives. It is particularly important to make sure that children can understand the differences between friends and acquaintances.

Friends are people a child plays with and are known and trusted by the family. Acquaintances are people whose names and faces are known to the child. They range from people who say "hello"

> *Once children understand how they feel about bad or uncomfortable touch, they need to know that they have the right to try and stop it.*

like store clerks to people who may spend time with the child regularly like bus drivers but that parents do not know well enough to trust for unsupervised activity.

2. *Understanding and using the right to say "no."* Once children understand how they feel about bad or uncomfortable touch, they need to know that they have the right to try and stop it. This is a crucial concept in sexual abuse prevention, and one that is very important for children with disabilities.

It is often tempting to try and anticipate all of the needs of disabled children and to take care of them before a request is made. Over time, this encourages children with disabilities to feel little control or responsibility for their bodies and lives, and increases their feelings of dependency on others. It is helpful for exceptional children to use whatever abilities they may have to express their wants and preferences, and to experience as much control over their bodies as they possibly can.

Even daily routines like toileting or dressing can be learning experiences. Whenever possible, parents and teachers can let children do as much as they are able to in requesting help, explaining or showing what they need done, and expressing their feelings as to how they want to be touched or assisted.

When children feel in control of what happens to them, it becomes easier for them to learn assertive ways to respond to unwanted touch. These responses can be as simple as learning to say a strong "No!" or "Stop that!" whenever they feel bothered or threatened. Non-verbal children can also learn assertive responses—a strong shake of the head, turning away, frowning, waving a hand from side to side, anything they can do which will let potential offenders know that they will not find a passive or compliant victim.

3. *Recognizing and avoiding dangerous situations.* Exceptional children who have independent mobility need to have enough information to recognize places and situations that hold risks for abuse and assault. In addition, they may need help learning how to generalize to new situations when they occur. For example, knowing that they should

not accept a ride from a stranger may not keep them from getting into a car with someone who has been nice to them at the corner store. Or knowing that they should not walk through the alley behind the grocery store may not keep them from walking alone across a dark playground.

Again, many opportunities can be found to introduce discussion and practice. Passing the playground can be a prompt for discussing the reasons why it would not be a safe place to be after dark ("No one could see you if you needed help.") Children can be encouraged to think of their own reasons why it would be unsafe, and try to give examples of other unsafe places.

"What if" questions and role plays allow children to act out and practice their responses to unwanted approaches and other potentially dangerous situations:

What if someone you just met at the store asked to take you home in his car?

What would you say if someone asked you to come into the house when you were alone?

What if someone put a hand on your knee and you did not like it?

Situations like these can be discussed and acted out by family members, with children given opportunities to practice appropriate responses. As with all self-protection skills, repetition reinforces learning.

4. *Understanding the need to report abuse.* Children need to know that they must tell a trusted adult immediately about any unwanted touching or attention from anyone. They are more likely to do this when they have previously experienced support for expressing their feelings about touch (even if that support means denying Grandma a perfectly innocent peck on the cheek because a child said "no" or "I don't want to.")

Encouraging Children to Tell

Role playing situations should combine practice of the assertive "no!" with simulated reporting of the incident to an adult. Children also need to be prepared for the possibility that they might not be believed initially when they report something. It is helpful to talk about all the adults—not just parents, but teachers, counselors, relatives, clergy, etc.—to whom the child might turn.

Discussion and role plays also need to deal with the possibility that the child may be threatened or bribed by an offender to keep silent ("I'll hurt you if you tell." or "I'll be your boyfriend if you keep this a secret.") All children need frequent reassurance that they will be protected and supported whenever they report abusive behavior.

Education for Prevention

Programs about sexual abuse are actually strengthened when they are combined with "positive" sex education. When children learn about uncomfortable or bad touch, they also need to know that most touch is good touch, as long as it is wanted and comes at an appropriate time and place. Knowing about the parts of their bodies and those of the opposite sex will facilitate their ability to discriminate the different kinds of touch—and will give them the vocabulary to report abuse should it ever occur.

Lack of information or misinformation about sexual feelings can cause some young people to be overly shy, compliant, affectionate, or aggressive—all behaviors which might encourage sexual exploitation. A complete sex education and abuse prevention program needs to stress the teaching of appropriate behavior and social skills, not just body parts and functions.

The biggest mistake is not to teach anything at all. The sexual abuse of children is never an easy subject for parents to talk about. Yet parents of exceptional children need to talk about it—to each other, to the teachers and administrators of their schools, and especially to their children.

Recognizing the vulnerability of exceptional children is a difficult but necessary first step. Teaching and reinforcing prevention skills both at home and in school are next. With these skills, children with disabilities will be better prepared to recognize the first indications of sexual abuse, to respond assertively, and to seek help immediately. ■

Janice Daar Watson was formerly the special education department chairperson and resource specialist for the Bassett Unified School District. Since 1981, she has been teaching sexual abuse prevention skills to special education students. She currently does workshops and seminars on sexual abuse prevention for parents, teachers, and administrators.

CHAPTER 51

When It's Time to Let Go

by Joan K. Blaska

Whether we want to face it or not, there comes a time when we must let go of our disabled child. We watch our other children grow, develop, and finally leave the nest. Likewise, we must try to be prepared to have our special needs child leave also.

The difficulty for us in this situation is that some of our disabled children are never fully ready or able to take care of themselves. However, this does not mean that they are not ready to leave home.

We must ask ourselves whether home is always the best place for our children to grow and develop. Our son, David, who is mentally retarded, was fifteen years old when we were faced with this question. I had planned on having him live at home until he was about twenty-one. In that way, he could move to a group home at about the same age that most children leave home. I believed that I could care for him and love him as no one else could, because I am his mother!

> We recognized that the only educational program available to our son was not meeting his needs.

Changes
David began having a difficult time controlling his behavior after he transferred to middle school. This was partly due to a staff that was reluctant to accept children with special needs, and also due to his hyperactive behavior.

My husband and I decided it was time to take a careful look at what was happening at school and at home. David had done quite well in elementary school, although mainstreaming was always difficult because of his high activity level. At middle school, David's behavioral problems became more apparent. Passing in the halls, eating in the lunchroom, and riding the bus provided so much stimulation that David was unable to control his impulsive behavior. As a result, he was unable to be in the mainstream, and spent many hours alone in the classroom with an aide. It was then that we available to our son was not meeting his needs.

David also became more disruptive at home, often teasing and fighting with his younger brother. There was more defiant behavior toward daily routine and following directions. For example, he decided he no longer liked to shower and shampoo his hair. We had to argue with David in order to get this task accomplished. And, he began swearing to let us know how he felt.

Lack of Friends and Activities
Because we felt that he needed someone to set limits and provide some structure to help him control his behavior, David was not allowed to go anywhere outside of the neighborhood without adult supervision. As a result, David began to realize that he was being treated differently. One day he asked why he could not play on the basketball team with his younger brother. We tried to explain how playing the game with these boys would be too hard for him. As he became older, it was more difficult for him to understand why he was not included in many activities.

David had few of his own friends. He usually played with his younger brother and his friends. As we looked at David's life, my husband and I questioned how a child could live happily without friends. We recognized that we could do many things for David as his parents, but we could not be his friends. We were also worried about the impact of his continual disruptions on our other two sons.

A Difficult Decision
My husband and I had several long discussions. Although we knew that we were meeting David's physical needs, we had to admit that someone else could do as good a job. Educationally, our school district did not have an effective program for him, and socially, David was dependent on his brothers.

It became apparent to us that we could no longer meet David's needs at home. If we were going to provide the best possible environment for our son where he could develop to his maximum capacity, it was time for him to leave home.

Although intellectually the decision was made,

the thought of packing his things and knowing he would never live with us again was almost more than I could endure. During the two weeks following our decision, I cried every time I thought of David leaving. Since David did not yet know of our plans and would not understand my tears, I would seek refuge in the locked bathroom. I tried to be strong.

Once our decision was made, the long search for an appropriate group home began. We decided to wait before telling David of our plans until they were more specific. After two months of phone calls, meetings, and visits, that time arrived.

Breaking the News

Sitting with David on his bed, I began to explain about the group home. My heart was racing, and beating so loudly that I could almost hear it. I had to take deep breaths to keep my voice steady. "David," I said, "You'll live at the group home and go to a new school that has special classes that will help you learn." I compared it to his cousins living away from home and going to college. He seemed to understand. I felt it was extremely important that David know he was still loved and wanted by us.

"At the group home, you'll live with other kids your age," I continued. "With these friends, you will have a lot of fun things to do. You'll go bowling, swimming, to the movies, and do many things that you are unable to do here. And you'll come home very often to be with us, every two to three weeks."

David looked at me sadly, and sounded as though he might cry. "I don't want to go," he said, "I want to be home with you." Although my heart was breaking, I tried to stay calm as I explained again how much fun it would be to live with his new friends, and reassured David that he would still come home to us very often.

Afterwards, I sat with my arms around my special son, wanting to tell him how sorry I was that it had to be this way. I knew that I could not though—that it would only confuse him and make it more difficult for both of us.

I knew that if this was upsetting for me, it must also be very difficult for David, even if he could not openly express his feelings. As difficult as this was, I knew it was the right choice.

David looked up at me with sad eyes. I gave him a kiss, and told him again how much I loved him. After a few more minutes, he wanted to go outside and play, almost like any other day.

When I explained the situation to his brothers, my eyes again flooded with tears. They seemed to understand why this was the best choice for their brother. The two of them had lived with David's disruptive behavior for years, and knew how hectic it often was at our house. At the same time, they knew of his difficulties at school, and how he was always looking for friends. They were the ones that came to his rescue when neighborhood kids would tease.

The visits and interviews continued, but now David was with my husband and me. When a specific group home became a possible choice, the three of us would visit. In all, David visited three group homes, and stayed overnight on two different occasions. Nine months after this process began, David moved into a group home with seven other mentally retarded adolescents, about thirty-five miles from our home.

The Right Decision

After five months, David adjusted to living with his new friends. Although he loves coming home and wants his calendar marked so he is ready for each visit, he willingly returns to the group home. Furthermore, he is kept busy with an excellent school program and many exciting activities in the evenings. Our youngest son says he is jealous of David because he gets to see so many movies.

David also goes bowling every week. He called us after one of his outings sounding very excited. "You'll never guess what I got," he exclaimed! "It's like that thing at home on the bookcase." Questioning him further, I suddenly realized it was a trophy he was talking about. "Yah, that's it!" he shouted. "I got a trophy because I bowled so good!" The happiness and excitement in his voice was another warm reassurance that we had made the right choice in letting go. ■

Joan K. Blaska lives in Minnesota with her husband, John. They have three children, Steven, David, and Michael. Ms. Blaska is a council member and former chairperson of the St. Francis Council for Special Needs Kids—a local group responsible for organizing and funding Special Olympic activities, as well as other social activities for special needs children in the community.

CHAPTER 52

A Teenager Comes Home
A Dilemma for the Family

John Harris was about to enter the local high school after many years at a residential school for physically disabled children. Because of their own doubts, his parents wanted a professional to represent them at the school's planning meeting.

In many ways, we were told what a miracle it was that he survived.

"**We would like you to represent** us at the meeting when our son, John, is discussed." Mrs. Harris, a slender, dark haired woman in her late forties spoke quickly. "John is very physically handicapped. He has been living at the state school for handicapped children for the last six years. He's fourteen, and next year he will be entering high school.

"Last fall, Dr. Kollman, a new pediatrician, was put in charge of the medical care at the school. Since Christmas, he has been urging Tom and I to transfer John to our local public high school. When he first brought up the idea, we thought he was a little crazy.

"Dr. Kollman has spent a lot of time talking to us about this, trying to convince us. He's committed to having every child educated while they live at home and go to their local schools. He's quite a crusader, but we don't want our son merely to be a soldier in his crusade. It may be good for the doctor's career but it may be terrible for John, and for us too.

"When John came home for Christmas, we began to take a new look at him. He spends most of the year at school, and I hate to say it, but it's been a big relief for the family. We have three older children, and only one, Jimmy, who's a senior in high school, still lives at home. He'll be going to college starting this fall.

"But when John was born, we had an active household to manage. I had three other children who ranged in ages from three to ten. Not only was there Jimmy, but an older sister, Joan, and a brother, Michael. As you can imagine, we were all in a state of shock after John's birth.

"It seems so long ago. With John away at school so much of the time, I find myself wondering sometimes if it ever really happened. At other times, it seems like just yesterday that he was born.

"When I got back to my own room at the hospital after John's birth, my husband came in with our pediatrician and obstetrician. I knew something terrible had happened. I could see it on their faces. It had been a long, hard delivery, even though all my other deliveries had been easy. They couldn't even begin to describe what I was going to see when I could get to see my baby. He was in an intensive care nursery because they weren't sure that he was going to live.

"He came home about a month after I did. It was our first encounter with what seems to me like science fiction. When I would look at John through the window in the nursery, he would be hooked up with gadgets and monitoring devices that I had never seen or heard of before.

"In many ways, we were told what a miracle it was that he survived. John was fortunate enough to be born in a hospital with an intensive care service for newborns. If he had been born someplace else, he might not have lived.

"I hate to say it, but all the time that John was in the nursery, we weren't sure what we wanted. I

> *The only thing I regret is that I wish we talked more sometimes about how we all felt.*

certainly wasn't. We talked about whether we would all be better off if he died. But when he came home, he became more real to us. We could hold him; he was our child. As difficult as it was, we wanted the best for him.

"He is what people call a 'multiply handicapped' child. John is crippled, so he couldn't walk or move very much as a baby. He did make a lot of noise, and you could almost see the spirit in him fighting to do something. We all spent a lot of time being upset.

"We were lucky to have Dr. Gale as our pediatrician. Everybody else seemed to be afraid of us. Whenever we would approach somebody, you could almost see them shrinking. But, Dr. Gale spent a lot of time with me when I was in the hospital, and she has been available whenever I've called. I think in the first six months that John was home, I probably drove the poor woman out of her mind. She always had time to listen to me and to make me feel that somehow it was all worthwhile.

"The next years were spent trying to make some kind of judgement as to how much John would grow and be able to learn; what physical therapy activities would be helpful; and what kinds of programs would be best for him. We were always picking and choosing. If I heard of anything going on within a fifty mile area—once I even went ninety miles—of some parent doing something or some program that might be good for John, I would drive out and look.

"It was a strange period for the family. In a lot of ways, I think I did the poorest for my husband and my other children. At the same time, I feel that it was the best time for us. The only thing I regret is that I wish we talked more sometimes about how we all felt. Everybody pitched in. We did the best we could and we did o.k.

"The kids were growing, and I really didn't have to ask them to take care of themselves. Everybody accepted the fact that my time was going to be taken up with John. Because of their attitudes and help, I was able to take him pretty much everywhere I went.

"Tom and I went to the children's athletic events, school plays, and graduations while John was with us. Sometimes, I was uncomfortable and I felt a lot of people didn't want to see us there, but the kids never said a word. I take that back—they said without speaking that it was all right. Maybe my other children felt a little ashamed or embarrassed about their brother, but they always encouraged Tom and me to bring him with us. Sure it was hard, but they love him.

"The doctors debated for a number of years as to how damaged John was. I began to think that he was pretty bright. He was alert. He couldn't talk so that I could understand him, but he seemed to know what I was doing and what I wanted. When he was about three, they had one of these programs they called 'early stimulation' as if our family wasn't stimulating enough.

"They brought in some people with real ability. They had a speech teacher who struggled to try and help John speak more clearly. After a while, I realized I could understand John better than she could. So the three of us worked together.

"They began a bunch of programs to try and strengthen whatever physical barriers he had. One of John's hands is pretty free but the other one is harder for him to control.

"Then we got a hold of a special wheelchair. It was one that fitted him well, and provided the support he needed. It was pretty portable, too. The other ones that seemed to be any good weighed a ton. John had an easier time with this chair. He was able to sit up better, and seemed to notice more things as a result.

"When he was about six, they told us about the school run by the state. The new law was coming in, but everyone said that a child as handicapped as John could never be in the mainstream. I had already heard about the school, and my husband and I knew that this was going to be best for John. In the past, we never had enough energy to bring ourselves to go through the steps of applying, but somehow we managed to complete all the forms and go through the interviewing process. I didn't like talking to people who wanted me to explain myself. To tell you the truth, I'm not sure how much better I feel here and now.

"With the school came a new freedom for our family. It was sort of funny. It was as if everyone had put off being cranky until John left. I began to have more disagreements with everybody. Some of it was because the kids were teenagers and were about to say, 'No,' anyhow. But for a while there, little things seemed to set everyone snapping at one another. There was a period of time when I didn't know what I was going to do. Almost as rapidly as the tension started, it seemed to subside.

"We all were trying to figure out what we were going to do with the time we had. My husband went back to the Rotary group that he had abandoned when John was born. At first, I resented him going, and he felt a little guilty, too. Finally, we both realized that there were a number of things we hadn't done and friends that we had seen very little of since John was born.

"The last six years I have gone back to work full time. I'm a secretary at the local high school. I love it. I enjoy being around the kids and the activities and the enthusiasm there.

"From my vantage point, John has done well at school. He's benefited from all the scientific advances. He's really quite a bright, independent young man at this point. He's got a communication device so that when he has to turn in papers or talk to people who don't know him very well—particularly in the classroom—he is able to communicate what is in his head and what he knows. Actually, his grades have been very good. Beyond the grades, the scores he's taken on tests that other kids take around the country have also been above average. I think they're going to continue to improve.

"As Tom and I began to think about it, we weighed the pros and cons of having him come back to the local school. The pros can be listed easily, and the cons seem overwhelming. One day I'll support the idea and my husband will object, and the next day it will be my husband who thinks it's a great idea and I'll object.

"We went to our pediatrician for advise, and she said that it wasn't her field. She suggested we talk to you—that you could figure out what John could do in school. She thought that until we could get our act together and resolve how we feel about John coming home, we wouldn't be the most help to our son. That's why we've come."

I guess I'm the accountant in the family." Mr. Harris laughed as he spoke. "The pros about John transferring schools seems to be mostly theory, but at the same time, it seems right. Yet, I can't quite say why and neither can Jean.

"This new doctor could whistle the birds out of the trees. He keeps telling us that some day John is going to have to live out in the world and the sooner he gets to learn how other people are going to react to him, the better off he will be. And sometimes that sounds right.

"Someday the normal kids leave the house, and you can't really protect them from the difficult things, but John has never been normal. If kids have had a good grounding, they may still have trouble, but sooner or later, it all works out.

"As our two oldest kids have gone to college and out on their own, Jean and I worry. We can think of each kid and say, 'Well, this is what their strengths and weaknesses are and this is what they're going to have to deal with,' and that's the way it's going to go." Of course, they had some experience living away from home at college.

"The interesting thing is that you're always right and you're always wrong. It always seems such a surprise when they manage well. They're a lot better organized than I was when I got my first apartment. You wonder where they learned it.

"I began to realize that my wife and I really don't know John. Well, I think my wife does, but I don't. I didn't spend much time with him when he was a little kid. I don't know if I've ever come to peace with why Johnny is the way he is. It's funny. from the time we began to think about him coming to live with us, I started to have nightmares. I had terrible thoughts that I haven't been able to talk to Jean about. I'll be in the midst of a meeting and my mind will turn to John and I'll wonder why God did this to us or to him.

"My image of John is still—I can't describe it—but it's sort of like a baby who is never going to grow up. I feel like that idea is still in my head and is never going to die. I read the reports, and I see him when he comes home, but I can't seem to match the report with my son. I see the gadgets that he has and I see the gadgets that they're fooling around with in the school and it seems like a Star Wars movie to me. These devices do terrific things.

"It's amazing how smart John is—I see the papers that he gets done on that portable computer he has on his wheelchair. I can hardly believe it.

"What are we going to do if he comes home? Who will take care of him? I don't even know how much care he really requires. He's always a guest when he comes home. How do you go from treating someone like a guest to treating them like your own kid? He's done so well at school. Why should he have to leave it?

"My wife talks about how great the public high school is, but she's always talking about the kids who get scapegoated or teased. I remember that from my childhood—we said terrible things about kids like John.

"Sometimes, when he comes home it bothers me for the first few minutes. I can imagine how it might be for a group that didn't love him. People aren't always nice when they're upset. It's not that kind of a world.

"Then I wonder what kind of a man I am. I want to do what's best for my son, but how do we proceed? How do we know what to do? We know the school will be trouble, but unless we get our act together, how are we going to be able to help?"

"My mother told me you would be coming to talk to me." John sat slumped backwards in his wheelchair. He had a microphone attached but it was often difficult to understand what he was saying.

"I asked Mrs. Green to stay with us because I know when I get excited, it's hard to understand me. She knows me so she can help me calm down. Sometimes I use my special typewriter to tell people what I want to say.

"I used to dream of going to school from my

house, but I never thought it was possible. I've been here a long time. I've got a lot of friends here, and I've learned here. I like the teachers.

"I stopped dreaming that it was going to be possible a long time ago. Dr. Kollman came in the fall and he's been talking to me about going to live at home.

It's very scary. When I go home now, if my brothers and sister aren't around, it's very lonely. I don't have any friends and the kids in the neighborhood know who I am. Except for the kids next door, nobody ever comes over to say hello. I know I'd be all by myself a lot of the time.

"People stare at me when my mother takes me shopping. The kids do too. At school, I talk to my friends about what we should do. Sometimes I want to do something nasty, but what good would it do? Besides, it would probably embarrass my parents.

"Dr. Kollman tells me that I shouldn't want to spend my whole life shut away from the world—that sooner or later I'm going to have to get used to other people. He thinks I'm smart enough to do well in regular school. My teachers think so too. I get all A's here. Sometimes I wonder if they would be A's outside.

"I can't figure out whether my mother and father really want me home either. I watched them when Dr. Kollman talked to them. At first I thought they were irritated. I watched their faces and they didn't look happy. In fact, they looked very worried. My mother said to me that she wants the best for me. If Dr. Kollman thinks it's the best, maybe they will take the chance.

"Last week my mother called up and said that she had talked to you about helping figure out a school plan and how to deal with making sure I got into the right classes and everything. You had told her that maybe we ought to have my opinion, too.

"I don't know what my opinion is. Some days I'm very excited. It's the greatest thing in the world to think of going to the high school. Other days, I get very scared. All I know about high school is what I've seen on television. I don't expect to be invited to the parties. I'm like the kids they play tricks on. My brothers and sister had a good time in high school. They say that school is rated very good, and helps you get into good colleges. I think I can do the school work, but I don't know what I would do without my friends who are here."

The Harrises came to discuss the educational future of their physically disabled son, John. His entire academic career had been at a residential facility for physically disabled children. As he was finishing the eighth grade, the new medical director at the school was strongly urging the family to have John in the local, public high school, and live at home.

Mrs. Harris wanted a professional person at the meetings where John's academic program would be discussed and finalized. In her position as a secretary at the public high school, she believed that a number of children were kept in special classes within the school because of "convenience" rather than educational necessity. She also believed that her position in the school made it awkward for her to take an active part in a formal school meeting.

At the same time, both she and Mr. Harris were aware of their own doubts about having John come back to live at home with the family. Each was concerned about the changes that would be necessitated in family life. Mrs. Harris found that her life was fuller in terms of friendships, activities, and her relationship with her husband and other children since John left home.

Mr. Harris discussed how little he had been involved in planning John's life. At the time that John was born, Mrs. Harris played the major role of working with the professionals involved with John. Mr. Harris felt like he had given up any belief that John could grow up normally in any way. Although he was aware that John had been able to learn in school and that his communication skills had improved considerably, he had not thought about what John could potentially achieve either academically or socially.

Although school attitudes and climates have changed over the past decade, educators often have difficulty communicating with parents in the role of potential decision makers. They find it easier to discuss matters with other professionals. Professionals often find it difficult to recognize when their communication to parents contains jargon that they use with each other, and can obscure their message. The person employed by the parents can help "translate" these messages whenever necessary.

After the school planning session, this professional can remain a positive link between school and parents by remaining available anytime there seem to be misunderstandings that could interfere with the working relationship between the parents and the school.

All parents adjust to the continuing growth and independence of their children. When a child is placed at an early age, the parents do not have the daily continuous experience that helps change their image of the young child who is helpless and dependent.

In the case of John Harris, the various scientific breakthroughs in communication devices have made it possible for him to achieve at a much higher level than anyone ever considered. The Harrises were faced with the anxiety and problems that come when new hope is arroused. Now that they understood that John had some potential, no one could be certain how much further development was possible. Even if he succeeded in high school, could John profit from more education? Would they then have to stop hoping again?

The full time return of a youngster to a family can be a very difficult process for everyone involved. Every family has its own style of dealing with the everyday problems of living together and of deciding how to take care of everyday household tasks.

When a youngster comes home after living at college, the family can assume that this is a transition to independent living, and the resulting problems they have living at home often prove why independence from one another is necessary. When an individual with a disability returns home, the family's concern about never ending dependence can be very upsetting. Becaue it is upsetting, it is not fully discussed and therefore the problems may never be resolved.

After my meeting with John to discuss his thoughts about returning home, the Harrises realized he was capable of being included in family discussions. They were surprised at his awareness of their concerns and his ability to articulate his own.

The Harrises were not sure how they would be able to help John with self-care over an extended period of time. They were encouraged to hear that John had discussed these issues with the guidance counselor at his school. John had expectations of independence—staying out late, going places on his own—that was an interesting contrast to his parent's belief that they would have to do everything for him.

Mr. and Mrs. Harris and John went to the high school to explore the problems of physical barriers, and to meet the guidance counselor who would be responsible for coordinating John's program. Again, they were surprised and pleased both by John's ability to identify problems and his ideas for solving them.

The school personnel at the planning meeting were still unsure about integrating John into classes. After meeting him, they were optimistic about what they would and could do.

I suggested that John and his parents meet with me regularly during the school year to have a forum for discussing and solving mutual problems. I also planned to meet with the school personnel at the end of each planning meeting so that John's progress could be actively monitored. ∎

—M.J.S.

CHAPTER 53

Residential Placement— A Problem for Parents

by Paula Haramis

I should have felt relief, but instead there was just that awful, gut pain—the guilty feelings. I had "abandoned" my disabled child.

Not being able to care for a child is one of the most difficult problems any parent must face.

Ms. Haramis describes the problems and doubts she experienced when sending her brain injured child to a residential treatment facility.

I find it almost unbearable at times to enter my daughter's room. As I stand there, her toys and stuffed animals scrutinize me with somber faces as they wait for their mistress and friend to return. They long to be tossed around the house again. I almost yearn for the mess she could make so easily. The room now seems too straight and orderly for that free-spirited child of mine.

I have memories of tearful nights in that empty bed. I tortured myself with the absence of the one thing in life that meant more to me than anything else in the world—my child. There were the bittersweet phone calls to hear her faint, half words to me. Her group home "parent" assured me that Tara was doing fine. She missed her mommy, but she was doing fine.

Tara's Absence

I remember the brief enjoyment of my first found freedom Tara's absence allowed me. There were no hourly phone calls home to a frantic babysitter on my rare evenings out; no more bus to wait for or run home to catch; no more daily discussions with agitated therapists, teachers and day care providers. I should have felt relief, but instead there was that awful pain—the guilty feelings. I had "abandoned" my disabled child.

Had I given up, failed at the awesome responsibility of motherhood? My friends could do it—raise their children at home—but they were normal. *Normal*. What a funny word that becomes in the world of people with disabilities. A world where normal means the accepted ways of behaving and getting social approval. Normal, as if God had put qualifications on a big blackboard in heaven.

My Daughter's Empty Room

"You're so strong, Paula," words that seem comic from my well-meaning friends. They mean what they say, and it might appear so to them, but you, this empty room, know better. You have seen the magnitude of my fears and my tears. You have heard my angry accusations to God, the bitter words projected from my mouth. Yes, lonely, empty, still room, you know the truth.

You also can boast of the joy and the excitement when a new word was spoken from her small, all but silent mouth. You saw the tears of joy that ran down my cheeks when Tara put together a puzzle properly, or just when she got out of this bed on her own and found mine one morning without panic and confusion.

You have heard the soulful begging I did to my autistic-like child when I tried to get her to sleep—the well meant reasoning that fell on those seemingly deaf ears. The anger I felt well up when I came close to losing my temper. The frustration of the nights of staying up with high brain fevers, storms, or incorrectly measured medicine.

Just simple excitement could keep her up all night moaning and humming that monotone hum that could drive even a saint to her limits. Oh bed, do you forgive me as I stare at you and thrash through my mind at our memories? You, room, you have been through it all. What do you think of me? Saint or sinner? What will it be, strong or weak, or just a lonely, confused mother? This is no easy job, and the answers are not easy ones either.

Single Parents

Divorce runs high among parents of special children. It happened to me too. Although I cannot blame my ex-husband for leaving, there are many times when I wish I did not have to face the pain alone. The loss alone. The trials and tribulations and even the joys alone. How nice it would be to share those newly spoken words with another caring person, other than the therapists and psychologists I report to regularly. The joy and sense of accomplishment is genuinely shared by them, but it is not the same as sharing with someone close to you.

It has been hard to face the good as well as the bad alone. Sharing the accomplishments sometimes takes as much explaining as the difficult times, maybe even more. "Well, yes, a child of five should be potty trained, but Tara is brain injured. A dry day is a big achievement for my little girl. I'm sure your daughter has been toilet trained for years, or riding a bike, or walking, or rolling over, or... listen, this is a big deal for my kid, and I'm proud."

My Friends

There are some who have tried very hard to understand. These people are my support, my true friends. These are the ones who are still around, the ones who survived my hysterical phone calls in the middle of the night. Ones who I made late for work as I kept them on the phone across the country because I was falling apart and they dared not hang up until I could pull myself together again.

There is even one friend who survived a draining, day long brain study in a hospital. There are a special two who flew across the country to a hospital where Tara and I were stranded long past our expected stay. Another friend came many times to my rescue when I was exhausted and needed a brief respite. Yes, I am one of the lucky parents of a disabled child who has supportive friends.

I sometimes forget the friends who slipped away while I was busy reading up on my child's condition. Maybe they thought I had flipped. After all, no one in their right mind would drop everything to fly miles away to see a specialist who had an idea or just some interest in Tara. I cannot blame them. I must have looked as crazy to them as I do to this empty bed and room that I am talking to.

Closing Thoughts

The world of parents of children with disabilities is filled with sharp ups and downs. Many of them walk around proud, looking like the epitomy of strength. There are many who do not make it, or who are desperately trying to overcome that nagging feeling of guilt. There are parents who torment themselves unnecssarily.

Others are the wounded parents of children who do not make it or never improve. That is a struggle that is hard to bear. The sense of failure is overwhelming. How many of us are like the walking wounded who pace the floor through sleepless nights, and lean on empty walls, in empty rooms, and talk to empty beds, just like me?

This room will come alive again some day, and so will I. ■

How many of us are like the walking wounded?

TECHNOLOGY

It has only been in the past decade that contempory technology has been applied to the problems encountered by individuals with disabilities. This section first presents the use of computers for general teaching and learning. Then the utilization of computer technology for devices that enable children to communicate both visually (through typed messages) and orally (through sound) is presented.

CHAPTER 54

FAMILY LIFE

"Can You Imagine Feeling That Way About Your Own Helpless Kid?"
Mixed Feelings About New Opportunities

The Fines had come for counseling. Mr. Fine had stopped talking after he and his wife had seen a new communication device for their nine year old, brain damaged son, Jimmy.

"I don't know how well you remember us." Mrs. Fine, a tall, slender woman in her early thirties with prematurely grey hair, spoke quietly.

"We came to see you four years ago when we were trying to decide what to do about our nine year old son, Jimmy. He was five then and he couldn't do very much at all. My husband, Hal, and I disagreed about whether to find a place to send him or to try to keep him at home in our own community.

"Jimmy is our second child. He has an older sister, Jane, who is now fifteen, and a younger sister, Connie, who is three and a half and has just started nursery school.

"Jimmy was born with brain damage as near as we can figure out. He was an awfully quiet baby and our pediatrician and obstetrician were worried about him from the day he was born. They didn't tell us exactly what they thought was wrong, but they told us that Jimmy would be slow in growing up.

"My husband and I were overwhelmed. We really were in a kind of a fog for at least the first year of Jimmy's life. He was such a quiet baby and sort of easy to take care of, but he did everything slowly. He ate slowly; he moved slowly, and he was slow to develop in every way you could think of.

"Sometimes I wondered whether he was deaf or dumb or worse. We would go back to the pediatrician who would keep telling us that it was too early to know and that when various tests were appropriate, he would get them done for us.

"Although Jimmy walked late, he was able to do it. He's still very awkward, though. I never thought that the toilet training would ever be accomplished but he learned how to take care of himself, and to wash and feed himself.

"At three, he still wasn't talking. We became more and more desperate—me in my way and my husband in his. At that time, Hal began to argue that Jimmy so dominated our family's time and energy that we had little time for our own interests. He thought that we ought to find some place that could take care of him.

"He also felt that we were both spoiling him, and thought that someone who could take a firmer hand might be able to do more. We had Jimmy in a day school program for mentally retarded kids. My husband and I found that as depressing as anything else. The children were severely retarded and some of them were much older than Jimmy. My husband kept saying, 'Look at how little these kids can do. What can we really expect from Jimmy unless we get him into a program that can do something?'

"Hal kept pressuring so much that our pediatrician suggested that we talk to you. We came twice and never returned, and never even called. That is why we weren't sure whether we should or could come back to you.

"I remember you pointing out how depressed we both seemed because of this situation with Jimmy. You particularly talked to me about the fact that I had all kinds of questions about what had gone wrong in the pregnancy and who was to blame and I seemed to be so guilty and fearful. I had wanted to go back to the obstetrician and ask him what had happened but I never could. You suggested that I might profit from getting some attention and help for myself. That was very helpful to hear.

"When we left the meetings, Hal began to feel better and felt that you had given us some perspective about what we might expect. We decided it would be better to wait and find a place for Jimmy when he was older, because everybody, including his sister, would feel better if we gave it our best try.

"Jimmy has been in the public schools since. There has been a great change over the past four years, a lot more activities for the kids. It seems to me the teachers and therapists have learned a lot. Jimmy certainly has profited from being home. I think we have, too.

"I found myself a therapist and spent a couple of years struggling with my own problems. It was very good for me. Now I can separate out which problems really belonged to me and which ones had to do with the entire family.

"Things improved so much that we had another child. Connie started nursery school in the fall and I'm thinking about either going back to business school part-time or finding some kind of employment. My husband says that we really don't need the money and that there is so much responsibility with the children at home that I shouldn't do it. I think I need to do it for my sanity.

Jimmy's speech is still unintelligible. Hal has become obsessed with this problem. It is almost as if he believes that our mission as parents would be accomplished if Jimmy could really learn to speak. He seems to think that our ultimate goal would be to have Jimmy improve his ability to communicate with other people.

"Something very important happened a month ago. We were visiting some friends who told us about these new communication devices that are run by computers. I don't know how they work, but they work.

"We went to see one at the school for severely handicapped children in our community. To me, they seemed like a miracle. Many of these kids are a lot worse off than Jimmy, and by pushing things with pictures or symbols, the machine somehow prints the message or activates something that speaks. The voice may be a monotone, but the teachers say it seems to improve the way the youngsters are able to make their needs known or respond in class.

"I thought my husband would be excited since his major wish might be taken care of—that Jimmy speak. But we have hardly talked about it since we came back from the school, and it's almost like the way we were when we came four years ago.

"I was so upset, I went back to see my own therapist. He didn't think it was a good idea to see the two of us because he already had a long, working relationship with me. He thought Hal might feel awkward meeting with him. Instead, Hal and I agreed that you might be more neutral.

"We only saw you twice, but I thought we got a lot out of it."

Mr. Fine, a tall, heavy set man sat slouched forward in his chair.

"You were very direct about what you thought, and it gave us a pretty clear picture of what the story was. You also seemed so direct that I was afraid that you would just tell us what to do. I guess I'm the kind of person that always gets uptight when I think people are going to tell me what to do without giving me a chance to think it over.

"That's sort of how I felt after we saw those communication devices at that school. Julie came out very excited and said that we would get one and that this is what we'll do. All of a sudden, I felt I better call a halt, just to see what was going on.

"I spend most of my time trying to think problems through by myself. Since I don't talk about my ideas, other people can't see that I'm upset or concerned.

"This is not the best way of dealing with things because it leads to greater and greater misunderstandings. I think Julie thinks I'm mad at her. Actually, most of the time I'm upset about myself and how and what I think.

"First I thought that we had gotten used to Jimmy as he is. He gets along reasonably well with other kids, and at home. Somehow, all of a sudden, I thought about what might have been if he had been all right. Suppose he had been able to talk from the time he was a baby.

"The more I thought of what might have been, the sadder and sadder I got, and the more I got down on myself—not only at home but at work as well. I don't think I've gotten anything done in the last month. I'm tired, even though I sleep a lot. And, I don't enjoy Julie's cooking the way I used to.

"Then, I found myself feeling resentful. Jimmy had taken up so much time and money. What might have been if there had been no Jimmy? The more I thought that, the worse I felt. Can you imagine feeling that way about your own helpless kid? It isn't his fault. And yet the more I thought of it, the angrier I got.

"I had another terrible thought—if only Jimmy were gone. When he got to be thirteen or fourteen we would find a place for him, some kind of a farm, or a farm school—someplace where he could work and they could teach him things to do that weren't too complicated. I was hoping we could find a place that would take care of him for the rest of his life. This way, we would have some freedom. We could have time for ourselves and for our other kids.

"All of a sudden, this device comes along. Who knows how far this will take him? Sometimes I figure he can't talk because he doesn't understand too well. If you understand like a two or three year old, how can you talk? Other times I realize that he knows what's going on. He hears things. He sees things. He can remember. So what are the limits?

"The more the device helps, the longer he'll stay home. The longer he stays, the longer we'll wonder about what we could do. And we'll continue to wonder, what has happened to Jimmy and to our family?

"It's a crazy idea that the thing that can make you the happiest for your kid is also the thing that can make you miserable.

"I also have to wonder how much time and energy will Jimmy have to use to figure out how to use this thing. It seems like he could be trapped. I know he can use it while he's sitting down. But does he carry it around with him or what? Who knows?

"This thing didn't exist ten years ago, and who knows what will exist five years from now. Yet, I feel trapped. I can't get myself out of it, and I didn't know how to talk about it with Julie or with Jimmy. How do we figure out what is right for our kid?"

My husband and I were overwhelmed. We really were in a kind of a fog for at least the first year of Jimmy's life.

The Fines came because of difficulty in their marriage. This new crisis started shortly after they had seen a new communication device which might be helpful for their nine year old, brain damaged son, Jimmy. Mr. Fine stopped talking to his wife and children and spent a great deal of time either in front of the television set or in his bedroom, preoccupied with his own thoughts. Mrs. Fine saw this as a problem in their marriage and did not want her husband's behavior blamed on her son.

The Fines had come with a similar problem four years earlier. At that time, they were in serious disagreement about what to do with their son, Jimmy, who was then five. Mrs. Fine had wanted Jimmy to live at home. She felt that they would be able to find educational and social programs in the community. Mr. Fine thought that the community had already failed, and wanted to place Jimmy in a residential school where they had relevant programs.

Mr. Fine had withdrawn from his wife, and become relatively uncommunicative. They had come to see me at the recommendation of their pediatrician. After two visits, they did not return or reply to a letter.

Both parents thought they had gotten a lot out of the earlier meetings. They had resolved their disagreement about their son. The Fines agreed to keep Jimmy at home, and not look for an alternative, at least until he was an adolescent.

Mrs. Fine said she had decided that she ought to deal with her own feelings of depression and found a psychotherapist who had helped her. Mr. Fine said he felt better after they had reached a decision about Jimmy, and therefore did not see any reason for further meetings at that time. His energy returned, and Mr. Fine became more active in his marriage as well as at work.

When the current problem emerged, Mrs. Fine had gone back to her own therapist. The therapist felt that the Fines should consult a professional about their marriage problem, and suggested they see someone, other than herself, who Mr. Fine would not see as his wife's ally. Mr. and Mrs. Fine were not sure that I would see them again because of the way they had left.

Mr. Fine seemed surprised that his not talking to his wife and children, his difficulty sleeping, his preoccupation with his son's problem, and his guilt about angry thoughts were all symptoms of depression. He had assumed that that was his style of dealing with problems. That is, after he had a chance of reviewing things by himself, he was going to be able to take steps that were necessary for his family. He did not recognize the extent to which his behavior upset his wife and children. Mr. Fine could not believe that they all assumed he was blaming them for the difficulties.

He was most confused by his negative feelings about his son.

All parents have expectations about what their child will become, even before she or he is born. During their growing years, these dreams of the child's future are modified by what the child's real abilities and opportunities are. The parental expectations are challenged immediately if a child is born with a disability. Since there are seldom clear guidelines for mapping out what the child's future development might be, parents expect the worst, and their dreams for the future are often postponed indefinitely. Their original dreams lie out of awareness, and therefore are not modified by the growing understanding of the child's abilities and potential. In this way, the original expectations continue to influence the parent's feelings and behavior in ways that can be troubling.

When any child with a disability passes through a new milestone, such as starting school, the original dreams that their parents had for them can be aroused. Whatever depression or despair the parents experienced when they were confronted with the child's limitations can also re-emerge.

In the Fine family, when Jimmy was about to enter school, his parents argued whether he would be best cared for at home or at a residential school. After agreeing to keep Jimmy home, Mrs. Fine decided to do something about her intense feelings of depression. Mr. Fine was relieved that their conflicts had ended, and did not want to do anything further about his own concerns.

The new communication device represented an

opportunity for real growth for Jimmy. However, it reminded Mr. Fine of his dreams for his son that had never been resolved. As a middle-aged man, Mr. Fine was at a point when adults are struggling with issues related to what has happened in their own lives. Their dreams of their futures, both in their work and with their family, now have to be evaluated in terms of what really has happened. Knowing that Jimmy would always be dependent made Mr. Fine feel as though he had failed as a parent.

Although he was reluctant to get help for himself, he was concerned about what he had been doing to his wife and children, and accepted a referral to another psychotherapist for himself. Mr. Fine understood that this might also help his relationship with Jimmy.

The parents were both excited about the possibility of a new communication device for their son. Although they were cautious, they had great hopes about how this might improve his chances to lead a more independent life. ■

CHAPTER 55

HI! MY NAME IS DANIEL

by Nancy Schmalz

Waiting with my son, Daniel, for the pharmacist to fill a prescription, I was pleased when a young woman introduced herself to me. She had noticed the pad I made for my son's wheelchair tray, which states in big red letters, "Hi! My name is Daniel." The woman also had a son named Daniel who is in a wheelchair.

After we had exchanged addresses and phone numbers, as well as information about homemade wheelchair ramps, I picked up my prescription, and walked home with Daniel, feeling richer by two new friends.

Reaching Out

Daniel's tray pad was intended as an experiment to see whether some of the people who stared curiously at him or looked away when we approached would respond differently if they knew his name. The experiment has confirmed my belief that many people have a sincere interest in disabled children, but are not comfortable enough in their presence to initiate a conversation. They avoid any encounter, rather than risk being embarrassed or saying the wrong thing. They may also be afraid of "bothering" the child or her or his parent.

Interpreting this silence as hostility or disgust, many parents leave their disabled children at home, or hurry through the shopping with them, avoiding the eyes of other shoppers. This reinforces the isolation which often traps families of children with disabilities. I was determined not to let myself and members of my family accept that isolation.

The Tray Pad

With that goal in mind, I designed a covered foam pad to replace the folded ragged towel which was always falling off Daniel's tray. The pad is made of washable fabric placed over foam cut to fit the surface of Daniel's tray. It has a velcro strap which fastens underneath. The letters are in bright red capitals, appliqued with a machine zigzag stitch. For practicality, I added a flashy yellow washcloth fastened with red buttons which can be easily washed without laundering the whole pad.

The basic design of the pad has been successful, but since making it, I have thought of variations which may be helpful for other children. A textured fabric (corduroy or fake fur) for the letters would be especially appropriate for children who are visually impaired, or those who enjoy feeling unusual surfaces. Beads, ruffles, lace, and yarn could be added to make the surface of the pad decorative, as well as stimulating for children who like to use their hands.

Finding Friends

The first few times I took Daniel out with the new pad, I was concerned that people would be disappointed when he did not respond to their greetings. My fears were unfounded. People extended their friendship with no apparent expectation that Daniel should reciprocate. By providing the visual message to strangers that my child welcomes their friendship, I am doing for him one more thing that he would do for himself if he could. I feed, bathe and undress Daniel; I can also help him to experience the pleasure of initiating friendships.

"Guess what happened while we were shopping today!" is a frequent opening line for our family conversations. We have learned to expect surprises when we take Daniel out, and to allow time for the conversations which inevitably ensue.

Often, someone will pass us and then back up to reread Daniel's tray. The spontaneous smile which follows is warm and often relieved, as if an invisible barrier has been broken.

Children are usually freer than adults to ask their questions and to make observations. The bright colors of the tray pad are appealing to them, and they are interested in how it is made, what it is for, and who Daniel is. It seems easy for them to accept the idea that someone can be happy without smiling, or can be a friend without saying so. Many a thoughtful conversation with a four or five year old has been sparked by their questions about Daniel's tray.

Children's Questions

The line of questioning used by young children is straightforward and logical, within the limits of their experience. It often goes like this:

"Why is he in that chair?"
"Because he doesn't walk."
"Did he break his leg? Did he fall out of a tree?"
"No, he just hasn't learned to walk yet."
"Why not? My baby sister knows how to walk."
"He learns more slowly than you do, and walking is one of those things he hasn't learned yet."
"Oh. Can I push his chair?"
"Yes, you may help me. Daniel really likes to go for rides in his chair."

Usually this amount of information is satisfying to the children. They sometimes want to join us for walks, and are comfortable with mere descriptions of Daniel's differences explained in ways that they can understand. As they grow older, they will be prepared to handle questions at a more sophisticated level: Why does he learn so slowly? What will happen when he grows up? In the meantime, most children accept Daniel for who and what he is, a kid in a wheelchair who likes to be outside with them.

Other Needs

All of my idle hours are not spent planning new opportunities for Daniel to greet the public. Some days I just do not feel like being cheery, answering questions, or pushing a wheelchair. Sometimes this mood is due to problems related to Daniel, sometimes it is not. But, I now know that other people feel the same way, and that nobody will be upset if I send someone else to the store, if Daniel misses a walk, or if the neighborhood kids hang on to their questions until another day.

The need for reflective time that parents of disabled children have is often overlooked as we attend to the never ending job of being a parent. It is easy to overextend our energy as we strive to maintain the cheerful, optimistic bouyancy which we feel is a part of our role. This reservoir of strength is, in fact, one of the coping mechanisms which parents of "demanding" children never know they have until they need it.

I have learned that this energy level cannot be maintained indefinitely without renewal, and that it is the responsibility of each parent to recognize when it is time to slow down and gather strength for another day. Rejuvenation of this kind is not a luxury, but an essential part of an individual's physical and mental health. The knowledge that these dark days pass in their own time—sometimes without any conscious awareness of a problem having been solved or even identified—has helped me to use them as occasions to get in touch with myself again.

When by taking care of my own needs as well as those of my family, I have collected a store of energy and good cheer enough to see me through the next few days, then it is time to take Daniel out for a walk. You never know who we might meet! ■

Nancy Schmalz has written before for THE EXCEPTIONAL PARENT. *(Is That Your Brother? Our Family's Response, Dec. 82)* She graduated from Lawrence University with a degree in music, and now teaches flute and piano. Ms. Schmalz lives in Oshkosh, Wisconsin, with her husband, Peter, and their children, Brian, Daniel, and Heidi.

CHAPTER 56

Communication Devices and an Enriched Life
An Autobiography

by Lake N. Kissick, Jr.

The rapid advances in communication devices continue to improve the lives of many severely disabled people. The ability to communicate our thoughts and feelings to others is a basic human need. For years, people with severe handicaps were often unable to let others know what was inside them, and bright individuals were often viewed as vegetables— institutionalized or classified as uneducable. Today, many of these individuals are attending colleges, living in their own apartments, and having social lives.

Lake Kissick's autobiography is an active demonstration of the changes that are possible.

My life began in a suburb of Chicago on a beautiful June day thirty-three years ago. I probably would not be alive if my aunt, Nancy, who is a nurse, had not been in the delivery room. She saved my life by giving me mouth-to-mouth resuscitation after the doctors gave up.

I had a smile for the first few months, but was unusually silent. Although I reacted to people talking to me, the only sound that I could make was, "uh." My laughter was described as "explosive." I am sure it was then that my dad gave me the first of many nicknames—Laughing Boy.

My mother took me to our family doctor when I was seven months old because I had bronchitis. The doctor was horrified by how I was tensing up on the table. Except for using the strange term, "cerebral palsy" to describe my condition and prescribing phenobarbitol, the doctor did not know what to do. As a result of that drug, my mother and father had a dish rag for a baby for a year because I was so doped up all the time.

In addition to my lack of vocalization, my folks noticed I was not progressing like other babies my age. I was not grasping at toys, trying to walk, or starting to talk. At eighteen months my grandfather found a doctor who was supposed to know about cerebral palsy. My mom and dad took me to the doctor's office in Chicago. The doctor told my parents, "Put him into an institution because he will be a vegetable. Just forget about him and have other children."

My mom argued, "But his eyes tell me he is mentally alert and can be taught."

The doctor came back with, "Well, does he understand what we are talking about?"

"Of course not!" my mom said. "Would any eighteen month old child?"

After a long discussion, the doctor convinced my folks that the state hospital was a good option because supposedly I would learn, and be cared for by trained people. Naturally, that sounded good to my parents, so they went ahead getting the court order to commit me to a state hospital outside of Chicago.

My parents thought it would be a good idea to tour the hospital before placing me, and I sure am glad they did. As my mother tells it, "We took one step into the hospital and knew we were going to keep you with us. The place smelled, there wasn't any training, and they had older patients caring for younger ones."

To say the least, my entire family was steaming mad at that doctor. I still get chills when I think about it. My mother read a few years ago that the Illinois Health Department closed that state hospital.

The Next Step

My mother describes the next step in figuring out how to take care of me. "One day after I cried myself to sleep about you," she told me, "I woke up suddenly with the answer. I called Dad and told him about it, and called our regular doctor, Dr. Shnute, to ask him when he could examine you. Although he usually didn't go to his office on the weekends, he said we could come that Saturday."

In a letter to the doctor who had recommended the state hospital for me, our doctor wrote that although I had some spasticity, I appeared to be a healthy two year old boy. He also thought that I did not have much mental delay. In other words, he wrote in that letter that he was not in favor of institutionalization unless the situation was really impossible for my family. Fortunately, my family was extremely interested in my care. Dr. Schnute set us on the right track with exercises, some equipment, and support.

In July of 1952, Dr. Schnute sent us to the Chicago Metropolitan Unit of the Illinois Association for the Crippled to enroll me in the preschool cerebral palsy program. There, I had physical, speech and occupational therapy. My speech therapist only tried to teach me to talk instead of also working on a back up communication so I could at least begin to communicate in the meantime. It really burns me when I think of the years that speech therapists refused to play with alternative communicating methods for me.

Moving To a Small Town

Early in 1953, I had to leave the program I was in because my dad got a new job in Bloomington, Indiana. My parents became very frustrated in Bloomington after living in Chicago where there was a lot of help for us. There was nothing for me in our new home!

Instead of giving up, my folks went to work with two new friends who had an older son with cerebral palsy. The four of them looked for other parents with disabled children, and convinced them that having disabled children was not the end of the world. They started a nursery on the Indiana University campus in 1954. They also began a parent's group. Both projects flourished, and the nursery school is now a part of the public school system.

During the process of getting the school started, my dad got involved with the Monroe County Easter Seal organization. A fellow member told the state organization about what my mom and dad were doing. After someone came to see personally, they honored my family and me by choosing me as the 1955 Easter Seal Child.

My picture was all over just like the other Easter Seal children before and after me. Because of the "ham" that I have always been, that year was a lot of fun for me. I remember one particular day when I went to the capitol and gave the first Easter Seals to the Governor of Indiana. We moved to Findlay, Ohio after I finished being the Easter Seal child because my dad was transferred again.

Trying to Learn and Communicate

When I was six, after a lot of searching and praying, my mother found someone in Findlay who agreed to be my home tutor. The town of Findlay would only pay for five hours a week— which is not enough for anyone. My tutor made the five hours of home tutoring a week really fun! She moved the next year, so I had a different home tutor for the next two years.

Besides my tutoring two days a week, I had speech therapy thirty miles away two other days weekly. My mother still did my exercises with me each day. She was very busy working with me and taking me around to everything.

For the first ten years of my life, I could only communicate by pointing with my eyes, shaking my head "yes" or "no," or sticking out my tongue—a never ending game of twenty questions. It was slow and frustrating and no way to live. Although it was very difficult, both my mother and father patiently made sure that my mind did not go to waste.

My dear sister, Sheryl, helped in her own loving way. Sometimes when my mother or father could not figure out what I wanted—which did not happen too many times—they asked Sheryl to assist. Usually, she would get it. Other times when the two of us were playing together, she would go to our mom and dad to tell them that I wanted this or that. Again, she was usually right. Sheryl and I loved each other a lot, and we still do!

Although my lack of verbal communication must have had an affect on my getting friends in the neighborhood, I did not feel it until I was older. Sheryl and the kids in the neighborhood involved me in whatever they did. My boyfriends asked me to join their Cub Scout troop. My dad and the fellows in the troop helped me to do almost everything that Cub Scouts do.

Going Away to School

After three years living at home and living as normal a childhood as possible, my folks decided they could not give me enough schooling and therapies. They found the Anne Carlson's School For Disabled Children in Jamestown, North Dakota. Most of the places around the country which they had heard about put hospitalization ahead of schooling. The school in North Dakota scheduled therapies around classes.

In September, 1959, I started fourth grade at the new school. My occupational and speech therapists tried to get me to use my left fist to point to a big lap conversation board. That did not work, so they tried a dental mouth plate with a pointer sticking out of it. It kept falling out of my mouth simply because I could not keep my mouth closed.

My dad stepped in and solved most of my communication difficulties. Recognizing that I had more control of my neck and head, he invented the first head pointer for me in the school year of 1960-61. Even though it was crude, it worked!

When my fifth grade teacher and I started using the pointer with an electric typewriter, she discovered I could not write an intelligent sentence or spell. Realizing this, she took me all the way back to a first grade level in grammar, phonics, and spelling. She found reading books that were interesting to me. I was eleven years old. I could work at my own speed, so I finished six years in three, besides keeping up with my other subjects. When I was not at my typewriter, a conversation board took its place. I graduated from high school with honors in 1972.

Typing my way through two years of college one key at a time was not easy, but I made it with great determination and patience! It was not easy trying to make many close friends using a conversation board, either. In other words, there is a limit to what a pointer, typewriter, and board can do for a physically disabled person.

After those two years of college, I had to quit and go home to Ohio for six long years bacause my parents could not afford to pay my way *and* also pay for my attendants.

A Major Change

Even though I was deeply saddened by my dad dying in October, 1979, God had fantastic times ahead for me and my family beginning on the last Thursday of November, 1979.

My life began to soar! The best way to describe how much it took off is to compare it to taking one giant leap out of the Iron Age into the Space Age. For my mother, my friends, and me that is exactly how important that day will be forever. It was the day I received my Express 1—an electronic and technological communication system built by the Prentke Romich Company of Shreve, Ohio. My speed and social life changed greatly.

After my dad died, I realized I had to start taking charge much more of my own life than ever before. Quite frankly, that was a shock to realize suddenly. In February, 1980, about three months after I received the Express 1, I applied to the Courage Center—an independent training residential facility for physically disabled adults in Minneapolis, Minnesota.

I was accepted eight months later. And I did it all by myself. My mother just went with me for my interview. I am positive that my Express 1 was the deciding factor for my acceptance. With their help, I finally obtained an electric wheelchair from the state. Before my electric chair, I could not do half the things which now I am capable of doing by myself. When I left, I was a new person.

An Apartment

In February, 1982, I moved into a university health care center just until an apartment opened up. It was a nursing home in the city with a floor for young, handicapped adults. It was quite a shock to my ego to move there after the Courage Center. However, it was a great experience for me because I learned so much about myself.

Eventually, an apartment opened up on the twenty-seventh floor in a part of downtown Minneapolis. I moved in with a male attendant on November 1, 1982. After having two live-in attendants for a time, I now have a one bedroom apartment on the thirty-fourth floor where I live by myself. I have hired six part-time attendants. I schedule when they come, keep their hourly records, and approve them with my signature stamp each month so they can bill the state to get paid. It is like a small business that I am running. I really enjoy my living situation.

The Express System

What makes the Express I and the Express III much faster is that I can work them with a light device attached to my headband instead of having to operate a typewriter or computer headpointer. I do not have to lean forward to push anything. One of the standard features of the Express III is its ability to work easily with the Apple computers. That will increase my speed enormously.

Another standard feature of the Express III is its speech capability. It recognizes all standard words and names and pronounces them correctly. Unusual words can be constructed phonetically. I can dial phone numbers through the Express III instead of having to have an attendant make calls for me. It has a battery pack so I can carry it around with me on my wheelchair, and because of its speech capability, I do not have to carry around a bulky TV monitor. That will enable me to communicate much more easily.

Although the Express III has only 128 visible squares, that is really just the tip of the iceberg. Actually, I have an enormous amount of storage at my "fingertips." Each square has the capacity of not just one letter or one word, but whole paragraphs.

Aspirations

As I mentioned above, I am an aspiring writer, and have also started accounting classes at the Minneapolis Technical Institute.

Many have heard the expression, "a chain is only as strong as its weakest link." I do not have trouble taking in information nor thinking clearly. In the past, my weakest link has always been in getting what I wanted to say out quickly. I truly believe that the Express III is the bridge to my goals and more outside contact with society. ■

Lake Kissick, Jr. lives in Minneapolis, Minnesota in his own apartment. He is a consultant for the Prentke Romich Company, Shreve, Ohio.

CHAPTER 57

New Products

For the first time, we are featuring new products in THE EXCEPTIONAL PARENT. We debated about the suitability of this theme. Our dilemma about bringing new products to the attention of our readers parallels the concerns we have about advertising.

In 1971, when we began THE EXCEPTIONAL PARENT, we wondered for two years whether we should accept any advertising. We were cautious because our experience had led us to believe that many families had been taken advantage of by programs, products, and promises that were unrealistic. We discussed this question with our advisory board, and attempted to develop advertising guidelines.

An executive of a major, national publication, whose child has a physical disability, told us that he bought a number of foreign publications because they were the only places in which he could see products that might be useful. He confronted us with the inconsistency between our editorial philosophy of helping parents become informed consumers and our resistance to advertising. He suggested that we were being "overprotective" of parents by not giving enough credit to their abilities to discern what would be helpful for their children. It was the first of many times in which our readers confronted us with how our own prejudices limited the magazine's content. We now see advertising as part of our editorial material.

THE EXCEPTIONAL PARENT is cautious about accepting advertising without understanding the nature of the company, their ability to deliver, and the type of product. We still turn down specific ads or require our advertisers to re-edit their copy because it is unclear or over-promises. In addition, we have always acted on complaints from our readers about products they have purchased from advertisers.

Although we do not formally endorse any products or programs, we would not use the pages of the magazine for anything that we did not believe deserved attention. This is as true for paid advertising as it is for any items in the new products section.

This new feature gives us the opportunity to present to our readers those products that are available that might be important for them, as well as a way of identifying those areas in which new products need to be developed. We will continue to share new products in future issues.

Many of the new products we are featuring reflect the advancing state of technology. Items are available now that we could not even imagine a few years ago.

Problems and Prospects

The revolution in technology has been a main feature of the past quarter century. We have seen astronauts leave the earth, enter into outer space, and return. Time magazine identified the computer as its Man of the Year, so significant has its impact been. Most aspects of our daily life have been influenced by technological changes, whether we pay our bills by telephone, watch while our supermarkets automatically prepare a sales slip by moving items across a sensor, or use a word processor at our places of employment. The world is changing.

Our constant concern has always been that this knowledge be brought to bear on the challenges faced by individuals with disabilities. Until recently, the technology utilized in this area had been extremely outdated. Individuals with disabilities were not participants in everyday community life and could not communicate their needs directly. Therefore, it was difficult for the scientists, engineers, and inventors to observe or to understand how their knowledge and creativity was needed.

Often, changes were made because a creative—or desperate—individual wanted to help a disabled member of her or his family, and found traditional materials inadequate. A device was created in a basement to suit one person's needs. Ordinarily, these "advances" existed only in the stories told at parent meetings; rarely were they brought to the marketplace.

At other times, individual faculty members at universities or medical centers would be interested in entering this arena with a new idea, and would find little support from their colleagues. They would also describe the difficulty they encountered when trying to find a way to have their products reach potential users. Often, they simply could not find a willing manufacturer.

Slowly but surely with government support, we began to see the development of programs to train people in such fields as biomedicine and biotechnology. Individual entrepreneurs began to develop products. Some larger companies have entered the field as well.

Finally, whenever we think about this area, we worry about finding funds for research and development on the one hand, and the ability of families to pay for products developed on the other. THE EXCEPTIONAL PARENT invites you to write to us about products you have found helpful, your experiences in evaluating them, and suggestions about making products available to all in need. ■

—M. J. S., S. D. K.

CHAPTER 58

WIDE WORLD OF RECREATION

Wheelchair Design Changes
New Opportunities For Recreation

For many years, parents and professionals viewed people in wheelchairs as individuals who lived their lives indoors, or only traveling on hard, smoothed surface areas such as sidewalks, driveways, and paved playgrounds. However, thanks to many perservering young men and women who were determined to find ways to have active lives rather than be confined by their disabilities and the limitations of their wheelchairs, important changes have been made. Rather than accepting restrictions, these individuals began to adapt their chairs to suit their needs.

The designers and manufacturers of wheelchairs responded to the efforts of wheelchair owners and to changing opportunities for people with disabilities. Wheelchair design changes such as larger tires and lighter overall weight, now make it possible for many more children and adults to expand their worlds to include outdoor activities on natural turf.

Past Designs and Attitudes

For a long time, people complained that the only change in wheelchairs over the centuries had been shifting from wood as a primary material to steel and aluminum. Today, significant changes in design are coming about.

Wheelchair sports enthusiasts have provided some of the impetus for these changes. Often these people had been injured or wounded as teenagers or young adults after having been involved in sports and outdoor recreational activities. They remembered the joys of active recreation in their daily lives and were eager to find ways to return to these activities. Their attitude was to ask themselves, "How can I?" instead of saying, "I can't." Adaptability and persistence were the means they used to help bring about change.

One adult, in a wheelchair for over ten years since a skiing accident, observed that although he needs his chair to get around, he owns it, it does not own him. He *wears* his chair, his chair does not consume him. Both the tangible successes and the unrelenting efforts of individuals like this man are bringing about significant changes in attitudes concerning the capabilities of people with physical disabilities participating in outdoor activities.

Changes in Design

Many recent design changes increase the mobility of the wheelchair, as well as the amount of control the person in a wheelchair has. At the same time, more mobility is likely to mean less stability—and increased risk of accidents.

1. Casters.
Pneumatic tires. The front casters of the wheelchair are now available with pneumatic rubber tires. They are better able to tolerate bumps and other changes in terrain. The pneumatics are wider so they absorb shock, and are better able to "float" over unpaved surfaces. These tires pick up more mud, just as the grooves on someone's hiking boots would pick up material on the ground. When people first began requesting front pneumatics, some individuals thought it would be impractical. They are now such big sellers that few of the original thin, hard casters are sold anymore.

2. Wheels
Rear Pneumatics. Pneumatic rear wheels are also being manufactured, and have similar qualities and benefits as the pneumatic casters.
Rear Wheel Axle. By providing an adjustable rear wheel axle, the large wheel of the chair can be moved forward or backward to be more aligned with an individual's center of balance.

Putting the center of balance over the axles gives the user more control, and makes the chair easier to turn. The risk, however, is that as the chair becomes easier to move and turn, it is also easier for the chair to tilt over backwards or sideways. To compensate for this problem, one can have small wheels attached in the back to keep the chair from falling over if one starts to do a "wheelie." These will, however, slow down the chair somewhat.

The placement of the rear wheels underneath the person in the chair also takes weight off the front caster tires, and keeps them from sinking down into the soft ground. Also, it is easier to control the chair when going downhill if more of the weight is on the back tires.

Bearings. Improvements have also been made in the bearings of the wheels so that there is less friction. This means that less effort is required to move the chair.

Handrims. Handrims have been made smaller and easier to grasp. The combination of an adjustable rear wheel axle and a smaller handrim improves the ability of a person to push the chair. By having a smaller handrim, arm and hand movement can be more efficient.

In traditional wheelchairs with large handrims, an individual had to put his or her hands back to grasp the rim and then move the wheel forward by moving his or her hands parallel to the ground. With the smaller rim, a longer downward stroke of the hands and arms provides more power. This movement makes more effective use of the muscles in the arms and shoulders, and means that one can go further with the same number of strokes. This results in greater mobility.

3. Weight

Overall, wheelchairs have been made lighter as a result of changes in materials. This means that it is easier to move the chair around, as well as transport the chair when necessary. Some also come apart more easily, as well as fold. Taking a wheelchair along in the car can now be much less difficult.

The "Sports Chair"

The chairs described above are often referred to as "sports chairs" because, in the past, they had been used primarily by people participating in wheelchair sports. Now, many designers prefer to call them "lightweight chairs" since they are useful and practical for a wide range of individuals.

One problem with some of these wheelchairs is that the seat is smaller. A smaller seat design can mean that there is less support for a child who needs help with posture. It is also less modifiable for particular seating needs.

The changes in design in a lightweight chair mean a trade of stability for efficiency. The "sports chair" is more efficient, and gives the user more control and mobility. However, it is less stable. As with all adaptive aids, this means a comprehensive assessment of the individual and her or his ability to learn to use the aid is essential.

The Right Chair

With any kind of wheelchair, the most important thing for the child and the family to do is "test drive" it in the various settings in which the child spends her or his time. Wheelchair dealers are usually happy to cooperate with a family that wants to try out a wheelchair.

Having proper posture and seating support is essential so that the child sits properly and is balanced in the chair. When considering purchasing a wheelchair for a child, it is important to know which designs can accommodate specific sitting or postural adaptations or devices.

Along with proper seating posture and balance, the vulnerability of the child to skin problems needs to be considered. Depending on the type of seating posture and how long a child sits in a particular position, the child may be susceptible to pressure sores. It is helpful to discuss, both with your child's rehabilitation team and wheelchair dealers, the various cushions or seating supports available to provide comfort and prevent pressure sores.

It will take time for a child changing to a new, lightweight chair to learn the different principles of movement. Practice will be necessary before the child, the parent, and the team know how well the child can do. This new learning process is similar to an automobile driver going from a standard shift and ordinary steering to automatic transmission and power steering. While certain basics may be the same, there are some major differences in control and "feel" of the vehicle, and some retraining is necessary.

Reimbursement

Lightweight wheelchairs are usually more expensive than traditional designs. Reimbursement policies for wheelchairs used for outdoor play and recreation from family health insurance or public agencies vary. Ordinarily, under typical health insurance or public agency programs, when a physician prescribes a wheelchair as a medical necessity, the individual or family is reimbursed in full for the cost of the chair.

Physicians differ about the "medical necessity" of wheelchairs used for recreational activities. For those individuals who are able to use the lighter weight—and more expensive—wheelchair as a primary vehicle, some reimbursement programs will pay up to the cost of a traditional wheelchair.

Motorized Vehicles

There have been some design changes in motorized vehicles, and more vehicles are available. There are some four-wheel motorcycles being manufactured that can go almost anywhere. The rider must be able to get on and off the cycle, and drive it safely. One manufacturer has created a four wheel motorcycle side car that is operated with hand controls. An individual can drive his or her wheelchair up into the side car, and drive around with an able-bodied friend on the cycle next to the side car.

A tractor adjustment makes it possible for individuals in wheelchairs to participate in such activities as landscaping, farming, and snow removal. This adjustment can also be used to drive around in areas in which it is legal to drive a tractor.

Some small riding mowers operate with handles for going backward and forward or left and right.

As soon as someone lets go of the handles, the vehicle stops. These offer another way for the child to get around in the outdoors, as well as to help with the family chore of grass cutting.

In recent years, many electric powered vehicles have been developed that look similar to golf carts or motorized scooters. Not only do these vehicles move easily, but the riders are less likely to be stigmatized in the same way that wheelchair riders often are.

Activities

As a child with disabilities is able to become more mobile and thereby participate in more outdoor activities, the child is more likely to be interacting with other children, developing social skills, and enjoying activities in the outdoor world.

Participating in outdoor activities usually means that a child will have more opportunities to take chances. This can be stressful for parents who worry that their children may be hurt or that they will fail once again.

Many activities have been successfully adapted for people with disabilities. By learning about these, parents and children together can discover different activities, their joys, and their risks.

Warm Weather Fun

A variety of activities can be enjoyed in warmer weather. Hiking is much more possible in lightweight chairs with wide rubber tires that move over rougher terrain more easily. Jeep trails and other paths that have some grooming can be fairly accessible.

Poling is another activity that is a lot of fun. It gives people in wheelchairs the opportunity to exercise some muscles that are not usually used by basic wheelchair motion. Poling approximates skiing on the road. For this activity, poles approximately 120–140 centimeters long with carbide tips at the end are used to propel oneself in a wheelchair. An asphalt road is needed for poling since the carbide tips cannot get a good grip on cement. Able-bodied friends can jog or roller skate along side the person who is poling.

Canoeing is a pleasant activity that is accessible for some people who use a wheelchair. By constructing a "director's chair" or back support in the canoe, and going with someone able-bodied and in a life jacket, this summer activity can be enjoyed. A seat belt can be provided for individuals who require additional support.

Kayaking uses similar principles. With seating adaptations—a seat belt, a back support, and good cushioning—one can enjoy the pleasures of kayaking. It is not necessary to go on wild rapids; kayaking is pleasurable on calm waters as well. Activities like canoeing and kayaking enable the person in a wheelchair to get out of the chair and move around in a different environment.

Scuba diving is also possible as an activity. Properly trained and equipped, an individual could either go under water with someone who is able-bodied for some assistance, or could go alone if she or he had sufficient arm strength and swimming skills. Again, this is a wonderful opportunity to get out of one's chair, and explore an exciting, new environment.

White water rafting is a thrilling sport. Several people, some of them disabled and some of them able-bodied—all of them wearing life jackets—can fit onto a large raft, and conquer swirling waters. Seat belts and cushions could be provided for those who need some seating support.

Skateboarding (sitting down), sailing, and even water skiing have all been attempted successfully by people with physical disabilities. Imagination, determination, and some comfort with risk taking are all important factors in attempting these recreational endeavors.

Winter Sports

Several winter sports have been adapted for people who are mobility impaired. Some require purchasing relatively expensive equipment.

Sit skiing gives a great sense of speed because the skier is close to the ground. Even going ten miles per hour can feel much faster, and be very exciting. Sit skiing can be made relatively safe by using a tetherer. A tetherer is an able-bodied, experienced skier who skis behind the person sit skiing and holds about twenty-five feet of webbing attached to the sit ski. If the person in the vehicle starts to get out of control, the tetherer can pull the webbing to slow down the vehicle.

Ice sledding vehicles are sled frames with three or four blades on the bottom. By using poles about one meter long, a person with some arm control can propel him or herself along the surface of the ice without too much effort. Ice sledding is a good idea for those who feel frightened by downhill sit skiing because there is more control, and one moves more slowly.

Accomplishment

Most of the recreational activities described above can be done without competing against others. Ice sledding, kayaking, hiking, and others are all activities that can be enjoyed by one person or experienced via participating with family and friends in outdoor recreation.

Parents who like to fish, hunt, hike, camp, or ski now have options available to include their child with disabilities. The opportunity to share the excitement and joy of outdoor activities with the *whole* family is one of the most promising "products" of the changes in wheelchair design and in our attitudes toward people with disabilities. ■

—S.D.K.—

CHAPTER 59

LOGO Is For All Children
Learning With The Turtle

by Cleborne D. Maddux and Rhoda E. Cummings

LOGO is a common computer language used with school aged children. This article describes LOGO, and how it may benefit children with disabilities.

LOGO is a computer language now available for almost every computer capable of producing color on its screen. Companies which produce machines for which LOGO software is available are Atari, Apple, IBM, Commodore, Radio Shack, Texas Instrument, DEC, and others.

LOGO is really a multipurpose language which can be used to do just about anything any other computer language can do. What gives it its great potential for use with exceptional children, however, is the ease with which it allows children to create colorful and interesting graphics on the computer screen.

In fact, ease of learning is what really sets LOGO apart from other computer languages such as BASIC or FORTRAN. Even a very young child can begin to do interesting and fun things with LOGO after a five to ten minute introduction to the language. Most children never master BASIC, FORTRAN, or other computer languages because they require hours of intensive study before anything especially enjoyable can be done with them. LOGO will also retain a child's interest since it can be learned at many different levels of complexity.

Turtle Geometry

"Turtle Geometry" is at the heart of LOGO's graphics abilities. A LOGO turtle is usually a small triangular shape which initially appears in the center of the computer screen. The child can draw pictures by giving simple commands which move the turtle from one spot on the screen to another. As the turtle moves, it draws a line on the screen.

The child must learn only four simple commands in order to start making designs. These commands are FORWARD (FD), BACK (BK), RIGHT (RT), and LEFT (LT). The child can make the turtle go forward 30 turtle steps by typing in FD30. When the ENTER key is pressed, the turtle goes forward 30 steps and draws a line to that spot.

BACKWARD (BK) works similarly, and moves the turtle in reverse. To cause the turtle to move in directions other than up or down, the child must first change the turtle's orientation according to the points of the compass. In order to make the turtle point to the right, the child types RT 90. This rotates the turtle in place, 90 degrees to the right. The FD command will then cause the turtle to draw a line at right angles to the original line. The following commands would cause the turtle to draw a square: FD60
RT90
FD60
RT90
FD60
RT90
FD60
RT90

Since the turtle can be rotated in place any desired number of degrees, intricate designs can be created.

As the child gains experience with LOGO, other capabilities of the language are discovered. The child learns how to change the background color of the screen, how to change the color of the line drawn by the turtle, how to erase lines, etc.

Shortcuts are also learned. For example, the square drawn above could also be drawn by using the following commands: Repeat 4 [FD 60 RT 90]

LOGO's Different Modes

When a child first begins to learn LOGO, commands are entered in the "immediate mode." In this mode, the child types in a command and presses the ENTER key. The turtle then immediately carries out the command. After the immediate mode is mastered, the child learns that LOGO also has a "program mode." In the program mode, a series of commands— a program— are entered. After the entire program is written, the child returns to the immediate mode and runs the program. All commands are then carried out at once.

Some children may never progress far enough to learn to use the program mode. However, others will master it easily and move on to more and more sophisticated uses of the language.

Exceptional Children and LOGO

LOGO was invented by Seymore Papert, an MIT

computer scientist and mathematician. Before developing LOGO, Papert spent five years studying with the famous child psychologist, Jean Piaget. As a result, Papert has created a langauge firmly grounded in our knowledge of how children learn.

Papert believes that by learning to program with LOGO, children can actually move more quickly into adult thinking stages. We are reserving judgement on this particular issue. However, other less lofty reasons exist for making LOGO available to children with disabilities.

1. Many children have experienced so much failure within the regular academic program that they no longer view school positively. Years of difficulty with schoolwork and returned homework papers covered with red marks may make the child quite sensitive to adult criticism. Since LOGO provides immediate feedback, the child can readily correct mistakes without anyone else knowing that an error has been made. As a result, adult intervention and criticism are unnecessary, and the child's sense of failure is greatly reduced.

2. Children with disabilities are sometimes rejected or ignored by non-special education children. However, children who have learned LOGO can be assigned to teach it to other children in the regular school program. Research has shown that such interaction can improve the social status of previously rejected special education students.

If the student has access to LOGO at home, it is far more likely that he or she will develop expertise with LOGO since recent studies have shown that most elementary school children have access to school computers for only about one-half hour per week.

3. Because of physical handicaps, some children are restricted in their movements. As a result, these children often do not develop an awareness of spatial relationships. By planning movements of the turtle around the computer screen, the child is helped to understand such spatial concepts as forward, backward, left, and right.

4. Many special education students have short attention spans. This is not a barrier to learning LOGO, however, since the basic concepts can be learned in just a few minutes. In addition, LOGO is structured so that it can be operated in the immediate mode. In this mode, the turtle carries out each instruction as it is entered. If the child's attention wanders, there is no problem since he or she can easily resume where he or she left off.

5. Some children have difficulty with math. Part of this problem can be that they do not see the relevance of what they are learning. However, LOGO requires numbers and arithmetic to make the turtle do what one wants it to do. This supplies a powerful, concrete reason for using numbers, and provides important practice time.

6. Problem solving is difficult for many students. LOGO provides a lot of practice in activities such as trial and error attempts at problem solving. Since the child is provided with immediate feedback, an error is obvious when the turtle goes the wrong direction or distance after being given a command. Upon seeing the error, the child can restructure commands to the turtle, usually through trial and error, until they are carried out correctly.

7. Some special students have difficulty with handwriting and benefit from learning to type well. Typing in LOGO commands may supply the practice and motivation for many of these students to improve their typing skills.

Conclusion

LOGO seems ideally suited for home use with exceptional children. It is simple to learn, fun to use, and its capabilities far exceed the creation of interesting designs. Although there is nothing magical about LOGO, and some of the major claims regarding its effect upon the acceleration of learning may be exaggerated, it is still beneficial. LOGO's value comes from the ease with which it can be learned and from the sense of control gained by the child as the language is mastered. After a brief initial exposure to LOGO, a simple design such as a box or a house can be drawn. However, as the child gains experience, complex pictures such as an elephant or a frog can be created. For the child who has often experienced defeat and frustration, the ability to master and have control over a machine as technologically complex as a computer can provide great rewards. ■

Cleborne D. Maddux, Ph.D., is an Associate Professor and Chairperson of Special Education at Texas Tech University. He teaches courses in computer education and special education, and is the author of numerous books and articles on both subjects.

Rhoda E. Cummings is an instructor and research associate in the College of Special Education at Texas Tech University. She holds an M.Ed. in special education with an emphasis on learning disabilities. She and Dr. Maddux co-authored an article entitled, Parental Home Tutoring: Aids and Cautions for the August 83 issue of THE EXCEPTIONAL PARENT.

CHAPTER 60

Microcomputer Activities and Occupational Therapy

by Nancy Wall

Computers are becoming everyday tools providing health professionals with new ways of evaluating and treating patients. Nancy Wall stresses the need for a careful assessment of the individual child in order to match the versatility of the computer to the skills and understanding of the child.

This article is addressed to occupational therapists, but it is useful for parents and professionals because it summarizes the variety of computer applications that are currently available. It was originally published in **The American Occupational Therapy Association Newsletter.**

The entry of the microcomputer into the therapy and special educational setting provides occupational therapists with a whole new array of evaluation and treatment modalities and activities to help solve some of the problems of the developmentally disabled population.

These problems include physical impairments that restrict or eliminate access and control over one's environment as well as learning disabilities and related problems of attention, problem solving, perception, cognition, abstract thinking, memory and motivation. Microcomputers may also be used to address psychosocial needs that influence development, relationships to peers, group interaction skills, self concept, and work and school behaviors.

Microcomputer activities in occupational therapy offer unique and versatile opportunities. However, like any therapeutic activity or modality, the key to success as an evaluation and treatment tool is the therapist who uses it. It is the therapist's responsibility to define the person's needs and assets, to establish goals with an individual, to know the activity, to direct the application of the activity, to monitor the person's performance and to intervene when indicated.

The therapist's role and responsibility, of course, is nothing new. What is new is the activity itself—the computer and the variety of programs and capabilities it offers. Developing knowledge and skill in the use of microcomputers is part of our responsibility of keeping current in the profession.

The computer, with appropriate software, is patient, flexible, and can be individually tailored. It supports a variety of input and output devices that are adapted to the individual's physical and mental strengths and limitations. The computer keeps track of a user's performance and adjusts the skill level accordingly. It allows the user to define and solve a problem. It guides the problem solving process according to individual parameters set. The

Developing knowledge and skill in the use of microcomputers is part of our responsibility of keeping current in the profession.

computer offers the user a sense of mastery over a task, along with a feeling of success, independence, and creativity.

Computer Devices

There are many input and output devices available that allow users with physical impairments access to the computer and its capabilities. If physically disabled users cannot handle the standard keyboard, other input devices (tools used to place information into the computer) that can be used include joy sticks, game paddles, single, dual, or mercury switches, adapted keyboards, touch sensitive tablets, light pens, speech recognition modules, and light sensitive photo cells. Many of these devices can be mounted anywhere and usually do not interfere with normal keyboard use.

Special output devices (devices that enable the user to read the information in the computer) other than the monitor and printer include speech synthesizers, braille printers, environmental appliances, biofeedback machines, and robots.

In addition, special software and firmware products provide the added capability of using existing commercial programs by way of one switch control, adapted direct selection or scanning. For example, children with cerebral palsy may have only been able to watch their less involved peer's participation in activities. Now, with the use of one switch, these children can be active participants on a potentially equal basis, experiencing and demonstrating control, cooperation, competition, creativity and independence. It is easy to imagine that through the experience of this new physical control, there are now opportunities for children with disabilities to experience new social interactions, sensations, perceptions and cognitive concepts.

Computer Programs

Many commercial educational software programs are available for children and adults with learning difficulties. These programs include basic perceptual concepts of matching, recognition, discrimination of shapes, sounds, and rhythms, basic academic skills of number and letter recognition, math, grammar, and cognitive skills of problem solving, logic, sequencing and reasoning. More sophisticated programs are available that allow the adolescent and adult to solve problems relating to community life skills such as budgeting, shopping or check writing. Many of the input devices mentioned above enable the user with limited physical abilities to access these software programs.

Some programs do nothing more than display colorful graphics with sound that change dramatically at the touch of one key or switch. This seemingly simple program can be used to provide general sensory stimulation, or to reinforce or reward attention, functional motor movements, or purposeful keyboard use. The same concept of cause and effect can be applied to other environmental sensory stimuli. For example, a microcomputer can be hooked up to turn on and off a radio, a TV, or a fan in response to switches that the user activates. These switches can be put in positions that encourage purposeful movements while in bed, on a mat, or in a wheelchair.

LOGO

A powerful computer language, known as LOGO, allows the user to experience abstract ideas and concepts using concrete approaches and methods. The user moves a "turtle" about the floor or screen using one or two key commands. In this process of directing the turtle's movements, various shapes and designs can be created.

With the emphasis on the process rather than on the product, LOGO provides the user with the opportunity to define a problem, experiment with possible solutions, get feedback and use the feedback to try another solution. Many developmentally disabled children and adults have not developed or been able to demonstrate skill and ability in problem solving, an adequate attention span, appreciation of perceptual concepts, or the experience of control or success. LOGO provides an opportunity to practice, experiment and demonstrate an understanding of these concepts and a skill in implementing them into real life situations.

Other Applications

Identified psychosocial needs such as group interaction skills, work and school behaviors, and self concept can be addressed through such computer activities as educational programs and software games requiring more than one user or player. For example, a mystery story enables and encourages the users, as a group, to share their ideas, pool their resources, divide responsibilities, and compromise and cooperate in order to solve the problem. They enter their collective responses

> *The computer offers the user a sense of control and mastery over a task, along with a feeling of success, independence, and creativity.*

into the computer and the computer then presents the next clue. The computer is really a vehicle for promoting cooperative play and work with the added benefit of being objective, nonthreatening, patient and friendly. Many programs, though not specifically designed for group use, can be applied in this way.

Therapists frequently question what computer and software they should get. The question can really only be answered by first carefully identifying the needs to be addressed by a computer or computer activities. Meeting administrative needs of documentation or data base management through computer technology is very different than meeting learning or physical needs of a child with cerebral palsy or an adult with mental retardation. Once the specific needs and realistic objectives are defined, the decision as to what particular kind of computer and accompanying software to purchase will be easier.

The application of microcomputers to the developmentally disabled population is becoming an accepted part of health care. It is our role as therapists to join the computer age so that we can assist our clients in reaching their potential. ■

Nancy Wall is a full time lecturer at Tufts University, Medford, Massachusetts. She teaches a course in Microcomputers in Rehabilitation as part of Tufts new graduate program in Technology in Rehabilitation. This article appeared originally in the American Occupational Therapy Association Newsletter, Volume 7, No.1.

RESOURCES

It is difficult for anyone to keep up with the information, both practical and theoretical, that is continuously being developed. It is especially difficult for the parent who has to learn about an unfamiliar area. This section provides a directory of national organizations, parent, professional and governmental, dealing with disabilities. The section also presents other groups that make practical information available.

CHAPTER 61

WHAT'S HAPPENING

Public Affairs Pamphlet

In the pamphlet *Getting Help for a Disabled Child—Advice from Parents*, Irving R. Dickman and Sol Gordon discuss the feelings of parents when they learn that their child has a disability. The pamphlet offers suggestions on where parents can go for information, services, and personal support; the right of disabled children to an education, and parents rights.

The booklet, which includes a list of national organizations for additional information, is available for 50 cents from the nonprofit *Public Affairs Committee, 381 Park Avenue South, New York, New York 10016*.

Accessibility

Disney World's EPCOT Center is claimed to be one of the largest, most modern models of accessibility in the world. According to Disney World officials, accessibility was a key issue throughout EPCOT's development, design, and construction phases, and accessibility continues to be an operational and management priority. EPCOT Center opened last year as a part of the Walt Disney World Vacation Kingdom.

To assist disabled visitors, Disney World staff members have compiled an information guide which identifies various accommodations for disabled people. The guide also lists activities in the Kingdom in which people with mobility impairments may participate if they are able to transfer to what Disney officials call an "adventure vehicle."

Some disabled tourists have found EPCOT less than accessible. It is advisable to call Disney World before a visit to ensure that your disabled child's needs will be met so that she or he can enjoy a day of fun with the family.

To obtain more information concerning the EPCOT guide or accessibility, contact *Information, Walt Disney World, P.O. Box 40, Lake Buena Vista, Florida, 32830, (305) 824-2222*.

Shopper's Special

Retailers can be more sensitive to the emotional and physical needs of their disabled customers if they take a few tips from *Shoppers Special*, a brief checklist distributed by the Easter Seal Society.

The brochure has a dual purpose. It is intended to alert store managers to important features that can render their facilities accessible while, at the same time, enlighten sales personnel to the appropriate means of showing hospitality towards persons with specific disabilities.

If you are a retailer, or know of one who could use this leaflet, contact: *Gregory Sulgit, National Easter Seal Society, 2023 West Ogden Avenue, Chicago, Illinois 60612*.

Legal Aid

The Legal Resource Center for the Disabled is a new advocacy program which provides legal services for handicapped related issues. The center offers legal counseling and representation, training programs for professionals, volunteers, and consumers and information on pending laws, rules, and policies affecting the disabled.

The program is rather small, funded temporarily by grants from corporations and foundations, but will handle a limited number of inquiries. Contact: *Mr. David Popiel, Esq., 55 Washington Street, East Orange, New Jersey 07017*.

Attitudes

Every day more disabled people are moving into the mainstream by pursuing education, employment, and leisure activities. To acquaint those who have had little exposure to disabled persons, the Minnesota State Council for the Handicapped has published *Responding to Disability: A Question of Attitude*.

This well-illustrated booklet is designed to stimulate thinking and dialogue in a question and answer form. Uncomfortable or awkward situations are illustrated which allow the reader an opportunity to think about the situation involving disabilities, to respond, and then to consider the various responses more carefully. The first two copies are free of charge. A charge of $1.50 to cover printing and postage is requested for each additional copy. Contact: *Ms. Leslie Lane, Minnesota State Council for the Handicapped, 208 Metro Square, St. Paul, Minnesota 55101*.

Project REACH

An innovative program in Millbrae, California offers unique after-school recreation for physically and emotionally handicapped children. Project REACH (Recreational Experiences for Adults and Children with Handicaps), conceived in 1981 by recreation therapist Shirley Moore, is conducted on the school site where the children attend special education classes. This eliminates the difficulty of transporting them to a different location after school.

The program is five days a week, from 2:00 pm to 5:00 pm. Twenty-five children now participate, chosen from a parental interest survey, as well as school and community recreation center referrals.

The current site, Highlands School, is for severely emotionally disturbed children, some of whom have physical disabilities as well. Final plans are under way for a site for orthopedically handicapped children.

REACH emphasizes the freedom to choose activities. Participants are not forced to do anything; rather, they learn to decide how they want to spend their leisure time. They have an active planning role by rating the activities on a scale from "boring" to "very exciting."

Many of the activities are done in the local community. Participants go bowling, hiking, riding in buses, and eating at restaurants. The staff goes out with small groups of children (from two to five), which makes it easier to give individual attention and promote community acceptance. Several children, accompanied by a staff member, have even been integrated into a local recreation center.

Expenses for the program are minimal. REACH was initially grant-funded. The eventual goal is to give the recreation responsibility to the cities involved. Interns from San Jose State University make up the volunteer staff. There is one paid program coordinator, and three paid recreation specialists. Parents pay a monthly fee of fifty dollars. Money is available for those who cannot pay.

There has been a tremendous response from parents in reports of positive changes in their children's behavior. The program also serves as a respite for many working parents who otherwise have no place to take their child after school.

Janet Pomeroy, founder and director of the San Francisco Center for the handicapped, feels the great thing about REACH is that it is showing the community how a program like this can work, and is an excellent educational process for everyone involved.

For more information, write to *Project REACH, c/o Shirley Moore, 1008 Montgomery Drive, San Carlos, California 94070*

The HIP Report

HIP (Help for Incontinent People) was organized in the Winter of 1983 to assist the estimated ten million Americans and Canadians who have bladder control problems. The organizers of HIP maintain that although incontinence is not a subject people like to discuss, those who suffer from its effects are relieved and encouraged when they discover they are not alone.

The HIP Report, the free quarterly newsletter published by the group, is edited by Dr. Katherine Jeter, a well-known enterostomal therapist, and author of *These Special Children: The Ostomy Book for Parents of Children with Colostomies, Ileostomies, and Urostomies.*

In August, 1983, The HIP Report was first plugged in a "Dear Abby" column, and HIP received 35,000 requests in the first week after the column appeared. The overwhelming response was indicative of the great need for information and support on this subject.

In 1984, HIP projects the formation of self-help groups that will function as chapters of HIP, Inc. They hope this will encourage a more open discussion of incontinence. The readers of the HIP Report claim that they would feel more comfortable talking to others who have experienced the same or similar situations.

Other areas HIP hopes to encourage are an increased awareness of the problem among health professionals; improved communication between the patient and others involved in providing care and comfort items; improved products that reflect the needs of the consumers; and modified legislation to gain insurance reimbursement for the absorbant products and accessories needed by incontinent people.

For further information, or to receive the free newsletter, write to *HIP, P.O. Box 544, Union, South Carolina 29379.*

New Catalog

More than 350 household, business, technological and recreational items making life easier for blind and visually impaired people are listed in the American Foundation for the Blind's free catalog, *Products for People With Vision Problems.*

Available in print or braille, the publication lists canes, watches, clocks, calculators, games, tools, housewares and medical equipment, as well as many new products. The catalog also includes more than fifty sales items.

For a copy of the new catalog, including instructions and forms for ordering, write *Consumer Products Division, American Foundation for the Blind, 15 West 16th Street, New York, New York 10011.*

Disability Newsletter

Irving K. Zola, Brandeis Sociology professor and member of THE EXCEPTIONAL PARENT editorial advisory board, has recently created and is the editor of *The Disability and Chronic Disease Newsletter.* The newsletter is free, and is published quarterly.

The newsletter is designed to provide information to the health professional about research, conferences, funding, and other resources, and reviews literature and documentaries pertaining to people with disabilities.

If you are interested in receiving the newsletter, write to *The Disability and Chronic Disease Newsletter, Irving K. Zola, Ed., Department of Sociology, Brandeis University, Waltham, Massachusetts 02254.*

Role Models

Partners, a Boston organization based on similar principles as Big Brother/Big Sister, addresses the need for the child with disabilities to develop a supportive relationship with a caring adult who has the same or similar disability.

The purpose of the partnership is to inspire the disabled child to develop his or her talents and abilities by means of an appropriate role model who has experienced the same frustrations and fears, and has experienced success.

Volunteers twenty years of age and older are recruited through human service programs and organizations that address the concerns of the handicapped in the Boston area. Each applicant is screened through an interview process in an effort to determine personality, needs, commitment, interests, and resources. This process helps in the efforts to determine the best match of adult and child.

The disabled children are referred to Partners through programs for the handicapped, and by parents, friends, and teachers.

Partners serves children with disabilities in the Boston area. For further information contact *Regina Snowden, Partners, 87 Summer Street, Boston, Massachusetts 02110.*

Wheelchair Etiquette

The Schoitz Medical Center in Waterloo, Iowa has prepared a pamphlet called, *"What Do I Do When I Meet A Person In A Wheelchair?"* It offers the following suggestions for non-wheelchair users who encounter people using wheelchairs:

- Always ask the wheelchair user if she or he would like assistance before you help. Your help may not be needed or wanted.
- Don't hang or lean on a person's wheelchair. It is part of the user's body space.
- Speak directly to the person in the wheelchair, not to someone nearby as if the user did not exist.
- If conversation lasts more than a few minutes, consider sitting down or kneeling to get yourself on the same level as the user.
- Do not demean or patronize the wheelchair user by patting him or her on the head.
- Give clear directions, including distance, weather conditions and physical obstacles that may hinder the user's travel.
- Do not discourage children from asking questions about the wheelchair. Open communication helps overcome fearful or misleading attitudes.
- It is O.K. to use expressions such as "running along" when speaking to the wheelchair user.
- Be aware of a wheelchair user's capabilities. Some users can walk

with aid and use wheelchairs because they can conserve energy and move about more quickly.

• Do not classify people in wheelchairs as "sick."

• Do not assume that using a wheelchair is in itself a tragedy. It is a means of freedom that allows the user to move about independently.

The Schoitz Medical Center will be happy to send a free pamphlet to anyone who requests one. Send a legal size, self-addressed, stamped envelope to, *Public Relations Office, Schoitz Medical Center, Kimball and Ridgeway Avenues, Waterloo, Iowa 50702.*

Networking Project

The YWCA of New York City is launching a Networking Project for Disabled Women and Girls, designed to address the lack of visible role models for disabled girls.

This project will involve the development of a network of successful disabled women in the New York City area, and the use of this network to provide role models for disabled junior and senior high school girls. A first local networking conference will develop and organize strategies for effective role-modeling work with disabled girls.

A second conference will be held for the girls themselves, who will meet and gain access to relevant contacts and resource materials. The successful disabled women who participate will serve as mentors and facilitators for the girls, to expand their educational and career aspirations, and encourage them to join ongoing peer support groups and other follow up activities.

For the purpose of this project, the organizing committee is considering disabled girls and women to be those who have an impairment of vision, hearing, mobility, or body structure.

At present, the committee is in the process of identifying successful disabled women in various fields. They ask that if anyone knows of such women who might be willing to participate in the mentorship aspect of the project, or in a more limited way, through filling out a questionnaire for their research on successful disabled women, to please send their names and addresses to the Networking Project.

Write to, *Harilyn Rousso, Networking Project For Disabled Women and Girls,* *YWCA of the City of New York, 610 Lexington Avenue, New York, New York 10022.*

Support Dogs

Support Dogs for the Handicapped is a privately funded organization which provides specially trained dogs to disabled persons at no charge to the individuals or their families.

The dogs are trained to aid people with such activities as climbing stairways, opening heavy doors, getting up from chairs, retrieving dropped objects, and, in some cases, walking.

Support dogs are usually large-boned dogs such as German Shepherds, Collies, Labradors, Newfoundlands, and some mixed breeds as well. The dogs come from such different sources as breeders, private individuals, and the Humane Society. They first go through a basic training period of eight to twelve weeks, and then specialty training for three to six weeks during which time the recipient and the trainer work together.

A support dog can be for anyone who is physically disabled, desires independence, and has the capabilities to function well with a dog. Individuals with disabilities may apply for a support dog along with their doctor's written approval. After the initial application, a committee will decide if the individual is qualified.

Support dogs can help the disabled conquer previously non-negotiable barriers, and, as one recipient said of her support dog, "It gave me the strength and support, both emotional and physical, but most important, my independence."

For further information, write to *Support Dogs for the Handicapped, P.O. Box 28457, Columbus, Ohio 43228-0457*

Parent Group Expands

Ross Laboratories has extended a grant to Parents of Premature and High-Risk Infants International, Inc., which will significantly assist the organization in supporting parents with babies in intensive care nurseries. In the United States each year, close to three hundred thousand infants require intensive care at birth.

The outlook for these babies is often hopeful, but each family must deal with terrible uncertainty about the future. Questions about disabilities and serious health problems may remain unanswered for months or years. The emotional and practical impact on families can be devastating.

Parents of Premature and High-Risk Infants International, Inc. (PPHRII) was formed in 1982 by parents and prenatal professionals. Its purpose is to provide information, referrals and support to parent groups, families and professionals concerned with infants who require special care at birth. They provide a quarterly newsletter, resource directory, and information and referral services.

For more information about the organization, contact *Maureen Lynch, Parents of Premature and High-Risk Infants International, 33 West 42nd Street, New York, New York 10036*

Fetal Alcohol Syndrome

Excessive use of alcohol by pregnant women can lead to a variety of serious defects in their offspring, including facial deformities, central nervous system dysfunction, heart disorders, and skeletal problems or growth deficiencies. It is estimated that two to two and a half million children a year are born with some effects of Fetal Alcohol Syndrome (FAS), which makes it the third most common cause of mental retardation. All of this condition is preventable, although it is irreversible.

Safe levels of drinking have not been positively identified and researchers are certain that the probability of having a baby with FAS increases with the amount and frequency with which a pregnant woman drinks alcohol. The U.S. Surgeon General has advised pregnant women and women who wish to become pregnant to avoid all alcohol because of the potential danger to the fetus.

In 1977, the Eunice Kennedy Shriver Center was designated as the New England Regional Resource for FAS education and service by the federal government. The program has two basic components—to prevent future cases of FAS and to identify and treat those already affected. Although FAS cannot be cured, proper treatment can improve initial expectations of the child's ability.

The Shriver Center's FAS Clinic offers free screening and diagnoses of children suspected of having FAS. In addition, the Fetal Alcohol Program Coordinator speaks to school groups, health clinics, civic organizations, and other agencies. The program serves as a national clearinghouse for information on FAS.

For more information, contact *Ms. Lorraine Mastropieri, The Shriver Center, 200 Trapelo Road, Waltham, Massachusetts 02154*

Leukemia Support Programs

The Leukemia Society has recently initiated a pilot family support program that provides free education, information and expanded referral services for the families of leukemia victims.

The program's design is based on a successful support group that the Leukemia Society's Southern New Jersey Chapter established in 1981. This group began with six families; today, sixty-five patient's families are included, and as many as two hundred people have attended the meetings at one time.

Attendance is open to parents, spouses, siblings, grandparents and others close to the patient who feel the need to discuss similar circumstances and feelings. The meetings provide a forum in which to air many of the fears, anxieties, and other issues that the disease generates. People are free to attend as they choose.

Chapters of the Leukemia Society that have expressed the greatest need have been given priority assistance in setting up a group. It is hoped that the Society eventually will have an ongoing group in each chapter's locale.

For further information, contact *The Leukemia Society of America, 800 Second Avenue, New York, New York 10017*

Advocacy Project

The American Bar Association plans to launch a year-long project aimed at improving advocacy on behalf of children with learning disabilities involved with the nation's juvenile and family courts.

The project is designed to improve practical legal skills in order to help assure that children involved in the juvenile or family court—whether for acts of delinquency, non-criminal behavior, or victims of parental maltreatment—will receive appropriate remedial educational services to help them deal with their disabilities.

Howard Davidson, Director of the Child Advocacy Project, explained that a significant percentage of court-involved children have learning disabilities which may significantly interfere with their academic and social functioning, as well as their self-esteem.

With the assistance of a $43,000 grant from the Foundation for Children with Learning Disabilities, the project will develop an advocacy skills manual to aid attorneys in understanding federal and state laws, court procedures, and educational agency policies related to the subject.

The project will also work to encourage state and local bar groups to feature educational programs and training sessions on the subject and to encourage lawyers in private practice to participate in programs providing legal assistance to such children.

The American Bar Association grant is part of a national effort by the Foundation for Children with Learning Disabilities to sensitize lawyers, judges, probation officers and court workers to the link between undetected learning disabilities and juvenile delinquent behavior.

The Foundation has also awarded a grant to the National Council of Juvenile and Family Court Judges to conduct training sessions for over one thousand judges, and another grant to the Research and Development Training Institute to develop self-help manuals for probation officers in the juvenile justice system.

For further information, contact *The American Bar Association Child Advocacy Center, 1800 M Street, N.W., S-200, Washington, D.C. 20036.*

Rubinstein-Taybi Support Group

Parents of children with Rubinstein-Taybi syndrome who want contact with other parents or who have any information on the syndrome—particularly new developments—are invited to contact *Garry and Lorrie Baxter, 416 N. Washington, Smith Center, Kansas 66967*

Community Partnership

The National Organization on Disability has issued a comprehensive handbook of guidelines for organizing community partnership programs to expand the participation of people with disabilities in the community.

The thirty page, illustrated handbook, *Organizing Community Partnership Programs*, provides detailed guidelines on several subjects:

Forming a community partnership program;

Organizing a community partnership committee meeting;

Setting goals for your community;

Developing media cooperation;

Fundraising techniques;

Working with government agencies;

How to involve your congressional representatives and senators;

Avoiding "words that hurt."

Single copies of the publication, in both printed and recorded versions, are available free of charge by writing to the *National Organization on Disability, 2100 Pennsylvania Avenue, N.W., Suite 234, Washington, D.C. 20037*

☐ The National Organization on Disability (N.O.D.) will be carrying out its third Annual Community Partnership Awards Program.

This program recognizes communities for setting and pursuing community goals designed to improve the lives of people with disabilities. The awards will be presented to thirteen winning communities in March 1985.

The National Organization on Disability is a private, non-profit organization concerned with all disabilities for all age groups. N.O.D.'s approach to developing solutions to the issues and concerns of people with disabilities is through its volunteer networks in community groups, corporations, national organizations, and liaisons in all fifty states.

This network carries out programs to improve public attitudes and increase acceptance of disabled people, to promote greater opportunities in education, housing, employment, transportation and recreation, and to prevent disabling conditions.

For further information about the

1984 Awards Program or the National Organization on Disability, write to *The National Organization on Disability, 2100 Pennsylvania Avenue, N.W., Suite 234, Washington, D.C. 20037*

Sudden Infant Death Syndrome

The National Center for the Prevention of Sudden Infant Death Syndrome has published a brochure entitled *Facts on Sudden Infant Death Syndrome* for new and expectant parents.

The brochure is the collaborative effort of scientists, physicians and representatives of counseling and parent groups. It contains medical facts about Sudden Infant Death Syndrome, more commonly known as "crib death," the nation's leading cause of death for infants beyond two weeks old.

The brochure is available upon request, free of charge. To order, write to *The National Center for the Prevention of Sudden Infant Death Syndrome, 330 North Charles Street, Baltimore, Maryland 21201*

Program on Childhood Cancer

Based on their belief that a patient's return to a normal, full life can be facilitated through the informed understanding of his or her peers, the Children's Cancer Research Institute in San Francisco has developed a health unit which gives a broad overview of the physical and psychological aspects of cancer on an elementary school level.

The entire unit can be presented in a five day health or science lesson. It includes illustrations for overhead reproduction and activities for students. The unit can be used as a tool for general elementary education or in a school re-entry program for pediatric patients.

The content includes lessons on: normal cells; cancer cells; treatments (chemotherapy, radiation, surgery); how it really feels to have childhood cancer; and anticipated emotional response of the patient.

The educational goals and techniques include developing understanding, using problem solving skills and creative thinking, and developing attitudes.

For more information, contact *Lori Haynes, Education Outreach, Children's Cancer Research Institute, 2351 Clay Street, Suite 512, San Francisco, California 94115*

Abilities Unlimitied

The 1985 International Abilities Unlimited Exposition, with the latest in technology, products, and services for the disabled, seniors, and professionals working with them will take place in April at the Los Angeles Convention Center,

The Exposition draws exhibitors and visitors from many nations. There will be approximately two hundred exhibitors featuring all types of products, services, organizations, recreational activities, job opportunities, artistic creations, and technology, all designed to enhance the quality of life for people with disabilities and senior citizens.

The Exposition is open to the public and is free of charge to all visitors. This is an opportunity for those who attend giving them a chance to comparison shop for their particular needs in one location.

Anyone wanting to be placed on a mailing list for annual information about the Exposition, or information regarding exhibiting should write to *RCW Productions, Inc., 1106 2nd Street, Suite 118, Encinitas, California*

Parent Handbook Available

The E.E.N. Triangle of Support—A Guide for Parents explains how decisions are made about disabled children's education and how parents can be involved in their children's identification, evaluation, and placement. Other sections discuss the I.E.P., disagreements, complaints, and due process.

Originally developed in 1983, the handbook has been revised and now includes a listing of organizations for parents of children with disabilities. It is especially helpful for parents whose school districts do not have their own handbooks for parents of exceptional children, but can be a helpful reference for anyone. It is written in a clear, readable style.

Five or fewer copies are avilable for free from *Kathryn Cavil, Department of Public Instruction, Division for Handicapped Children and Pupil Services, 125 S. Webster Street, P.O. Box 7841, Madison, Wisconsin 53707*. Copies of multiples of ten are avilable for $1.00 each from the Department of Public Instruction's Publications Unit.

Reading Service For the Blind

In Touch, a New York closed-circuit network that offers a free reading service for the blind announced plans to take its services nationwide.

Satellite Syndicated Systems of Tulsa, Oklahoma is donating part of the space on its communication satellite for distribution of the reading service to all areas of the United States. Any cable system or FM station that wishes to broadcast the service may do so without charge. In Touch expects over 300,000 new listeners will receive the broadcasts within the next year.

In Touch broadcasts twenty-four hours on weekdays and fourteen hours a day on weekends. The service is provided by more than three hundred volunteers, who read from selected newspapers and magazines.

For more information, contact *In Touch, 322 West 48th Street, New York, New York 10036*

Deaf Hotline

TRIPOD, a non-profit organization committed to giving families information about deafness, has established a toll-free hotline—the GRAPEVINE.

The GRAPEVINE was designed to provide counseling and information on deafness, as well as referrals to professionals and resources in the caller's local community. TRIPOD also mails individualized information packets in response to each request.

TRIPOD's Advisory Board consists of nineteen professionals and parents familiar with deafness. The Board is a working group that will provide individual counseling, depending on the GRAPEVINE caller's needs.

For further information about the other services available from TRIPOD, write to *TRIPOD, 955 North Alfred Street, Los Angeles, California 90069*.

The toll-free number is (800) 352-8888. In California, call (800) 346-8888.

National Poster Distribution

Sixteen year old Matthew Starr of Baltimore, Maryland is the subject of a new national poster being distributed by the National Organization on Disability.

Matthew has Down syndrome. His poster is the latest in a series of a nationwide public awareness campaign marking the Decade of Disabled Persons. Each poster depicts achievements and participation by a disabled person.

The Matt Starr poster shows him reading from the Torah at his Bar Mitzvah three years ago. He also recited his Haftorah portion and gave a short speech which he wrote himself.

Having a Bar Mitzvah was Matt's idea. He had seen his younger brother's Bar Mitzvah, and wanted to have one himself. Matt began the preparations six months ahead of time. With tape recordings of his Torah and Haftorah portions, he practiced the entire service twice a day, every day. His speech therapist at school coached him with his Bar Mitzvah speech—which Matt wrote himself.

"Down syndrome can be tough," says Matthew, "but I feel that I can do almost anything. I can and will become the best person I can be."

Matt belongs to the Boy Scouts, has taken acting and piano lessons, has run in the Special Olympics, and has learned to operate a computer. He enjoys folk music, mystery stories and television.

Ten thousand copies of the Matthew Starr poster are being distributed by the National Organization on Disability, a private, non-profit organization promoting increased public acceptance of disabled people and their further participation in national and community life.

The posters are being distributed to NOD's Community Partnership Committees in all fifty states, national organizations, corporations, state governors, agencies of the federal government, and other affiliated groups.

Single copies are available free of charge. Additional copies are $1.00 each. Write to *The National Organization on Disability, 2100 Pennsylvania Avenue, N.W., Washington, D.C. 20037*

Travel Center

Moss Rehabilitation Hospital in Philadelphia has been helping disabled travelers for twelve years with its free Travel Information Center.

During the past year, the Moss Travel Center has helped more than fifteen hundred disabled people plan trips both here and abroad.

The Center includes an extensive collection of materials on such topics as accessible hotels, restaurants, transportation and cultural facilities, airline regulations, and cruises for people with disabilities. Equipped with thorough information, travelers find they can eliminate or significantly diminish potential difficulties.

Unlike a travel booking agency, the Center provides necessary data so that disabled vacationers can plan their own excursions. The Center asks that requests be specific and include an outline of cities or areas the traveler wants to visit as well as tourist attractions of interest.

The Travel Center will then send appropriate available information, including data on suitability or accessibility. The Center also supplies names of people or agencies that might be able to provide further information.

A brochure is available describing the Center's services. For the brochure or for travel information, contact *Travel Information Center, Moss Rehabilitation Hospital, 12th Street and Tabor Road, Philadelphia, Pennsylvania 19141*

Magazine for Adoptive Parents

OURS magazine features articles by adoptive parents, practical information, as well as descriptions of children waiting for adoption.

Although the material in *OURS* does not deal solely with special needs children, there are several stories from parents who have adopted children with disabilities.

OURS is published bi-monthly by a non-profit adoptive parent support group. A one year subscription is $13, $24 for two years, $35 for three years. Canadian and foreign membership: $15 a year.

For further information, write to *OURS, 3307 Highway 100 North, Suite 203, Minneapolis, Minnesota 55422*

Muscular Dystrophy Brochure

The Muscular Dystrophy Association has recently published a brochure entitled *Duchenne Muscular Dystrophy*, providing up-to-date information on this form of muscular dystrophy.

The booklet describes the disease, explaining how it is genetically transmitted and how diagnosis is achieved. The brochure also explores theories about the cause of Duchenne muscular dystrophy and reviews current research and therapy.

In its final section, the booklet describes the course of the disease and discusses practical measures to improve the quality of patients' lives.

Copies are available free. Write to *Muscular Dystrophy Association, 810 Seventh Avenue, New York, New York 10019*

Getting About

A thirty-six page guide containing tips, hints and suggestions on ways individuals with disabilities can better function within their homes as well as travel comfortably and safely around their neighborhoods and across the country has been published as a public service project by Electric Mobility Corporation.

Getting About discusses the importance of positive mental attitudes to enable individuals with physical limitations to gain optimal independence in their daily lives.

The booklet also contains detailed information on special facilities available from airlines, hotels, national parks, railroads, car rental firms, bus lines, campgrounds and public transit systems to meet the needs of disabled travelers.

A complete bibliography as well as addresses and telephone numbers of firms and organizations offering free information of value to people with disabilities is also included.

Single copies are available without cost by writing to *Public Affairs Department/1213, Electric Mobility Corporation, #1 Mobility Plaza, Sewell, New Jersey 08080*

Muscular Dystrophy Research

A scientific investigation partially funded by the Muscular Dystrophy Association (MDA) has taken a major step toward the discovery of the defective gene that causes Duchenne muscular dystrophy, the most severe form of the disease.

Duchenne muscular dystrophy is a fatal muscle-wasting disorder caused by a defective gene on the X-chromosome—one of the two chromosomes that determine sex. Like other "sex-linked" genetic diseases such as hemophilia and color blindness, Duchenne affects males and only rarely females who generally do not have symptoms of the disease although, as "carriers," they may pass the disorder on to their sons.

The research team discovered the general location of the gene on the x-chromosome that is positioned closer to the Duchenne gene than any other "marker" to date. Although the precise distance between the two genes cannot yet be determined, pinpointing the exact location of the newly-found gene will bring scientists closer to finding the exact location of the elusive Duchenne gene.

The gene uncovered by the research team produces ornithine transcarbamlase (OTC), an enzyme essential to the metabolism of protein. Male infants born with a defective OTC gene rarely survive the first week of life.

Knowledge of the general location of the OTC gene may be useful in detecting carriers of Duchenne muscular dystrophy. Currently, there is no reliable carrier-detection test for the disease. MDA President, S. Mouchly Small, M.D., stated that such a test would be of enormous benefit to thousands who may be carriers of the Duchenne gene.

MDA is a national voluntary health agency working to defeat forty neuromuscular diseases through worldwide research, a nationwide network of hospital-affiliated clinics, and far-reaching professional and public health education. For further information, contact *Muscular Dystrophy Association, 810 Seventh Avenue, New York, New York 10019*

Newsletter for Grandparents

A newsletter with information on topics of interest to grandparents of children who are developmentally disabled is now available from the King County (Washington State) Advocates for Retarded Citizens.

The free newsletter offers up-to-date information on medical and educational topics, therapeutic programs, recreational activities, respite care, estate planning, and legislation affecting the disabled child and his/her family. Written and edited by grandparents, the newsletter provides a forum for grandparents to share their concerns and personal experiences relating to life with a grandchild who is developmentally disabled.

The newsletter is part of a two year program providing support and information to grandparents. The Grandparent Newsletter is funded by a grant from the U.S. Department of Education, Office of Special Education and Rehabilitative Services.

The King County ARC is also interested in hearing from grandparents of children with special needs who would like to share their experiences, through the newsletter, with other grandparents.

For a free subscription or further information, write to *THE GRANDPARENT PROGRAM, King County ARC, 2230 Eighth Avenue, Seattle, Washington 98121*

Fears of Surgery

Children undergoing hospitalization, anesthesia, and surgery face five major fears that medical personnel must learn to deal with more appropriately, Dr. Charles H. Lockhart, a Denver anesthesiologist reported.

Health care professionals should attempt to eliminate surprises and become the child's ally and supporter during this highly stressful period. The bottom line is to think and care about the child as a person, and not just as a patient with an illness.

Health care professionals must also think about what is scary to the child and to prevent potentially bad experiences, while giving support and reassurance to the patient throughout his or her hospitalization.

The first fear is the fear of pain. Such things as shots, which many children fear more than surgery, can be avoided with oral medications. It is also important to reassure children that most scars will not be disfiguring. Children must understand that while they will not feel or remember anything during surgery, they will awaken after surgery is completed.

The second is the fear of separation from parents, trusted friends, or familiar surroundings. This can be minimized by having liberal visiting hours, parents staying overnight, keeping the teddy bear readily at hand, and shortening the duration of hospitalization whenever possible.

The third is the fear of the strange, the unknown, or the possibility of surprise. Familiarizing the child in advance with what s/he can expect, what will happen to him or her, where and why, can go a long way in diminishing this fear.

The fourth is the fear of not knowing what is acceptable behavior in the hospital. Can s/he get out of bed, leave the room to go to the bathroom, or visit down the hall? Defining the child's limits of behavior beforehand can increase his or her sense of belonging.

The fifth is the fear of loss of control. Children, and especially adolescents, need to demonstrate their competence and capability for autonomy. Allowing them some responsibility and engaging them in the decision making process where practicable can be a confidence builder.

Developing plans to prepare children for hospitalization, including informational pamphlets for parents, and prehospitalization tours for the patient, can significantly reduce the child's stress.

Sports Complex

The facilities of the Joseph Bulova School's Health/Sports Complex in Woodside, New York are open free of charge, seven days a week to any disabled person or disabled-oriented group.

The complex has an indoor heated pool, sauna, and gymnasium. All facilities are completely accessible. Various equipment, recreation consulting, access to organized athletic programs, and instruction in "adapted aquatics" are available.

Over seven hundred people with disabilities are currently benefiting from the Health/Sports Complex. Interested individuals or groups may contact William Meisner at *(212) 424-2929* for information regarding services and scheduling.

Open House

The American Foundation for the Blind held a series of open houses in late March designed to acquaint professionals, librarians, and consumers with the many services and materials available in the M.C. Migel Memorial Library and Information Center. The library was recently remodeled by Charles A. Moss, Jr., an architect known for his interest in making buildings accessible to people with disabilities.

In addition to housing the Helen Keller Archives, a rare book collection, several photograph collections, and a permanent print collection of over thirty-seven thousand books, periodicals, bibliographies, and other written material dealing with blindness, the library also owns high-technology machines which allow blind people total access to the print collection.

By operating a talking Apple Computer, a Kurzweil Reading Machine, or a Viewscan, Versabraille or Visualtek system, people with visual impairments can study the entire collection via synethic speech, braille or large print display.

The library also subscribes to SpecialNet, a data retrieval system which allows special educators throughout the country to communicate immediately on matters concerning legislation, employment, early childhood, and other subjects of interest to blind and visually impaired people.

Begun in 1926, the M.C. Migel Library and Information Center is a national resource center receiving thousands of requests yearly. It is located on the ground floor of the American Foundation for the Blind's New York City headquarters.

Requests for information and materials about blindness, including a recently completed comprehensive series of subject bibliographies may be made by telephone or mail. Materials circulate free of charge within the continental United States, and through interlibrary loan in Canada.

To contact the American Foundation for the Blind, write to *The AFB, 15 West 16th Street, New York, New York 10011.*

Children's Museum

The Children's Museum in Boston, Massachusetts conducts an individualized program for visitors with special needs each Wednesday during the school year. Visitors from a variety of classroom, medical and institutional settings ranging in age from toddlers to the elderly, are paired with museum staff for a one-hour guided program.

Serving as companions and guides, the staff accompany visitors through the exhibits, encouraging interaction, and providing interpretation, information and support—both physical and emotional.

Because most of the exhibits are "hands-on" and participatory, depending less on explanation than exploration, interaction takes place on many levels. Even the visitor who is severely disabled may derive satisfaction from the museum. Small group or one-to-one staffing allows the museum to serve the specific needs of the visitors.

Staff training for the program takes place on an ongoing basis, through orientation programs, weekly support meetings, workshops and multi-media materials.

The Special Needs Program is in its eighth year. Since its inception, the program has served thousands of visitors with special needs, and has strengthened the museum's capacity to work effectively and successfully with the disabled public—both in the structured context of the Wednesday program, and on an individual level.

For further information about this program, contact *The Children's Museum, Museum Wharf, 300 Congress Street, Boston, Massachusetts 02210.*

Information Center

The Department of Education recently established the National Information Center for Handicapped Children and Youth (NICHCY).

The clearinghouse will provide publications about specific disabilities, addresses of national, state and local support organizations, resource information, and "how-to" information to parents of disabled children, disabled adults, and professionals who work with them.

Information on NICHCY may be obtained from, *Jim Murphy, Information Services Manager, National Information Center for Handicapped Children and Youth, 1555 Wilson Boulevard, Rosslyn, Virginia 22209.*

Integrated Chorus

The Sing Along Chorus is a recreational program for special needs teenagers and young adults, and other interested non-handicapped young people in the community. The chorus is under the sponsorship of the Lexington, Massachusetts Recreation Department.

The primary goal of the program is to provide a pleasurable and stimulating activity for young people with disabilities in order to help them acquire the social skills and self-confidence which will enable them to participate in rewarding group and community experiences.

The chorus provides social interaction between the disabled and non-disabled participants, thus promoting opportunities for role-modeling and mutually meaningful relationships.

Throughout the year, the chorus presents sing-along concerts for the residents of local nursing homes. This outreach not only brings two groups together who are generally isolated, but it offers the young people a rare opportunity to provide community service. In addition, the chorus periodically invites other senior citizen groups to participate in musical and social events.

Since its inception in November 1983, the chorus has enjoyed a busy schedule of special events, as well as regular weekly rehearsals. For further information about the Sing Along Chorus, write to *Marilyn Able, 22 Partridge Road, Lexington, Massachusetts 02173.* ■

CHAPTER 62

Directory
Organizations and Agencies Serving Children and Adults with Disabilities and their Families

The addresses of the agencies and organizations listed in this directory are compiled from the most up-to-date information we have been able to obtain. If you are aware of any address changes or additional agencies and organizations not listed in this directory, please write to us. We hope to expand our directory of the year.

AC MRDD (The Accreditation Council of Services for Persons with Mental Retardation & Other Developmental Disabilities)
4435 Wisconsin Avenue, N.W.
Washington, D.C. 20016

Alexander Graham Bell Association for the Deaf
3417 Volta Place, N.W.
Washington D.C. 20007

Allergy Foundation of America
19 West 44th Street
New York, New York 10036

American Academy for Cerebral Palsy and Developmental Medicine
2315 Westwood Avenue
P.O. Box 11083
Richmond, Virginia 23230

American Foundation for the Blind
15 West 16th Street
New York, New York 10011

American Occupational Therapy Association
1383 Piccard Drive
Rockville, Maryland 20580

American Physical Therapy Association
1156 15th Street, N.W.
Washington, D.C. 20005

American Alliance for Health, Physical Education, Recreation and Dance
1900 Association Drive
Reston, Virginia 22091

American Association on Mental Deficiency
5101 Wisconsin Avenue
Washington, D.C. 20016

American Coalition of Citizens with Disabilities
1346 Connecticut Avenue, N.W.
Suite 1124
Washington, D.C. 20036

American Council for the Blind
1211 Connecticut Avenue, N.W.
Washington, D.C. 20006

American Printing House for the Blind
P.O. Box 6085
Louisville, Kentucky 40206

American Society for Deaf Children
814 Thayer Avenue
Silver Spring, Maryland 20910

American Speech and Hearing Association
10801 Rockville Pike
Rockville, Maryland 20852

Arthritis Foundation
3400 Peachtree Road, N.E.,
Suite 1101
Atlanta, Georgia 30026

Association for Children with Learning Disabilities
4156 Library Road
Pittsburgh, Pennsylvania 15234

Association for Education of the Visually Handicapped
919 Walnut Street, Fourth Floor
Philadelphia, Pennsylvania 19107

Association for Retarded Citizens of the United States
2501 Avenue J
P.O. Box 6109
Arlington, Texas 76011

Canadian Association for the Mentally Retarded/National Institute on Mental Retardation
4700 Keele Street
Downsview, Ontario, Canada M3J1P3

Canadian Cerebral Palsy Association
55 Bloor Street East
Suite 301
Toronto, Ontario, Canada M4W1A9

Canadian Diabetes Association
78 Bond Street
Toronto, Ontario, Canada M5B2J8

Canadian Hearing Society
60 Bedford Road
Toronto, Ontario, Canada M5R2K2

Canadian Hemophilia Society National Office
P.O. Box 2222
100 King Street West
Hamilton, Ontario L8N3R2

Canadian National Institute for the Blind
1929 Bayview Avenue
Toronto, Ontario, Canada M4G3E8

Canadian Rehabilitation Council for the Disabled
1 Young Street, Suite 2110
Toronto, Ontario, Canada M5E1A5

Coalition on Sexuality and Disability
122 East 23rd Street
New York, New York 10010

Compassionate Friends
(for bereaved parents)
P.O. Box 1347
Oak Brook, Illinois 60521

Committee for the Promotion of Camping for the Handicapped
P.O. Box 973
Traverse City, Michigan 49685

Council for Exceptional Children
1920 Association Drive
Reston, Virginia 22091

Cri-du-Chat Society
Department of Human Genetics
Medical College of Virginia
P.O. Box 33, MCV Station
Richmond, Virginia 23298

Cystic Fibrosis Foundation
6000 Executive Boulevard, Suite 510
Rockville, Maryland 20852

Disabled Living Resource Center
Kinsmen Rehabilitation Foundation
2256 West 12th Avenue
Vancouver, British Columbia
Canada B6K2N5

Down Syndrome Congress
1640 West Roosevelt Road
Chicago, Illinois 60608

Down Syndrome Guild
P.O. Box 1505
Scarborough, Maine 04074

Dysautonomia Foundation, Inc.
370 Lexington Avenue
New York, New York 10017

Dystonia Foundation
425 Broad Hollow Road
Melville, New York 11747

Ephphatha Services for the Deaf and Blind
P.O. Box 15167
Minneapolis, Minnesota 55415

Epilepsy Foundation of America
4351 Garden City
Landover, Maryland 20784

Foundation for Children With Learning Disabilities
99 Park Avenue, Second Floor
New York, New York 10011

Friedreich's Ataxia Group in America
P.O. Box 11116
Oakland, California 94611

International Spinal Cord Research Foundation
4100 Spring Valley Road
Suite 104 LB3
Dallas, Texas 75234

John Tracy Clinic
(deafness/hearing impairments, deaf-blind)
806 West Adams Boulevard
Los Angeles, California 90007

Juvenile Diabetes Foundation
60 Madison Avenue
New York, New York 10010

Little People of America, Inc.
Box 126
Owatonna, Minnesota 55060

Lowe's Syndrome Association
607 Robinson Street
West Lafayette, Indiana 47906

Leukemia Society of America
800 Second Avenue
New York, New York 10017

March of Dimes Birth Defects Foundation
1275 Mamaroneck Avenue
White Plains, New York 10605

Muscular Dystrophy Association
810 Seventh Avenue
New York, New York 10019

National Amputation Foundation
12-45 150th Street
Whitestone, New York 11357

National Association of the Deaf
814 Thayer Avenue
Silver Spring, Maryland 20910

National Association for Down Syndrome
P.O. Box 63
Oak Park, Illinois 60303

National Association of the Deaf-Blind
12573 S.E. 53rd Street
Bellevue, Washington 98006

National Association of the Physically Handicapped
76 Elm Street
London, Ohio 43140

National Association of Private Residential Facilities for the Mentally Retarded
6269 Leesburg Pike, Suite B5
Falls Church, Virginia 22044

National Association of Private Schools for Exceptional Children
P.O. Box 34293
West Bethesda, Maryland 20817

National Association for Sickle Cell Disease
3460 Wilshire Boulevard, Suite 1012
Los Angeles, California 90010

National Association for the Visually Handicapped
305 East 24th Street
New York, New York 10010

National Ataxia Foundation
600 Twelve Oaks Center
15500 Wayzata Boulevard
Wayzata, Minnesota 55391

National Center for a Barrier-Free Environment
1115 15th Street, N.W., Suite 700
Washington, D.C. 20005

National Center for Education in Maternal and Child Care
3520 Prospect Street, N.W.
Washington, D.C. 20057

National Center for Law and the Handicapped
University of Notre Dame
P.O. Box 477
Notre Dame, Indiana 46556

National Cleft Palate Association
P.O. Box 2647
Hutchinson, Kansas 67501

National Committee on Arts for the Handicapped
1825 Connecticut Avenue, N.W.
Suite 418
Washington, D.C. 20009

National Congress of Organizations of the Physically Handicapped, Inc.
1627 Deborah Avenue
Rockland, Illinois 61103

National Easter Seal Society
2023 West Ogden Avenue
Chicago, Illinois 60612

National Federation of the Blind
1346 Connecticut Avenue, N.W.
Suite 212, Dupont Circle Building
Washington, D.C. 20036

National Foundation for Asthma
P.O. Box 30069
Tucson, Arizona 85751

National Foundation of Dentistry for the Handicapped
1250 14th Street, Suite 610
Denver, Colorado 80202

National Foundation for Ileitis and Colitis
444 Park Avenue South, 11th Floor
New York, New York 10016

National Genetics Foundation
555 West 57th Street, Room 1240
New York, New York 10019

National Hearing Aid Society
20361 Middlebelt Road
Livona, Michigan 48152

National Hemophilia Foundation
19 West 34th Street, Room 1204
New York, New York 10001

National Icthyosis Foundation
P.O. Box 252
Belmont, California 94002

National Lymphatic and Venous Foundation, Inc.
P.O. Box 80
Cambridge, Massachusetts 02140

National Mental Health Association
1021 Prince Street
Alexandria, Virginia 22310

National Multiple Sclerosis Society
205 East 42nd Street
New York, New York 10017

National Neurofibromatosis Foundation
70 West 40th Street, 4th Floor
New York, New York 10018

National Organization for Rare Disorders
c/o National Huntington's Disease Association
1182 Broadway, Suite 402
New York, New York 10001

National Paraplegia Foundation
333 North Michigan Avenue
Chicago, Illinois 60601

National Rehabilitation Association
633 S. Washington Street
Alexandria, Virginia 22314

National Retinitis Pigmentosa Foundation
Rolling Park Apartments
8331 Mindale Circle
Baltimore, Maryland 21207

National Society for Autistic Children
1234 Massachusetts Avenue, N.W.
Suite 1017
Washington, D.C. 20005

National Spinal Cord Injury Group
369 Elliot Street
Newton Upper Falls, Massachusetts 02164

National Tay-Sachs and Allied Diseases Association
92 Washington Avenue
Cedarhurst, New York 11516

National Wheelchair Athletic Association
40-24 62nd Street
Woodside, New York 11377

North America Riding for the Handicapped Association, Inc.
P.O. Box 100
Ashburn, Virginia 22011

Office of Special Education Programs
400 Maryland Avenue, S.W.
MES Building, Room 3086
Washington, D.C. 20202

Orton Dyslexia Society
724 York Road
Baltimore, Maryland 21204

Prader-Willi Syndrome Association
5515 Malibu Drive
Edina, Minnesota 55436

Rehabilitation Education Center
University of Illinois
1207 South Oak
Champaign, Illinois

Sex Information and Education Council of the U.S. (SIECUS)
84 Fifth Avenue, Room 407
New York, New York 10001

Society for the Rehabilitation of the Facially Disfigured
560 First Avenue
New York, New York 10016

Spina Bifida Association of America
343 South Dearborn Street
Room 317
Chicago, Illinois 60604

TASH (The Association for the Severely Handicapped)
7010 Roosevelt Way, N.E.
Seattle, Washington 98115

Task Force on Life Safety and the Handicapped
P.O. Box 19044
Washington, D.C. 20036

Tourette Syndrome Association
41-02 Bell Boulevard
Bayside, New York 11361

Tuberous Sclerosis Association of America
339 Union Street
P.O. Box 44
Rockland, Massachusetts 02320

Turner Syndrome Support Group
700 Easton Avenue
Somerset, New Jersey 08873

United Cerebral Palsy Associations, Inc.
330 West 34th Street, 13th Floor
New York, New York 10001

United Leukodystrophy Foundation
714 Pioneer Drive
Indianapolis, Indiana 46217

United Ostomy Association
2001 West Beverly Boulevard
Los Angeles, California 90057

Government Agencies

Administration on Developmental Disabilities
Office of Human Developmental Services
Department of Health and Human Services
330 Independence Avenue, S.W.
Room 3194
Washington, D.C. 20201

American Association of University Affiliated Programs for the Developmentally Disabled
(35 interdisciplinary facilities working with the Department of Health, Education and Welfare)
110 17th Street, N.W. Suite 908
Washington, D.C. 20026

Architectural and Transportation
Barriers Compliance Board
330 C Street, S.W.
Room 1010, Switzer Building
Washington, D.C. 20202

Division of Assistance to States
Office of Special Education
400 Maryland Avenue, S.W.
Donohoe Building
Washington, D.C. 20202

National Information Center for
Handicapped Children and Youth
P.O. Box 1492
Rosslyn, Virginia 22209

National Library Service for the
Blind and Physically Handicapped
Library of Congress
1291 Taylor Street, N.W.
Washington, D.C. 20542

Office of Deafness and
Communicative Disorders
Department of Education
Room 3416, Switzer Building
400 Maryland Avenue
Washington, D.C. 20202

President's Committee on
Employment of the Handicapped
Department of Labor
1111 20th Street, N.W., #600
Washington, D.C. 20036

National Network of Parent Coalitions

Southern region

ACCEPT (Advocacy Center for
Children's Education and Parent
Training)
2204 Market Street
Wilmington, North Carolina 28043
(919) 762-3451

ADOM (Association of
Developmental Organizations of
Mississipi, Inc.)
6055 Highway 18, South
Jackson, Mississippi 39212
(601) 922-3210

Arkansas Coalition for the
Handicapped
1700 W. 13th Street, Suite 349
Little Rock, Arkansas 72202
(501) 376-3420

Asociacion de Padres Pro-Bienestar
de Ninos Impedidos de Puerto Rico
Box Q
Rio Piedras, Puerto Rico 00928
(809) 765-0345

BOLD (Bolder Opportunities for the
Learning Disabled)
9451 West Broadview Drive
Bay Harbor Island, Florida 33154
(305) 866-6939

Parents' Educational Advocacy
Center
Governor's Council for Persons with
Disabilities
116 W. Jones Street
Raleigh, North Carolina 27611
(919) 733-9250

Parent Educational Advocacy
Training Center
228 South Pitt Street, Room 300
Alexandria, Virginia 22314
(703) 836-2953

PEP (Parents Educating Parents)
Program
Georgia Association for Retarded
Citizens
1851 Ram Runway, Suite 104
College Park, Georgia 30337
(404) 761-2745

Midwestern region:

Coordinating Council for
Handicapped Children
220 South State Street, Room 412
Chicago, Illinois 60604
(312) 939-3513

Designs for Change
220 South State Street, Suite 1616
Chicago, Illinois 60604
(312) 922-0317

PACER (Parent Advocacy Coalition
for Education Rights) Center
4826 Chicago Avenue, South
Minneapolis, Minnesota 55407
(612) 827-2966

PEP (Parent Education Project)
Coalition
United Cerebral Palsy of
Southeastern Wisconsin, Inc.
152 West Wisconsin Avenue, Suite
308
Milwaukee, Wisconsin 53202
(414) 272-4500

Parent-Tel and Pilot Parent Program
444 South 44th Street
Omaha, Nebraska 68131

SOC (Southwestern Ohio Coalition
for Handicapped Children)
3333 Vine Street
Cincinatti, Ohio 54219
(513) 861-2400

Task Force on Education for the
Handicapped
812 E, Jefferson Boulevard
South Bend, Indiana 46617
(219) 234-7101

Northeastern region:

Federation for Children with Special
Needs
312 Stuart Street, 2nd Floor
Boston, Massachusetts 02116
(617)482-2915

New Hampshire Parent Information
Center
P.O. Box 1422
Concord, New Hampshire 03301

New York State Coalition
267 West 70th Street
New York City, New York 10023
(212) 873-6094

Parents' Campaign for Handicapped
Children and Youth
1201 Sixteenth Street
Washington, D.C. 20036
(202) 822-7900

Western region:

Hawaii Coalition
200 North Vinyard Boulevard
Room 402
Honolulu, Hawaii 96817
(808) 533-7130

PAVE (Parents Advocating
Vocational Education)
1516 North Orchard
Tacoma, Washington 98406

Southern Nevada Association for the
Handicapped
3333 West Washington
Las Vegas Nevada 89107
(702) 646-0275

TASK (Team of Advocates for
Special Kids)
1800 East LaVeta Avenue
Orange, California 92666
(714) 771-6542 ■